W9-BQI-364

JUL 1970
RECEIVED
OHIO DOMINICAN
COLLEGE LIBRARY
COLUMBUS, OHIO

ROBERT BROWNING

THE SELECTED POEMS
of
Robert Browning

Introduction by PIERRE LOVING

Published for the Classics Club by

WALTER J. BLACK · NEW YORK

PRINTED IN THE UNITED STATES OF AMERICA

Contents

Dramatic Romances

Men and Women

Dramatis Personae

Prologue from Fifine at the Fair

From Pacchiarotto, with Other Poems

La Saiziaz and The Two Poets of Croisic

Introduction

ROBERT BROWNING was a poet who used his own strong emotions, imagination, and curiosity to delve into the hearts of men and women whom he found endlessly fascinating, and not least because they were heirs of human frailty. To this eminent Victorian, every human being was unique, a self-contained organism instinct with the power for good and evil. Foibles and tastes, talents and weaknesses, were necessary elements of the total man. Apparently trivial on the surface, they often nourished the seeds of growth and personal destiny.

Steeped in the European literature of his day, Browning nevertheless belonged to no literary movement. He was an omnivorous newspaper reader, and although he favored the North during the Civil War and sympathized with Garibaldi and Mazzini in their struggle for Italian freedom, he took no part in politics. He had a formidable appetite for the unusual, the absurd, even the grotesque, particularly in human character. It was natural that he should reject the idea, as expressed in his sonnet, *Why I am a Liberal,* that men could be herded, branded, and owned. He held, above all, that a poet, who is commanded to look in his heart and write, had the duty to tear the mask from egoisms and catchwords. Democracy urges us to be one and yet multiple. Because he had faith in the individual, Robert Browning was a spokesman for the conscience of democracy, which upholds the dignity of man.

With an enormous zest for people, he hoped to find in everyone, if he could but probe deep enough, some virtue of originality. Men, he knew, justify themselves in devious ways, and so he chose the dramatic soliloquy as the carry-all best fitted to his use. And in this form he has given us an unforgettable gallery of portraits: duchesses, poets, painters, priests, statesmen, savants, quacks, and average men and women.

Robert Browning was born on May 7, 1812, at Camberwell, London. On both his mother's and father's side his was a middle class family. Earlier Brownings had settled in Wiltshire and Dorsetshire. The poet's mother was the daughter of William Wiedemann, a German merchant who had chosen to live in Dundee, where he married a Scottish girl. The elder Browning held a clerkship in the Bank of England for fifty years. On his retirement, he went to live on the French coast, dying there in 1866. The Brownings had a sufficient income for the education of their children—a daughter, Sarianna, was born in 1814—as well as for the exercise of cultivated tastes.

Camberwell was a quiet suburb during Browning's childhood and youth. The family was closely knit by deep affection; the home circle was at once stimulating and happy. Browning's father was a musical amateur and a painter on Sundays; his library was well-stocked and he was fond of reading aloud. Mrs. Browning played the piano, taught her children music, and attended the Independent Chapel. The children played duets and matched rhymes. In grotesque rhyming, at which they soon became adept, Browning senior set them an example, and the gift was stretched to virtuosity by the son.

Robert Browning composed verses before he knew how to write. At the age of twelve he put together a book of poems called *Incondita,* which Sarah Flower, a friend of his mother, copied out and locked in a cabinet. Years later she brought out the manuscript to the embarrassment of the mature poet. This manuscript was in existence in 1871, to be eventually destroyed by the poet.

Thus the boy was given thorough training at home in music, art, and poetry. He had the run of his father's library; his gifts, in consequence, unfolded naturally and he was given every encouragement by his parents. Robert presently came to believe that he could use everything as grist, everything that fed his mind and stirred his heart. In a late poem, *Development,* his childhood comes flooding back, and he gives us this delightful picture of the Camberwell scene:

My father was a scholar and knew Greek.
When I was five years old, I asked him once
"What do you read about?"
"The siege of Troy."
"What is the siege of Troy?"
Whereat
He piled up chairs and table for a town,
Set me atop for Priam, called our cat
Helen, enticed away from home (he said)
By wicked Paris, who crouched somewhere close
Under the footstool, being cowardly. . . .

He went to school in the neighborhood until he was fourteen, had boxing, riding, and fencing lessons, and was tutored in French. At the age of eighteen he attended some Greek lectures at London University and the rising interest in science prompted him to enroll in anatomy classes at Guy's Hospital.

Lord Byron, who had died fighting for Greek freedom at Missolonghi in 1824 when Browning was twelve years old, was the idol of the young poets of the period. Browning came under his magnetic spell. He said to Elizabeth Barrett during their courtship that he would go to Finchley any day to see a curl of hair or one of Byron's gloves, but that he "could not get up enthusiasm enough to cross a room if at the other end of it all Wordsworth, Southey, and Coleridge were condensed into the little China bottle yonder."

In 1830, when the Byronesque dandy came into fashion, both Tennyson and Browning succumbed to the romantic pose, but not to the extreme degree of young Disraeli and Edward Bulwer, later Lord Lytton, who cut dashing figures in clubs and country houses. Even Charles Dickens aped Beau Brummel in Fleet Street and in amateur plays. A thumbnail sketch of Browning as a young man has come down to us: finically dressed; coal-black hair; a becoming pallor; lemon-yellow gloves, which he stripped off, asking leave to play the piano while waiting for a friend who was out.

Soon Browning began to move in a world that had seen and met and talked and broken bread with Shelley and Keats. Leigh

Hunt, Severn, and Dilke recounted tender tales of their friends, John Keats and Percy Bysshe Shelley, twin stars of English poetry. Wordsworth, although retired to Rydal Mount in the Lake Country, was still among the living.

Browning's *Pauline* appeared anonymously in 1833. Not a single copy was sold. John Stuart Mill's review, which was never published, happened to reach Browning with a returned copy of the book. Mill's comment, that the author of *Pauline* (whoever he was) was sick with "a more intense and morbid self-consciousness than ever I knew in a sane human being," had a profound effect on the poet. Browning explained later that *Pauline* was not autobiography at all, but only one monologue in a series of dramatic poems, adding: "Only this crab remains of the shapely Tree of Life in this Fool's paradise of mine." The influence of Byron and Shelley is unmistakable in this early romantic poem, and to Shelley are addressed the famous lines:

> *Sun-treader, I believe in God and truth*
> *And love. . . .*

In the winter of 1833, Browning accompanied the Russian consul-general, George de Benckhausen, to St. Petersburg. On this trip he wrote *Porphyria's Lover* and *Johannes Agricola,* and his Russian impressions bore fruit many years later in the tale, *Ivan Ivanovich.* In the spring of 1834 he visited Italy for the first time. This was a turning point in his life and work, and henceforth Italy was to leave its impression on a great deal of his creative output.

In 1835 Browning published his drama *Paracelsus,* which portrays the clash of science with the sensuous and emotional elements in man. Paracelsus strives to acquire knowledge and thereby to command life and fails because he is devoid of love. In "Aprile," a Keatsian poet who loves beauty, Browning sums up the undefeated heart that goes in quest of love—and God.

Through *Paracelsus* the twenty-three-year-old poet gained a number of enthusiastic admirers and friends. Among them was John Forster, the critic, who said in his review: "Without the slightest hesitation we name Mr. Robert Browning at once with Shelley, Coleridge, and Wordsworth." The circle of the poet's friends soon widened to include Wordsworth, Tennyson, Dickens, Landor, and the famous tragedian, Macready.

Macready put off going to the United States where he had theatrical engagements and urged Browning to write a play for him. The result was *Strafford,* produced at Covent Garden in May, 1837. It ran for five performances and closed when the actor who played Pym dropped out. In 1840 appeared *Sordello* which alienated most of his champions and baffled even his most sympathetic friends. Although obscure, *Sordello* by no means lacks form, and it would be quite wrong to say that Browning gave no heed to form. He was of course aware of repeated charges against him on this score, and in the *Inn Album* he puts into the mouth of a character words which he must have heard or read:

> *That bard's a Browning; he neglects the form,*
> *But, ah, the sense, ye gods, the weighty sense!*

Sordello has given currency to a number of piquant anecdotes which, even if apocryphal, cast light on contemporary reaction to the poem. Carlyle wrote to Browning, whose friendship he enjoyed, that his wife had just read *Sordello* with great interest, and wished to know whether *Sordello* was a man, a city, or a book. Tennyson is reported to have murmured over to himself the first and last lines:

> *Who will, may hear Sordello's story told,*

and

> *Who would, has heard Sordello's story told.*

These lines, he announced, were the only two in the poem he could make out, and they were lies.

Small wonder, then, that *Sordello*—which contains so many exquisitely beautiful passages—delayed the poet's public recognition. Thanks to his resiliency and virile good humor, Browning did not let this temporary setback rankle. He soon grew accustomed to being taxed with unnecessary obscurity; he was lampooned and burlesqued; but he never abandoned his sense of humor, so that at a later date, when pressed for the meaning of a certain poem, he was able to give the amiable reply: "When that poem was written only two people knew what it meant—God and Robert Browning. And now only God knows what it means."

The stage production of *The Blot i' the 'Scutcheon* in 1843 at the Drury Lane Theatre led to a bitter quarrel with Macready, and as a result they were estranged for many years. Yet it was Macready's persuasiveness, in spite of the niggardly manner in which he mounted Browning's plays, that gave the poet the impetus to try his hand as a playwright. Between 1841 and 1846 he wrote *Pippa Passes, King Victor and King Charles, The Return of the Druses, Colombe's Birthday, Luria,* and *The Soul's Tragedy.*

Summing up Browning as a dramatist we may say, briefly, that he was a subtle analyst, a surgeon with a keen scalpel, rather than a builder of character by visible means. While he undoubtedly recognized the need to precipitate conflict, he failed in the theater partly because of his intricate use of language, but chiefly because he was impatient with the tricks and trappings of the playhouse and paid almost no attention to the exigencies of plot development. Under Browning's hand a soul grows, paradoxically, by analysis, not through cumulative and outward action. Yet the raw stuff of good drama is to be found in his plays. The doctored version of *The Blot i' the 'Scutcheon*—doctored by Macready—drew from Dickens this unrestrained outburst:

"I know no love like it, no passion like it, no molding of a splendid thing after its conception like it."

Between 1841 and 1846 Moxon, the publisher, brought out eight poetry pamphlets, including *Pippa Passes, Dramatic Poems,* and *Dramatic Lyrics,* under the title of *Bells and Pomegranates.* The title created a greater stir than the poems, the critics calling it affected. Later the poet explained to Elizabeth Barrett that the title meant, according to rabbinical lore, an alternation of the gay and the grave, pleasure and profit, poetry and prose.

The long-delayed meeting with Elizabeth Barrett, already a well-known poet, took place in 1845, and formed the beginning of a love idyll that has greatly enriched English literature. At that time Miss Barrett was almost forty, six years older than the urbane poet. A spinal injury suffered when she was a girl kept her a recluse in Wimpole Street. However, this did not prevent her from writing the poetry which drew Robert Browning's interest toward her.

She put off his repeated attempts to call, offering as an excuse the state of her health, although the eccentric attitude of her father was probably the main reason. Edward Moulton Barrett, a widower and dour patriarch, tyrannized over his three daughters, his love and solicitude taking the form of jealous despotism. He had forbidden his daughters to marry, as though such a step would constitute an unfilial rebuff to himself.

The situation was delicate, but Browning managed through John Kenyon, a school friend of his father's and a second cousin of Miss Barrett's, to make his first call in May 1845. Handsome and charming in manner, he brought into the sickroom an air of the world. Subsequently Browning described their first meeting, conjuring up "a little figure which did not rise from the sofa, pale ringletted face, great eager wistful eyes." Elizabeth, telling of this first visit, said, "He never went away again."

His earliest letter to her, although it referred to one of her recent poems, opened with the prophetic words: "I love. . . ." And soon afterward, when he became a frequent caller, her room was brightened by the fresh flowers he sent her. Mr. Barrett was kept in ignorance of these visits: Browning was smuggled in and out of the house on Wimpole Street by Miss Barrett's sisters.

A daily exchange of letters was kept up; Browning proposed; Elizabeth hesitated from a sense of her own inadequacy; he pressed for a decision. The way she arrived at one might have served as the raw material for a psychological poem by her lover. On that day in August 1846, the woman who had been hailed as the most masculine of women poets enacted the most feminine—or perhaps the most realistic—poem of her career. The invalid drove to the park in the family carriage, accompanied by her dog Flush. Alighting, she stood under a tree for several minutes, touching the bark with her hand and poking the ferrule of her parasol into the green turf. When she got back to her father's house her mind was irrevocably made up: she would no longer be the victim of her own physical frailties or of her father's domineering whims. She would marry Robert Browning.

In spite of Mr. Barrett's irrational prejudice, Browning wished the wedding to be public, but Elizabeth insisted that it be kept secret. During the summer her health had taken a turn for the better and on September 2, 1846—with Browning's cousin as sole witness—they were married at the St. Marylebone parish church. Elizabeth remained under the paternal roof until September 19 when with her maid and her dog she left Wimpole Street for good and joined her husband. They traveled directly to Paris.

Edward Moulton Barrett never forgave his daughter, and among his posthumous papers was an unopened letter from Elizabeth in which she had written of the birth of her son.

With slender funds at their disposal, the couple traveled from Paris to Italy, selecting Siena as their first stopping place; then they went to Florence and settled in the famous Casa Guidi which became their home for the next fifteen years. Their placid, uneventful existence was broken only by occasional trips to England and France or to Venice and Rome. Tranquilly happy, they took a keen interest in the life about them, and particularly in Garibaldi's movement for the liberation of Italy, known as the *risorgimento.* Their only child, Robert Wiedemann Browning, was born in Florence in 1849.

As the *Sonnets from the Portuguese* show, Elizabeth Barrett Browning fulfilled herself in her marriage. We may picture the former sofa-ridden invalid, who had moved from one room to another with greatest difficulty, active as never before in her life: writing in the mornings, watching the crowds under their windows, going to market, caring for their child. She took occasional trips in a mule-cart, with her husband on horseback, through the olive groves and terraced vineyards of the Tuscan countryside. They made many friends, among them Nathaniel Hawthorne, William Wetmore Story, the American sculptor, from whom Browning took lessons in clay modeling, Charles Lever, the Irish novelist, and Margaret Fuller, literary critic of

Horace Greeley's *New York Tribune,* and first editor with Emerson of *The Dial.* Years before when Browning was largely unappreciated by the British public, Margaret Fuller had acclaimed *Bells and Pomegranates* in the *New York Tribune* as follows: "The plan of the sketches is original, the execution in many respects admirable, and the range of talent and perception they display, wider than that of any contemporary poet in England."

No flaws are to be found in the smooth domestic canvas of the Brownings; at least nothing more ominous than harmless differences of opinion. Mrs. Browning cherished three pet enthusiasms which her husband could not share: spiritualism, Napoleon the Third, and the cigar-smoking French novelist, George Sand, whose novels they both read as they came from the press.

Neither was opinionated, but toward these interests of his wife Browning developed a most uncharacteristic irritability. Threatened with a floating wreath about his own head, he upset a séance presided over by the famous medium, George Daniel Home. Following a visit to George Sand's salon in Paris, he did not scruple to voice his distaste for the red-capped bohemian set that buzzed around her. After Mrs. Browning's death, he published *Prince Hohenstiel-Schwangau,* an acidulous but quite fair portrait of the Third Napoleon who fancied himself the savior of mankind and whom Browning, with justice, completely distrusted. This distrust, incidentally, was shared by another poet, Heinrich Heine, who then lived as an exile in Paris.

Kindness and regard for others was deeply ingrained in Browning as son, brother, and later as husband. He who had escorted his mother to church, kissed her almost every night before going to bed until he was well over thirty, and accompanied his sister to concerts and lectures, came naturally to devote himself to his wife's comfort and well-being. They wrote letters to each other while living under the same roof, and Mrs. Browning was her husband's most dependable critic whose suggestions he accepted without question. Although by temperament gregarious, for ten years he refused invitations to dine out, because his wife was not well enough to go with him.

This unselfish devotion explains perhaps why the years in Italy, while extremely fruitful, did not advance his fame as rapidly as his wife's. However, with the publication in 1855 of the two-volumed work, *Men and Women,* his powers became widely recognized.

Elizabeth Barrett Browning died June 29, 1861, in her husband's arms. Of that last agonizing night in Florence he wrote Miss Isa Blagden: "Then came what my heart will keep till I see her again and longer—the most perfect expression of love for me within my whole knowledge of her. Always smiling happily, and with a face like a girl's, and in a few minutes she died in my arms, her head on my cheek." He wrote in a similar vein to his sister Sarianna. Browning has been accused of being insensible by reason of his meticulous descriptions of his wife's death in these two letters; but it must be recalled that he was writing to the persons closest to him and to his wife, and, moreover, that he did not look on death as the final term of existence. He found solace in the thought that death was, as he once put it, "merely the prolongation of that which we call life." The last image of the woman he loved was indelibly imprinted in his soul, and he felt that nothing could bar communion with his wife's spirit, for death was only "our churchyardy, crepe-like word for change and for growth."

When he had placed his son in school, he began again to go out into society. He took a house at Warwick Crescent in London and soon became a regular diner-out. A brilliant and profuse talker, he was in demand at country houses and in London drawing-rooms. His manner was hearty and unaffected, and Gladstone's daughter records that he was so wrapped up in the flow of his own talk that he brushed his whiskers against her cheek and puffed in her face. Browning was, as it were, an athletic conversationalist, not above slapping his listeners on the back. Now, if Browning had been an ivory-tower poet, one who trimmed and tended his wick in lonely aloofness, such a course might have worked to the detriment of the poetic impulse and its favorable expression. But Browning's best and deepest instincts linked him to people, to the thousand and one minutiae that make up the daily drama of life. Hence his creative vigor did not wane in the atmosphere of social appreciation. He was not in the slightest danger of being "all dinnered out," as some of his friends feared.

The University of Oxford awarded him an honorary fellowship, but he declined the rectorship of St. Andrews, an honor frequently reserved for literary men, for no better reason than that he had no stomach for public speeches. *Dramatis Personae,* which contains some of the finest of Browning's poems, was issued in 1864 and *The Ring and the Book,* a book-length poem, too long to be included in this selection, was published in the winter of 1868-69. *The Ring and the Book,*

> *A book in shape but, really, pure crude fact*
> *Secreted from man's life when hearts beat hard,*
> *And brains, high-blooded, ticked two centuries since,*

is based on a murder case tried in Rome in the seventeenth century, the record of which Browning came upon by chance on a vendor's stall in a public market in Florence, and from which, in the ripeness of his genius, he fashioned poetry of a very high order.

Browning passed his holidays in France, usually with his friend and admirer, Joseph Milsand, the critic, and on one of these trips he wrote *Gold Hair* and *Hervé Riel.* While he was visiting the mountains of Savoy, he was saddened by the sudden death of his dear friend, Miss Egerton-Smith. Speculating on personal life after death, he wrote *La Saisiaz.* He revisited Italy but could not bring himself to return to the familiar scenes in Florence. *Fifine at the Fair,* which also had a French background, appeared in 1872. A recurrence of his interest in Greek literature was shown in *Balaustion's Adventure,* an imaginary re-telling of Euripides' *Alcestis, Aristophanes' Apology,* and a translation of the *Agamemnon. Dramatic Idylls,* published in 1880 when Browning was sixty-eight years old, surprised even his most ardent votaries, for the new volume showed no diminution of his wonderful power and variety. Then came *Jocoseria, Ferishtah's Fancies,* and *Parleyings with Certain People of Importance,* all interspersed with lyrics that are shot through with a kind of unfading youthful fire.

He was in Venice with his sister, his son and daughter-in-law when, after a stroll in the night air, he fell ill with a severe bronchial affliction. His strength ebbed away swiftly, and on December 12, 1889, at the age of seventy-seven, he died. Just a few minutes before the end, he was told of the publication of his last volume, *Asolando.* "That is good," he commented, and passed away. He was buried in the Poet's Corner of Westminster Abbey.

After attending the Browning rites in the Abbey, Henry James summed up the essential attributes of the man and the poet: "His voice sounds loudest and clearest for the things we like best—the fascination of faith, and acceptance of life, the respect for its mysteries, the endurance of its changes, the vitality of the will, the validity of character, the beauty of action, the seriousness, above all, of the great human passion."

In the earlier stages of Robert Browning's career, roughly from 1833 to 1866, the poet suffered popular neglect and, save for Fox and Forster, criticism of his work was on the whole rather obtuse. In England and the United States his wife was hailed as a far greater poet than her erudite and somewhat obscure husband. Both Margaret Fuller and Edgar Allan Poe shared this view.

During the thirty years following the publication in 1869 of *The Ring and the Book,* which was at once acclaimed a masterpiece, Browning's fame advanced by leaps and bounds. Widely read and quoted, he was clothed with the mantle of a teacher, and his obscurity as well as his grotesquerie was accepted, generally, as the mark of his profundity if not of his sovereign gift as a poet. Criticism busied itself with his philosophy and his message and endeavored to make a seer out of him. Digging into Browning's poems for esoteric meanings became an intellectual pastime. The first Browning Club, instigated by the Shakespearean scholar, F. J. Furnival, got under way in 1881, and the cult soon spread over England and the United States. The poet took small notice of these incense bearers. Holding himself aloof, he neither approved nor disapproved of their publications devoted to exegesis. It was fruitless to bombard the aging poet with queries as to the intent of this or that passage. The truth was that he himself could not always recall his original meaning or mood. Once he wrote to Ruskin what must have struck that critic as a most astonishing dictum: "A poet's affair is with God, to Whom he is accountable, and of Whom is his reward."

In the Classics Club edition, introductory notes have been provided for those poems which seemed to require comment as to their source, content, or significance. A brief glossary has also been prepared for the convenience of readers. The notes and glossary may be consulted before or after reading the poem—or ignored entirely. Aestheticians would prefer readers to grapple with a work of art unaided before resorting to a commentator's help. The reader will of course follow his own taste in this matter, as does the concert-goer with his program notes.

By 1895 Browning was enshrined among the galaxy of famous Victorians, even though the irreverent younger writers of the 'Nineties judged him somewhat prosy and pompous. Oscar Wilde, for example, could not resist the quip: "Meredith is a prose Browning and so is Browning." After the turn of the century, there was a slight decline in his reputation, although he was never without hosts of fervid admirers.

Since the first World War, Browning has again been swept into the stream of living English poetry, a source of creativeness to many young poets who have dipped their pens in his nectar mixed with wormwood. Of modern appeal in particular is his conversational style and likewise his habit of choosing remote subject-matter and far-fetched association, and suggested rather than complete statement. Ezra Pound, E. A. Robinson, T. S. Eliot, and W. H. Auden owe him much. Others have caught from him the habit of using colloquial speech and elliptical mannerisms, while discarding his firm religious faith and strong sense of moral values.

Life was immensely absorbing to Browning even when it showed as evil, which he accepted along with the good. You could count on him to turn down a by-street no matter how scrubby and mean it looked. He had, like the poet of Valladolid in *How it Strikes a Contemporary,* a "scrutinizing hat," and he was, like him, "God's spy." His zest for the human scene was gargantuan, and he seemed to write for the pure joy of writing, to fling off a thought or a mood, or to seize a character. But he was equally fond of taking a classic and reworking it in modern terms. He borrowed forms from other lands and literatures, but what he took he always made his own. His versatility is shown in his use of more than a hundred different meters.

Browning had a keen interest in history, art, music, and literature, and Italy stimulated him in all these fields. Love as a force for good or evil was for him a subject of unceasing study. In *Men and Women* critical opinion has seen the fusing of all these elements with such ripeness of poetic expression that Browning has been hailed as the last eminent figure in the great tradition of English poetry.

He was bold, learned, and original. In *The Ring and the Book,* for example, with grandiose courage he risks telling his seventeenth-century murder tale in twelve books, and from the point of view of each of the principals. He needed many human lights on his horror story, to reveal the strangeness and the subtlety of human nature. In *Pippa Passes* he weaves a series of vignettes, stringing them on the thread of Pippa and her songs. He made use of his eccentric sense of form to reveal in an extremely personal way what he saw and felt and thought. This often gives his poems the appearance of the grotesque. Often the grotesque emerges in exaggerated relief when a landscape, a book, a face, is seen in microscopic detail. An airplane view misses jagged rocks, unsightly stumps, weeds, toadstools, newts and frogs: small things but created by God; and if you overlook them you cast away an incalculable opportunity to come close to life and nature. These minute phenomena make the whole important. Hideously contorted as the gargoyle on the church cornice may be, still it fits into the design of the architectural and spiritual beauty of the cathedral.

The modern mind did not invent ugliness, nor was it the first to call attention to it. In the old Flemish painters, as in the primitives, shocking drolleries abound, drolleries which Browning, with his always questing antennae, appreciated highly:

men with pig's snouts; sirens with fish-tails; horned and crooked monsters; demons who flogged sinners in a rollickingly mad Walpurgis night. The poet valued the crude and grotesque in the same way that a painter might choose for his subjects dark and eerie landscapes or slum streets.

Browning's poetic method was influenced by his basic ideas. To Browning, said a humorist, life was a gymnasium where we could exercise our muscles for the everlasting track and field day. This figure is accurate, if somewhat irreverent. He was a firm believer in personal immortality. Incompleteness on earth gave promise of completeness in the life beyond. Ugliness, self-denial, sorrow—themes of human lament—are, he held, human prerogatives: they form the crucible of experience, provide the testing ground for growth. Browning, the so-called optimist, bared his senses and his heart to so much evidence of misery in the world that we may well wonder he did not issue from the ordeal a thoroughgoing pessimist. Another might have succumbed, but he clung fast to his vision, seeing the hand of God in all creation:

> *The beauty and the wonder and power,*
> *The shapes of things, their colors, lights, and shades,*
> *Changes, surprises—and God made them all!*

In Browning's view, every act of creation implied a struggle, and the aim of the creative mind is laid bare step by step in the process. Just as God's handiwork reveals itself in small things as in great, the poet reveals himself in every word; and this may explain in part why Browning strove to load every rift with the ore of his meaning. His opinion of the role of the poet he carried over to his concept of Deity. He concludes that God loves His creatures precisely as an artist loves his creation. Hence he finds it reasonable to pray to his Maker to remake him until he is complete, a god in the germ.

Browning's enormous energy exploded in verbal rockets but it also flowed in a quiet beauty derived from his healthy belief in men and women, and from his devotion to progress. He never faltered in his faith in a divine plan. But man achieves heaven through trial: good is inescapably bound up with evil. "Good struggles, but evil reigns," he tells us, a statement which supplements rather than contradicts

God's in his heaven—
All's right with the world!

PIERRE LOVING

THE SELECTED POEMS
of
Robert Browning

Concluding Lines from *Pauline*

1832

Pauline *is a long and confused outpouring in which are revealed the vague dreams, passions, and aspirations of an idealistic youth. Shelley is the "Sun-treader" to whom these last lines of* Pauline *are addressed. The words "I believe in God and truth and love" have that robust and dynamic quality so characteristic of the mature poet and sound the keynote of his life and work.*

Sun-treader, I believe in God and truth
And love; and as one just escaped from death
Would bind himself in bands of friends to feel
He lives indeed, so, I would lean on thee!
Thou must be ever with me, most in gloom
If such must come, but chiefly when I die,
For I seem, dying, as one going in the dark
To fight a giant: but live thou for ever,
And be to all what thou hast been to me!
All in whom this wakes pleasant thoughts of me
Know my last state is happy, free from doubt
Or touch of fear. Love me and wish me well.

Four Songs from *Paracelsus*

1835

Published when Browning was twenty-three, Paracelsus *was hailed by his contemporaries as "a marvelous production of youthful genius." The protagonist of this long poetic drama is the great Renaissance physician and chemist, Paracelsus, whose adventures and real achievements stirred Browning profoundly. The poem dramatizes the vanity of Paracelsus' search for knowledge without love. The poet Aprile, who symbolizes love as a way of life, sings in the following song of those who fail to heed the inner voice or to use the gifts God gave them.*

I

I hear a voice, perchance I heard
Long ago, but all too low,
So that scarce a care it stirred
If the voice were real or no:
I heard it in my youth when first
The waters of my life outburst:
But, now their stream ebbs faint, I hear
That voice, still low, but fatal-clear—
As if all poets, God ever meant
Should save the world, and therefore lent
Great gifts to, but who, proud, refused
To do his work, or lightly used
Those gifts, or failed through weak endeavour,
So, mourn cast off by him for ever,—
As if these leaned in airy ring
To take me; this the song they sing.

"Lost, lost! yet come,
With our wan troop make thy home.
Come, come! for we
Will not breathe, so much as breathe
Reproach to thee,

Knowing what thou sink'st beneath.
So sank we in those old years,
We who bid thee, come! thou last
Who, living yet, hast life o'erpast.
And altogether we, thy peers,
Will pardon crave for thee, the last
Whose trial is done, whose lot is cast
With those who watch but work no more,
Who gaze on life but live no more.
Yet we trusted thou shouldst speak
The message which our lips, too weak,
Refused to utter,—shouldst redeem
Our fault: such trust, and all a dream!
Yet we chose thee a birthplace
Where the richness ran to flowers:
Couldst not sing one song for grace?
Not make one blossom man's and ours?
Must one more recreant to his race
Die with unexerted powers,
And join us, leaving as he found
The world, he was to loosen, bound?
Anguish! ever and for ever;
Still beginning, ending never.
Yet, lost and last one, come!
How couldst understand, alas,
What our pale ghosts strove to say,
As their shades did glance and pass
Before thee night and day?
Thou wast blind as we were dumb:
Once more, therefore, come, O come!
How should we clothe, how arm the spirit
Shall next thy post of life inherit—
How guard him from thy speedy ruin?
Tell us of thy sad undoing
Here, where we sit, ever pursuing
Our weary task, ever renewing
Sharp sorrow, far from God who gave
Our powers, and man they could not save!"

2

Paracelsus sings this song as he is dreaming of the distant travels of his youth.

Heap cassia, sandal-buds and stripes
  Of labdanum, and aloe-balls,
Smeared with dull nard an Indian wipes
  From out her hair: such balsam falls
  Down sea-side mountain pedestals,
From tree-tops where tired winds are fain,
Spent with the vast and howling main,
To treasure half their island-gain.
And strew faint sweetness from some old
  Egyptian's fine worm-eaten shroud
Which breaks to dust when once unrolled;
  Or shredded perfume, like a cloud
  From closet long to quiet vowed,
With mothed and dropping arras hung,
Mouldering her lute and books among,
As when a queen, long dead, was young.

3

In the form of a fable Paracelsus here tells his friend Festus of the unwillingness of searchers for truth to admit mistakes or tear down the shrines they have built.

  Over the sea our galleys went,
With cleaving prows in order brave,
To a speeding wind and a bounding wave,
  A gallant armament:
Each bark built out of a forest-tree,
  Left leafy and rough as first it grew,
And nailed all over the gaping sides,
Within and without, with black bull-hides,
Seethed in fat and suppled in flame,
To bear the playful billows' game:

So, each good ship was rude to see,
Rude and bare to the outward view,
  But each upbore a stately tent
Where cedar-pales in scented row
Kept out the flakes of the dancing brine,
And an awning drooped the mast below,
In fold on fold of the purple fine,
That neither noontide nor star-shine
Nor moonlight cold which maketh mad,
  Might pierce the regal tenement.
When the sun dawned, oh, gay and glad
We set the sail and plied the oar;
But when the night-wind blew like breath,
For joy of one day's voyage more,
We sang together on the wide sea,
Like men at peace on a peaceful shore;
Each sail was loosed to the wind so free,
Each helm made sure by the twilight star,
And in a sleep as calm as death,
We, the voyagers from afar,
  Lay stretched along, each weary crew
In a circle round its wondrous tent
Whence gleamed soft light and curled rich scent,
  And with light and perfume, music too:
So the stars wheeled round, and the darkness past,
And at morn we started beside the mast,
And still each ship was sailing fast!

Now, one morn, land appeared!—a speck
Dim trembling betwixt sea and sky:
"Avoid it," cried our pilot, "check
  The shout, restrain the eager eye!"
But the heaving sea was black behind
For many a night and many a day,
And land, though but a rock, drew nigh;
So, we broke the cedar pales away,

Let the purple awning flap in the wind,
  And a statue bright was on every deck!
We shouted, every man of us,
And steered right into the harbour thus,
With pomp and paean glorious.

A hundred shapes of lucid stone!
  All day we built its shrine for each,
A shrine of rock for every one,
Nor paused we till in the westering sun
  We sat together on the beach
To sing because our task was done.
When lo! what shouts and merry songs!
What laughter all the distance stirs!
A loaded raft with happy throngs
Of gentle islanders!
"Our isles are just at hand," they cried,
  "Like cloudlets faint in even sleeping;
Our temple-gates are opened wide,
  Our olive-groves thick shade are keeping
For these majestic forms"—they cried.
Oh, then we awoke with sudden start
From our deep dream, and knew, too late,
How bare the rock, how desolate,
Which had received our precious freight:
  Yet we called out—"Depart!
Our gifts, once given, must here abide.
  Our work is done; we have no heart
To mar our work,"—we cried.

4

Festus sings this simple lyric to the dying Paracelsus.

Thus the Mayne glideth
Where my Love abideth.
Sleep's no softer: it proceeds
On through lawns, on through meads,
On and on, whate'er befall,

Meandering and musical,
Though the niggard pasturage
Bears not on its shaven ledge
Aught but weeds and waving grasses
To view the river as it passes,
Save here and there a scanty patch
Of primroses too faint to catch
A weary bee.

Six Songs from *Pippa Passes*

1841

The following songs from Pippa Passes *are probably the most effective and the best known parts of that rather complicated drama in verse. It is constructed on the same principle as* Grand Hotel *and* The Bridge of San Luis Rey: *several unconnected lives are transfixed at their crucial points by some outside agency. In this case the outside agency is Pippa, a girl worker in a silk mill at Asolo who spends her single holiday of the year roaming about the town singing. To several people her songs come as an omen, affecting their decisions on the life-and-death problems confronting them.*

I

This humble hymn to God, for whom no human being is insignificant, is prophetic in view of the part the unknown little Pippa will play in the lives of people she calls Asolo's Four Happiest Ones.

All service ranks the same with God:
If now, as formerly he trod
Paradise, his presence fills
Our earth, each only as God wills
Can work—God's puppets, best and worst,
Are we; there is no last nor first.

Say not "a small event!" Why "small"?
Costs it more pain that this, ye call
A "great event," should come to pass,
Than that? Untwine me from the mass
Of deeds which make up life, one deed
Power shall fall short in or exceed!

2

Sebald, the lover of the dazzling and adulterous Ottima, whose husband he had just killed, hears this song. With its ring of confident innocence it has the effect of turning him from a rather exalted contemplation of his crime to remorse and horror.

The year's at the spring
And day's at the morn;
Morning's at seven;
The hill-side's dew-pearled;
The lark's on the wing;
The snail's on the thorn:
God's in his heaven—
All's right with the world!

3

Pippa sings this song under the window of the arrogant, idealistic sculptor, Jules, whom his dissolute fellow students tricked into marrying the beautiful but common artist's model, Phene. She tells the story of a page who loved far above his station, which sets Jules to thinking of the happiness of loving a woman "with utter need of me," and makes him realize the futility of revenge.

Give her but a least excuse to love me!
When—where
How—Can this arm establish her above me,
If fortune fixed her as my lady there,
There already, to eternally reprove me?

("Hist"—said Kate the queen;
But "Oh"—cried the maiden, binding her tresses,
" 'Tis only a page that carols unseen
Crumbling your hounds their messes!")

Is she wronged?—To the rescue of her honour,
My heart!
Is she poor?—What costs it to be styled a donor?
Merely an earth to cleave, a sea to part!
But that fortune should have thrust all this upon her!
("Nay, list,"—bade Kate the queen;
And still cried the maiden, binding her tresses,
" 'Tis only a page that carols unseen
Fitting your hawks their jesses!")

4

The effect of this song about the fabulous saintly king of yore is to strengthen young Luigi's wavering decision to set out on a mission of tyrannicide.

A king lived long ago,
In the morning of the world,
When earth was nigher heaven than now.
And the king's locks curled,
Disparting o'er a forehead full
As the milk-white space 'twixt horn and horn
Of some sacrificial bull—
Only calm as a babe new-born:
For he was got to a sleepy mood,
So safe from all decrepitude,
Age with its bane, so sure gone by,
(The gods so loved him while he dreamed)
That, having lived thus long, there seemed
No need the king should ever die.

Among the rocks his city was:
Before his palace, in the sun,
He sat to see his people pass,

And judge them every one
From its threshold of smooth stone.
They haled him many a valley-thief
Caught in the sheep-pens, robber-chief
Swarthy and shameless, beggar-cheat,
Spy-prowler, or rough pirate found
On the sea-sand left aground;
And sometimes clung about his feet,
With bleeding lip and burning cheek,
A woman, bitterest wrong to speak
Of one with sullen thickset brows:
And sometimes from the prison-house
The angry priests a pale wretch brought,
Who through some chink had pushed and pressed
On knees and elbows, belly and breast,
Worm-like into the temple,—caught
He was by the very god,
Who ever in the darkness strode
Backward and forward, keeping watch
O'er his brazen bowls, such rogues to catch!
These, all and every one,
The king judged, sitting in the sun.

His councillors, on left and right,
Looked anxious up,—but no surprise
Disturbed the king's old smiling eyes
Where the very blue had turned to white.
'Tis said, a Python scared one day
The breathless city, till he came,
With forky tongue and eyes on flame,
Where the old king sat to judge alway;
But when he saw the sweepy hair
Girt with a crown of berries rare
Which the god will hardly give to wear
To the maiden who singeth, dancing bare
In the altar-smoke by the pine torch lights,
At his wondrous forest rites,—

Seeing this he did not dare
Approach that threshold in the sun,
Assault the old king smiling there.
Such grace had kings when the world begun!

5

This song is sung by one of the poor girls Pippa meets on the steps of the Duomo S. Maria. It is merely a graceful, simple love song with a faint tinge of melancholy.

You'll love me yet!—and I can tarry
  Your love's protracted growing:
June reared that bunch of flowers you carry,
  From seeds of April's sowing.

I plant a heartfull now: some seed
  At least is sure to strike,
And yield—what you'll not pluck indeed,
  Not love, but, may be, like!

You'll look at least on love's remains,
  A grave's one violet:
Your look?—that pays a thousand pains.
  What's death!—You'll love me yet!

6

Monsignor has come to Asolo to demand the account of his dead brother's estate from the latter's villainous steward. The steward tries to bribe him by offering to get rid of the rightful heir to the estate. At that moment of temptation comes Pippa's song telling of purity and the love of God; and the prelate repudiates his tempter.

Overhead the tree-tops meet,
Flowers and grass spring 'neath one's feet;
There was nought above me, nought below,
My childhood had not learned to know:
For, what are the voices of birds

—Ay, and of beasts,—but words, our words,
Only so much more sweet?
The knowledge of that with my life begun.
But I had so near made out the sun,
And counted your stars, the seven and one,
Like the fingers of my hand:
Nay, I could all but understand
Wherefore through heaven the white moon ranges;
And just when out of her soft fifty changes
No unfamiliar face might overlook me—
Suddenly God took me.

Dramatic Lyrics

1842

CAVALIER TUNES

While absorbing the lore of the English Civil Wars which formed the background of his poetic play, Strafford, *Browning wrote these stirring lyrics which he imagines being sung by the Cavaliers who fought for the King against Cromwell. Browning's sympathies, however, were not with these "great-hearted gentlemen," but with the Parliamentarians in their struggle against the "divine right of kings."*

Marching Along

I

Kentish Sir Byng stood for his King,
Bidding the crop-headed Parliament swing:
And, pressing a troop unable to stoop
And see the rogues flourish and honest folk droop,
Marched them along, fifty-score strong,
Great-hearted gentlemen, singing this song.

2

God for King Charles! Pym and such carles
To the Devil that prompts 'em their treasonous parles!
Cavaliers, up! Lips from the cup,
Hands from the pasty, nor bite take nor sup
Till you're—
CHORUS: *Marching along, fifty-score strong,*
Great-hearted gentlemen, singing this song.

3

Hampden to Hell, and his obsequies' knell
Serve Hazelrig, Fiennes, and young Harry as well!
England, good cheer! Rupert is near!
Kentish and loyalists, keep we not here
CHORUS: *Marching along, fifty-score strong,*
Great-hearted gentlemen, singing this song.

4

Then, God for King Charles! Pym and his snarls
To the Devil that pricks on such pestilent carles!
Hold by the right, you double your might;
So, onward to Nottingham, fresh for the fight,
CHORUS: *March we along, fifty-score strong,*
Great-hearted gentlemen, singing this song!

Give a Rouse

I

King Charles, and who'll do him right now?
King Charles, and who's ripe for fight now?
Give a rouse: here's, in Hell's despite now,
King Charles!

2

Who gave me the goods that went since?
Who raised me the house that sank once?
Who helped me to gold I spent since?
Who found me in wine you drank once?
CHORUS: *King Charles, and who'll do him right now?*
King Charles, and who's ripe for fight now?
Give a rouse: here's, in Hell's despite now,
King Charles!

3

To whom used my boy George quaff else,
By the old fool's side that begot him?
For whom did he cheer and laugh else,
While Noll's damned troopers shot him?
CHORUS: *King Charles, and who'll do him right now?*
King Charles, and who's ripe for fight now?
Give a rouse: here's, in Hell's despite now,
King Charles!

Boot and Saddle

1

Boot, saddle, to horse, and away!
Rescue my castle before the hot day
Brightens to blue from its silvery grey,
CHORUS: *Boot, saddle, to horse, and away!*

2

Ride past the suburbs, asleep as you'd say;
Many's the friend there will listen and pray
"God's luck to gallants that strike up the lay—
CHORUS: *Boot, saddle, to horse, and away!"*

3

Forty miles off, like a roebuck at bay,
Flouts Castle Brancepeth the Roundheads' array:
Who laughs, "Good fellows ere this, by my fay,
  CHORUS: *Boot, saddle, to horse, and away!"*

4

Who? My wife Gertrude; that, honest and gay,
Laughs when you talk of surrendering, "Nay!
I've better counsellors; what counsel they?
  CHORUS: *Boot, saddle, to horse, and away!"*

MY LAST DUCHESS

Ferrara

This famous monologue owes its inspiration to Browning's first trip to Italy in 1834. The hardness and cruelty of the Renaissance under its surface richness and polish is personified in the figure of the Duke of Ferrara. He is showing the portrait of his late wife, whom he had quietly done away with, to an intermediary sent by the father of the girl he expects to marry.

That's my last Duchess painted on the wall,
Looking as if she were alive. I call
That piece a wonder, now: Frà Pandolf's hands
Worked busily a day, and there she stands.
Will 't please you sit and look at her? I said
"Frà Pandolf" by design, for never read
Strangers like you that pictured countenance,
The depth and passion of its earnest glance,
But to myself they turned (since none puts by
The curtain I have drawn for you, but I)
And seemed as they would ask me, if they durst,

How such a glance came there; so, not the first
Are you to turn and ask thus. Sir, 't was not
Her husband's presence only, called that spot
Of joy into the Duchess' cheek: perhaps
Frà Pandolf chanced to say "Her mantle laps
Over my lady's wrist too much," or "Paint
Must never hope to reproduce the faint
Half-flush that dies along her throat": such stuff
Was courtesy, she thought, and cause enough
For calling up that spot of joy. She had
A heart—how shall I say?—too soon made glad,
Too easily impressed; she liked whate'er
She looked on, and her looks went everywhere.
Sir, 't was all one! My favour at her breast,
The dropping of the daylight in the West,
The bough of cherries some officious fool
Broke in the orchard for her, the white mule
She rode with round the terrace—all and each
Would draw from her alike the approving speech,
Or blush, at least. She thanked men,—good! but thanked
Somehow—I know not how—as if she ranked
My gift of a nine-hundred-years-old name
With anybody's gift. Who 'd stoop to blame
This sort of trifling? Even had you skill
In speech—(which I have not)—to make your will
Quite clear to such an one, and say, "Just this
Or that in you disgusts me; here you miss,
Or there exceed the mark"—and if she let
Herself be lessoned so, nor plainly set
Her wits to yours, forsooth, and made excuse,
—E'en then would be some stooping; and I choose
Never to stoop. Oh sir, she smiled, no doubt,
Whene'er I passed her; but who passed without
Much the same smile? This grew; I gave commands;
Then all smiles stopped together. There she stands
As if alive. Will 't please you rise? We 'll meet
The company below, then. I repeat,

The Count your master's known munificence
Is ample warrant that no just pretence
Of mine for dowry will be disallowed;
Though his fair daughter's self, as I avowed
At starting, is my object. Nay, we 'll go
Together down, sir! Notice Neptune, though,
Taming a sea-horse, thought a rarity,
Which Claus of Innsbruck cast in bronze for me!

INCIDENT OF THE FRENCH CAMP

There is no historical foundation for this tale of youthful heroism which is so popular with children. During the Napoleonic wars, however, the French did storm Ratisbon (now Regensburg, in Bavaria) under Marshal Jean Lannes.

1

You know, we French stormed Ratisbon:
  A mile or so away,
On a little mound, Napoleon
  Stood on our storming-day;
With neck out-thrust, you fancy how,
  Legs wide, arms locked behind,
As if to balance the prone brow
  Oppressive with its mind.

2

Just as perhaps he mused "My plans
  That soar, to earth may fall,
Let once my army-leader Lannes
  Waver at yonder wall,"—
Out 'twixt the battery-smokes there flew
  A rider, bound on bound
Full-galloping; nor bridle drew
  Until he reached the mound.

3

Then off there flung in smiling joy,
And held himself erect
By just his horse's mane, a boy:
You hardly could suspect—
(So tight he kept his lips compressed,
Scarce any blood came through)
You looked twice ere you saw his breast
Was all but shot in two.

4

"Well," cried he, "Emperor, by God's grace
We've got you Ratisbon!
The Marshal's in the market-place,
And you'll be there anon
To see your flag-bird flap his vans
Where I, to heart's desire,
Perched him!" The chief's eye flashed; his plans
Soared up again like fire.

5

The chief's eye flashed; but presently
Softened itself, as sheathes
A film the mother-eagle's eye
When her bruised eaglet breathes;
"You're wounded!" "Nay," the soldier's pride
Touched to the quick, he said:
"I'm killed, Sire!" And his chief beside
Smiling the boy fell dead.

SOLILOQUY OF THE SPANISH CLOISTER

Browning here gives us a glimpse of repressed hate seething beneath the surface serenity of monastery life. In a few short verses he builds up his two contrasting characters—the narrator, whose "interior monologue" reveals his warped, wry, cynical mind, and the pious, garden-loving monk whom he hates with such concentrated venom.

1

Gr-r-r—there go, my heart's abhorrence!
  Water your damned flower-pots, do!
If hate killed men, Brother Lawrence,
  God's blood, would not mine kill you!
What? your myrtle-bush wants trimming?
  Oh, that rose has prior claims—
Needs its leaden vase filled brimming?
  Hell dry you up with its flames!

2

At the meal we sit together:
  Salve tibi! I must hear
Wise talk of the kind of weather,
  Sort of season, time of year:
*Not a plenteous cork-crop; scarcely
  Dare we hope oak-galls, I doubt:
What's the Latin name for "parsley"?*
  What's the Greek name for Swine's Snout?

3

Whew! We 'll have our platter burnished,
  Laid with care on our own shelf!
With a fire-new spoon we 're furnished,
  And a goblet for ourself,
Rinsed like something sacrificial
  Ere 't is fit to touch our chaps—
Marked with L. for our initial!
  (He-he! There his lily snaps!)

4

Saint, forsooth! While brown Dolores
Squats outside the Convent bank
With Sanchicha, telling stories,
Steeping tresses in the tank,
Blue-black, lustrous, thick like horse-hairs,
—Can't I see his dead eye glow,
Bright as 't were a Barbary corsair's?
(That is, if he 'd let it show!)

5

When he finishes refection,
Knife and fork he never lays
Cross-wise, to my recollection,
As do I, in Jesu's praise.
I the Trinity illustrate,
Drinking watered orange-pulp—
In three sips the Arian frustrate;
While he drains his at one gulp.

6

Oh, those melons? If he 's able
We 're to have a feast! so nice!
One goes to the Abbot's table,
All of us get each a slice.
How go on your flowers? None double?
Not one fruit-sort can you spy?
Strange!—And I, too, at such trouble,
Keep them close-nipped on the sly!

7

There 's a great text in Galatians,
Once you trip on it, entails
Twenty-nine distinct damnations,
One sure, if another fails:

If I trip him just a-dying,
  Sure of heaven as sure as can be,
Spin him round and send him flying
  Off to hell, a Manichee?

8

Or, my scrofulous French novel
  On grey paper with blunt type!
Simply glance at it, you grovel
  Hand and foot in Belial's gripe:
If I double down its pages
  At the woeful sixteenth print,
When he gathers his greengages,
  Ope a sieve and slip it in 't?

9

Or, there 's Satan!—one might venture
  Pledge one's soul to him, yet leave
Such a flaw in the indenture
  As he 'd miss till, past retrieve,
Blasted lay that rose-acacia
  We 're so proud of! *Hy, Zy, Hine* . . .
'St, there 's Vespers! *Plena gratiâ*
  Ave, Virgo! Gr-r-r—you swine!

WARING

The original of Waring *was Alfred Domett, an intimate friend of Browning's when the two were young men in Camberwell. He was an ardent defender of Browning's poetry when it had few admirers. Domett was versatile and gifted; he wrote poetry, traveled widely, and eventually settled in New Zealand where he became prime minister. Browning, by adroit suggestion, builds up an impressionistic portrait of a many-sided, almost fabulous person—one who might have turned up anywhere on the globe, doing practically anything.*

I

1

What's become of Waring
Since he gave us all the slip,
Chose land-travel or seafaring,
Boots and chest or staff and scrip,
Rather than pace up and down
Any longer London town?

2

Who'd have guessed it from his lip
Or his brow's accustomed bearing,
On the night he thus took ship
Or started landward?—little caring
For us, it seems, who supped together
(Friends of his too, I remember)
And walked home thro' the merry weather,
The snowiest in all December.
I left his arm that night myself
For what's-his-name's, the new prose-poet
Who wrote the book there, on the shelf—
How, forsooth, was I to know it
If Waring meant to glide away
Like a ghost at break of day?
Never looked he half so gay!

3

He was prouder than the devil:
How he must have cursed our revel!
Ay and many other meetings,
Indoor visits, outdoor greetings,

As up and down he paced this London,
With no work done, but great works undone,
Where scarce twenty knew his name.
Why not, then, have earlier spoken,
Written, bustled? Who's to blame
If your silence kept unbroken?
"True, but there were sundry jottings,
Stray-leaves, fragments, blurrs and blottings,
Certain first steps were achieved
Already which"—(is that your meaning?)
"Had well borne out whoe'er believed
In more to come!" But who goes gleaning
Hedgeside chance-glades, while full-sheaved
Stand cornfields by him? Pride, o'er-weening
Pride alone, puts forth such claims
O'er the day's distinguished names.

4

Meantime, how much I loved him,
I find out now I've lost him.
I who cared not if I moved him,
Who could so carelessly accost him,
Henceforth never shall get free
Of his ghostly company,
His eyes that just a little wink
As deep I go into the merit
Of this and that distinguished spirit—
His cheeks' raised color, soon to sink,
As long I dwell on some stupendous
And tremendous (Heaven defend us!)
Monstr'-inform'-ingens-horrend-ous
Demoniaco-seraphic
Penman's latest piece of graphic.
Nay, my very wrist grows warm
With his dragging weight of arm!
E'en so, swimmingly appears,
Through one's after-supper musings,

Some Lost Lady of old years
With her beauteous vain endeavour
And goodness unrepaid as ever;
The face, accustomed to refusings,
We, puppies that we were . . . Oh never
Surely, nice of conscience, scrupled
Being aught like false, forsooth, to?
Telling aught but honest truth to?
What a sin, had we centupled
Its possessor's grace and sweetness!
No! she heard in its completeness
Truth, for truth's a weighty matter,
And truth, at issue, we can't flatter!
Well, 'tis done with; she's exempt
From damning us thro' such a sally;
And so she glides, as down a valley,
Taking up with her contempt,
Past our reach; and in, the flowers
Shut her unregarded hours.

5

Oh, could I have him back once more,
This Waring, but one half-day more!
Back, with the quiet face of yore,
So hungry for acknowledgment
Like mine! I'd fool him to his bent!
Feed, should not he, to heart's content?
I'd say, "to only have conceived
Your great works, though they ne'er make progress,
Surpasses all we've yet achieved!"
I'd lie so, I should be believed.
I'd make such havoc of the claims
Of the day's distinguished names
To feast him with, as feasts an ogress
Her sharp-toothed golden-crowned child!
Or, as one feasts a creature rarely
Captured here, unreconciled
To capture; and completely gives

Its pettish humours license, barely
Requiring that it lives.

6

Ichabod, Ichabod,
The glory is departed!
Travels Waring East away?
Who, of knowledge, by hearsay,
Reports a man upstarted
Somewhere as a God,
Hordes grown European-hearted,
Millions of the wild made tame
On a sudden at his fame?
In Vishnu-land what Avatar?
Or who, in Moscow, toward the Czar,
With the demurest of footfalls
Over the Kremlin's pavement, bright
With serpentine and syenite,
Steps, with five other Generals
That simultaneously take snuff,
For each to have pretext enough
To kerchiefwise unfold his sash
Which, softness' self, is yet the stuff
To hold fast where a steel chain snaps,
And leave the grand white neck no gash?
Waring, in Moscow, to those rough
Cold northern natures borne, perhaps,
Like the lambwhite maiden dear
From the circle of mute kings
Unable to repress the tear,
Each as his sceptre down he flings,
To Dian's fane at Taurica,
Where now a captive priestess, she alway
Mingles her tender grave Hellenic speech
With theirs, tuned to the hailstone-beaten beach,
As pours some pigeon, from the myrrhy lands
Rapt by the whirlblast to fierce Scythian strands
Where breed the swallows, her melodious cry

Amid their barbarous twitter!
In Russia? Never! Spain were fitter!
Ay, most likely 'tis in Spain
That we and Waring meet again
Now, while he turns down that cool narrow lane
Into the blackness, out of grave Madrid
All fire and shine, abrupt as when there's slid
Its stiff gold blazing pall
From some black coffin-lid.
Or, best of all,
I love to think
The leaving us was just a feint;
Back here to London did he slink,
And now works on without a wink
Of sleep, and we are on the brink
Of something great in fresco-paint:
Some garret's ceiling, walls and floor,
Up and down and o'er and o'er
He splashes, as none splashed before
Since great Caldara Polidore.
Or Music means this land of ours
Some favour yet, to pity won
By Purcell from his Rosy Bowers,—
"Give me my so-long promised son,
Let Waring end what I begun!"
Then down he creeps and out he steals
Only when the night conceals
His face; in Kent 'tis cherry-time,
Or, hops are picking: or, at prime
Of March, he wanders as, too happy,
Years ago when he was young,
Some mild eve when woods grew sappy
And the early moths had sprung
To life from many a trembling sheath
Woven the warm boughs beneath;
While small birds said to themselves
What should soon be actual song,
And young gnats, by tens and twelves,

Made as if they were the throng
That crowd around and carry aloft
The sound they have nursed, so sweet and pure,
Out of a myriad noises soft,
Into a tone that can endure
Amid the noise of a July noon
When all God's creatures crave their boon,
All at once and all in tune,
And get it, happy as Waring then,
Having first within his ken
What a man might do with men:
And far too glad, in the even-glow,
To mix with the world he meant to take
Into his hand, he told you, so—
And out of it his world to make,
To contract and to expand
As he shut or oped his hand.
Oh, Waring, what's to really be?
A clear stage and a crowd to see!
Some Garrick—say—out shall not he
The heart of Hamlet's mystery pluck?
Or, where most unclean beasts are rife,
Some Junius—am I right?—shall tuck
His sleeve, and forth with flaying-knife!
Some Chatterton shall have the luck
Of calling Rowley into life!
Some one shall somehow run amuck
With this old world, for want of strife
Sound asleep. Contrive, contrive
To rouse us, Waring! Who's alive?
Our men scarce seem in earnest now.
Distinguished names!—but 'tis, somehow,
As if they played at being names
Still more distinguished, like the games
Of children. Turn our sport to earnest
With a visage of the sternest!
Bring the real times back, confessed
Still better than our very best!

II

1

"When I last saw Waring . . ."
(How all turned to him who spoke—
You saw Waring? Truth or joke?
In land-travel, or sea-faring?)

2

"We were sailing by Triest,
Where a day or two we harboured:
A sunset was in the West,
When, looking over the vessel's side,
One of our company espied
A sudden speck to larboard.
And, as a sea-duck flies and swims
At once, so came the light craft up,
With its sole lateen sail that trims
And turns (the water round its rims
Dancing, as round a sinking cup)
And by us like a fish it curled,
And drew itself up close beside,
Its great sail on the instant furled,
And o'er its planks, a shrill voice cried,
(A neck as bronzed as a Lascar's)
'Buy wine of us, you English Brig?
Or fruit, tobacco and cigars?
A Pilot for you to Triest?
Without one, look you ne'er so big,
They'll never let you up the bay!
We natives should know best.'
I turned, and 'just those fellows' way,'
Our captain said, 'The 'long-shore thieves
Are laughing at us in their sleeves.'

3

"In truth, the boy leaned laughing back;
And one, half-hidden by his side
Under the furled sail, soon I spied,
With great grass hat and kerchief black,
Who looked up with his kingly throat,
Said somewhat, while the other shook
His hair back from his eyes to look
Their longest at us; then the boat,
I know not how, turned sharply round,
Laying her whole side on the sea
As a leaping fish does; from the lee,
Into the weather, cut somehow
Her sparkling path beneath our bow;
And so went off, as with a bound,
Into the rosy and golden half
Of the sky, to overtake the sun
And reach the shore, like the sea-calf
Its singing cave; yet I caught one
Glance ere away the boat quite passed,
And neither time nor toil could mar
Those features: so I saw the last
Of Waring!"—You? Oh, never star
Was lost here, but it rose afar!
Look East, where whole new thousands are!
In Vishnu-land what Avatar?

IN A GONDOLA

The starting point for this dramatic dialogue was a painting by Maclise called "The Serenade" which a friend of Browning's had seen and described to him. The scene was Venice, and since Browning had only lately returned from a visit to that city, he seized upon the idea of a pair of guilty lovers and developed it into this lyrical melodrama. After viewing the painting he added more verses.

He sings

I send my heart up to thee, all my heart
  In this my singing
For the stars help me, and the sea bears part;
  The very night is clinging
Closer to Venice's streets to leave one space
  Above me, whence thy face
May light my joyous heart to thee its dwelling-place.

She speaks

Say after me, and try to say
My very words, as if each word
Came from you of your own accord,
In your own voice, in your own way:
"This woman's heart and soul and brain
Are mine as much as this gold chain
She bids me wear; which (say again)
I choose to make by cherishing
A precious thing, or choose to fling
Over the boat-side, ring by ring."
And yet once more say . . . no word more!
Since words are only words. Give o'er!
Unless you call me, all the same,
Familiarly by my pet-name
Which, if the Three should hear you call,
And me reply to, would proclaim
At once our secret to them all.
Ask of me, too, command me, blame—
Do, break down the partition-wall
'Twixt us, the daylight world beholds
Curtained in dusk and splendid folds.
What's left but—all of me to take?
I am the Three's: prevent them, slake
Your thirst! 'Tis said, the Arab sage

In practising with gems can loose
Their subtle spirit in his cruce
And leave but ashes: so, sweet mage,
Leave them my ashes when thy use
Sucks out my soul, thy heritage!

He sings

1

Past we glide, and past, and past!
  What's that poor Agnese doing
Where they make the shutters fast?
  Grey Zanobi's just a-wooing
To his couch the purchased bride:
  Past we glide!

2

Past we glide, and past, and past!
  Why's the Pucci Palace flaring
Like a beacon to the blast?
  Guests by hundreds, not one caring
If the dear host's neck were wried:
  Past we glide!

She sings

1

The Moth's kiss, first!
Kiss me as if you made believe
You were not sure, this eve,
How my face, your flower, had pursed
Its petals up; so, here and there
You brush it, till I grow aware
Who wants me, and wide open burst.

2

The Bee's kiss now!
Kiss me as if you entered gay
My heart at some noonday,

A bud that dares not disallow
The claim, so all is rendered up,
And passively its shattered cup
Over your head to sleep I bow.

He sings

I

What are we two?
I am a Jew,
And carry thee, farther than friends can pursue,
To a feast of our tribe;
Where they need thee to bribe
The devil that blasts them unless he imbibe
Thy . . . scatter the vision for ever! And now,
As of old, I am I, Thou art Thou!

2

Say again, what we are?
The sprite of a star,
I lure thee above where the destinies bar
My plumes their full play
Till a ruddier ray
Than my pale one announce there is withering away
Some . . . Scatter the vision for ever! And now,
As of old, I am I, Thou art Thou!

He muses

Oh, which were best, to roam or rest?
The land's lap or the water's breast?
To sleep on yellow millet-sheaves,
Or swim in lucid shallows, just
Eluding water-lily leaves,
An inch from Death's black fingers, thrust
To lock you, whom release he must;
Which life were best on Summer eves?

He speaks, musing

Lie back; could thought of mine improve you?
From this shoulder let there spring
A wing; from this, another wing;
Wings, not legs and feet, shall move you!
Snow-white must they spring, to blend
With your flesh, but I intend
They shall deepen to the end,
Broader, into burning gold,
Till both wings crescent-wise enfold
Your perfect self, from 'neath your feet
To o'er your head, where, lo, they meet
As if a million sword-blades hurled
Defiance from you to the world!

Rescue me Thou, the only real!
And scare away this mad Ideal
That came, nor motions to depart!
Thanks! Now, stay ever as thou art!

Still he muses

I

What if the Three should catch at last
Thy serenader? While there's cast
Paul's cloak about my head, and fast
Gian pinions me, Himself has past
His stylet thro' my back; I reel;
And . . . is it Thou I feel?

2

They trail me, these three godless knaves,
Past every church that sains and saves,
Nor stop till, where the cold sea raves
By Lido's wet accursed graves,
They scoop mine, roll me to its brink,
And . . . on Thy breast I sink!

She replies, musing

Dip your arm o'er the boat-side, elbow-deep,
As I do: thus: were death so unlike sleep,
Caught this way? Death's to fear from flame, or steel,
Or poison doubtless; but from water—feel!
Go find the bottom! Would you stay me! There!
Now pluck a great blade of that ribbon-grass
To plait in where the foolish jewel was,
I flung away: since you have praised my hair,
'Tis proper to be choice in what I wear.

He speaks

Row home? must we row home? Too surely
Know I where its front's demurely
Over the Giudecca piled;
Window just with window mating,
Door on door exactly waiting,
All's the set face of a child:
But behind it, where's a trace
Of the staidness and reserve,
And formal lines without a curve,
In the same child's playing-face?
No two windows look one way
O'er the small sea-water thread
Below them. Ah, the autumn day
I, passing, saw you overhead!
First, out a cloud of curtain blew,
Then, a sweet cry, and last, came you—
To catch your lory that must needs
Escape just then, of all times then,
To peck a tall plant's fleecy seeds,
And make me happiest of men.
I scarce could breathe to see you reach
So far back o'er the balcony,
(To catch him ere he climbed too high
Above you in the Smyrna peach)

That quick the round smooth cord of gold,
This coiled hair on your head, unrolled,
Fell down you like a gorgeous snake
The Roman girls were wont, of old,
When Rome there was, for coolness' sake
To let lie curling o'er their bosoms.
Dear lory, may his beak retain
Ever its delicate rose stain
As if the wounded lotus-blossoms
Had marked their thief to know again!

Stay longer yet, for others' sake
Than mine! what should your chamber do?
—With all its rarities that ache
In silence while day lasts, but wake
At night-time and their life renew,
Suspended just to pleasure you
That brought against their will together
These objects and, while day lasts, weave
Around them such a magic tether
That they look dumb: your harp, believe,
With all the sensitive tight strings
That dare not speak, now to itself
Breathes slumberously as if some elf
Went in and out the chords, his wings
Make murmur whereso'er they graze,
As an angel may, between the maze
Of midnight palace-pillars, on
And on, to sow God's plagues have gone
Through guilty glorious Babylon.
And while such murmurs flow, the nymph
Bends o'er the harp-top from her shell
As the dry limpet for the lymph
Come with a tune he knows so well.
And how your statues' hearts must swell!
And how your pictures must descend
To see each other, friend with friend!
Oh, could you take them by surprise,

You'd find Schidone's eager Duke
Doing the quaintest courtesies
To that prim Saint by Haste-thee-Luke!
And, deeper into her rock den,
Bold Castelfranco's Magdalen
You'd find retreated from the ken
Of that robed counsel-keeping Ser—
As if the Tizian thinks of her,
And is not, rather, gravely bent
On seeing for himself what toys
Are these, his progeny invent,
What litter now the board employs
Whereon he signed a document
That got him murdered! Each enjoys
Its night so well, you cannot break
The sport up, so, indeed must make
More stay with me, for others' sake.

She speaks

I

To-morrow, if a harp-string, say,
Is used to tie the jasmine back
That overfloods my room with sweets,
Contrive your Zorzi somehow meets
My Zanze: if the ribbon's black,
The Three are watching; keep away.

2

Your gondola—let Zorzi wreathe
A mesh of water-weeds about
Its prow, as if he unaware
Had struck some quay or bridge-foot stair;
That I may throw a paper out
As you and he go underneath.
There's Zanze's vigilant taper; safe are we!
Only one minute more to-night with me?
Resume your past self of a month ago!

Be you the bashful gallant, I will be
The lady with the colder breast than snow:
Now bow you, as becomes, nor touch my hand
More than I touch yours when I step to land,
And say, "All thanks, Siora!"—
                                        Heart to heart,
And lips to lips! Yet once more, ere we part,
Clasp me, and make me thine, as mine thou art!

He is surprised, and stabbed

It was ordained to be so, Sweet,—and best
Comes now, beneath thine eyes, and on thy breast
Still kiss me! Care not for the cowards! Care
Only to put aside thy beauteous hair
My blood will hurt! The Three, I do not scorn
To death, because they never lived: but I
Have lived indeed, and so—(yet one more kiss)—can die!

CRISTINA

This poem expresses Browning's belief that certain souls are destined for each other through eternity. The immediate motivation was probably the forced abdication of Queen Cristina from the Spanish throne in 1840. After the death of her husband, King Ferdinand VII, in 1833 she had ruled as regent until her secret marriage to an army officer was discovered. The real Cristina was not an admirable character, but Browning has idealized the love story of this royal coquette in her lover's monologue.

I

She should never have looked at me
   If she meant I should not love her!
There are plenty . . . men, you call such,
   I suppose . . . she may discover

All her soul to, if she pleases,
  And yet leave much as she found them:
But I 'm not so, and she knew it
  When she fixed me, glancing round them.

2

What? To fix me thus meant nothing?
  But I can't tell (there's my weakness)
What her look said!—no vile cant, sure,
  About "need to strew the bleakness
Of some lone shore with its pearl-seed,
  That the sea feels"—no "strange yearning
That such souls have, most to lavish
  Where there 's chance of least returning."

3

Oh, we 're sunk enough here, God knows!
  But not quite so sunk that moments,
Sure tho' seldom, are denied us,
  When the spirit's true endowments
Stand out plainly from its false ones,
  And apprise it if pursuing
Or the right way or the wrong way,
  To its triumph or undoing.

4

There are flashes struck from midnights,
  There are fire-flames noondays kindle,
Whereby piled-up honours perish,
  Whereby swollen ambitions dwindle,
While just this or that poor impulse,
  Which for once had play unstifled,
Seems the sole work of a life-time
  That away the rest have trifled.

5

Doubt you if, in some such moment,
  As she fixed me, she felt clearly,
Ages past the soul existed,
  Here an age 'tis resting merely,
And hence fleets again for ages,
  While the true end, sole and single,
It stops here for is, this love-way,
  With some other soul to mingle?

6

Else it loses what it lived for,
  And eternally must lose it;
Better ends may be in prospect,
  Deeper blisses (if you choose it),
But this life's end and this love-bliss
  Have been lost here. Doubt you whether
This she felt as, looking at me,
  Mine and her souls rushed together?

7

Oh, observe! Of course, next moment,
  The world's honours, in derision,
Trampled out the light for ever:
  Never fear but there 's provision
Of the devil's to quench knowledge
  Lest we walk the earth in rapture!
—Making those who catch God's secret
  Just so much more prize their capture!

8

Such am I: the secret 's mine now!
  She has lost me, I have gained her;
Her soul's mine: and thus, grown perfect,
  I shall pass my life's remainder.

Life will just hold out the proving
  Both our powers, alone and blended:
And then, come the next life quickly!
  This world's use will have been ended.

JOHANNES AGRICOLA IN MEDITATION

Johannes Schneider, who took the name of Agricola, was a follower of Martin Luther, but later developed a sect of his own, known as Antinomianism, which held that a child of God cannot sin or fall from grace, a doctrine having points in common with predestination. This poem was originally published with Porphyria's Lover, *which follows it, under the heading of* Madhouse Cells. *Two men, each with a mental aberration, reveal their pathological trends: Johannes Agricola, the religious fanatic, and Porphyria's lover, who kills his mistress to preserve their love in all its perfection.*

There's heaven above, and night by night
  I look through its gorgeous roof;
No suns and moons though e'er so bright
  Avail to stop me; splendour-proof
  I keep the broods of stars aloof:
For I intend to get to God,
  For 't is to God I speed so fast,
For in God's breast, my own abode,
  Those shoals of dazzling glory passed,
  I lay my spirit down at last.
I lie where I have always lain,
  God smiles as he has always smiled;
Ere suns and moons could wax and wane,
  Ere stars were thundergirt, or piled
  The heavens, God thought on me his child;
Ordained a life for me, arrayed
  Its circumstances every one

To the minutest; ay, God said
  This head this hand should rest upon
  Thus, ere he fashioned star or sun.
And having thus created me,
  Thus rooted me, he bade me grow,
Guiltless for ever, like a tree
  That buds and blooms, nor seeks to know
  The law by which it prospers so:
But sure that thought and word and deed
  All go to swell his love for me,
Me, made because that love had need
  Of something irreversibly
  Pledged solely its content to be.
Yes, yes, a tree which must ascend,
  No poison-gourd foredoomed to stoop!
I have God's warrant, could I blend
  All hideous sins, as in a cup,
  To drink the mingled venoms up;
Secure my nature will convert
  The draught to blossoming gladness fast:
While sweet dews turn to the gourd's hurt,
  And bloat, and while they bloat it, blast,
  As from the first its lot was cast.
For as I lie, smiled on, full-fed
  By unexhausted power to bless,
I gaze below on hell's fierce bed,
  And those its waves of flame oppress,
  Swarming in ghastly wretchedness;
Whose life on earth aspired to be
  One altar-smoke, so pure!—to win
If not love like God's love for me,
  At least to keep his anger in;
  And all their striving turned to sin.
Priest, doctor, hermit, monk grown white
  With prayer, the broken-hearted nun,
The martyr, the wan acolyte,
  The incense-swinging child,—undone
  Before God fashioned star or sun!

God, whom I praise; how could I praise,
  If such as I might understand,
Make out and reckon on his ways,
  And bargain for his love, and stand,
  Paying a price, at his right hand?

PORPHYRIA'S LOVER

This poem is said to have been written during the poet's trip to Russia in 1834. It interests us for two reasons: it is Browning's first poetic monologue, the form which he was to develop so highly, and through its theme of love and death (which the young Shelley and Poe used so often), it reflects the Romantic mood of the period.

The rain set early in to-night,
  The sullen wind was soon awake,
It tore the elm-tops down for spite,
  And did its worst to vex the lake:
  I listened with heart fit to break.
When glided in Porphyria; straight
  She shut the cold out and the storm,
And kneeled and made the cheerless grate
  Blaze up, and all the cottage warm;
  Which done, she rose, and from her form
Withdrew the dripping cloak and shawl,
  And laid her soiled gloves by, untied
Her hat and let the damp hair fall,
  And, last, she sat down by my side
  And called me. When no voice replied,
She put my arm about her waist,
  And made her smooth white shoulder bare,
And all her yellow hair displaced,
  And, stooping, made my cheek lie there,
  And spread, o'er all, her yellow hair,
Murmuring how she loved me—she
  Too weak, for all her heart's endeavour,

To set its struggling passion free
  From pride, and vainer ties dissever,
  And give herself to me for ever.
But passion sometimes would prevail,
  Nor could to-night's gay feast restrain
A sudden thought of one so pale
  For love of her, and all in vain:
  So, she was come through wind and rain.
Be sure I looked up at her eyes
  Happy and proud; at last I knew
Porphyria worshipped me; surprise
  Made my heart swell, and still it grew
  While I debated what to do.
That moment she was mine, mine, fair,
  Perfectly pure and good: I found
A thing to do, and all her hair
  In one long yellow string I wound
  Three times her little throat around,
And strangled her. No pain felt she;
  I am quite sure she felt no pain.
As a shut bud that holds a bee,
  I warily oped her lids: again
  Laughed the blue eyes without a stain.
And I untightened next the tress
  About her neck; her cheek once more
Blushed bright beneath my burning kiss:
  I propped her head up as before,
  Only, this time my shoulder bore
Her head, which droops upon it still:
  The smiling rosy little head,
So glad it has its utmost will,
  That all it scorned at once is fled,
  And I, its love, am gained instead!
Porphyria's love: she guessed not how
  Her darling one wish would be heard.
And thus we sit together now,
  And all night long we have not stirred,
  And yet God has not said a word!

THE PIED PIPER OF HAMELIN

A Child's Story

Read and loved by generations of children, this is perhaps Browning's most popular poem. It was written for the small son of William Macready, the actor, who was sick at the time. As a child, Browning had heard versions of this old German legend whose basic plot is the revenge of a magician who has been cheated of his promised reward.

I

Hamelin Town 's in Brunswick,
  By famous Hanover city;
The river Weser, deep and wide,
Washes its wall on the southern side;
A pleasanter spot you never spied;
  But, when begins my ditty,
Almost five hundred years ago,
To see the townsfolk suffer so
  From vermin, was a pity.

2

  Rats!
They fought the dogs and killed the cats,
  And bit the babies in the cradles,
And ate the cheeses out of the vats,
  And licked the soup from the cooks' own ladles,
Split open the kegs of salted sprats,
Made nests inside men's Sunday hats,
And even spoiled the women's chats
    By drowning their speaking
    With shrieking and squeaking
In fifty different sharps and flats.

3

At last the people in a body
        To the Town Hall came flocking:
" 'T is clear," cried they, "our Mayor's a noddy;
        And as for our Corporation—shocking
To think we buy gowns lined with ermine
For dolts that can't or won't determine
What 's best to rid us of our vermin!
You hope, because you 're old and obese,
To find in the furry civic robe ease?
Rouse up, sirs! Give your brains a racking
To find the remedy we 're lacking,
Or, sure as fate, we 'll send you packing!"
At this the Mayor and Corporation
Quaked with a mighty consternation.

4

An hour they sat in council,
   At length the Mayor broke silence:
"For a guilder I 'd my ermine gown sell,
   I wish I were a mile hence!
It 's easy to bid one rack one's brain—
I 'm sure my poor head aches again,
I 've scratched it so, and all in vain.
Oh for a trap, a trap, a trap!"
Just as he said this, what should hap
At the chamber door but a gentle tap?
"Bless us," cried the Mayor, "what 's that?"
(With the Corporation as he sat,
Looking little though wondrous fat;
Nor brighter was his eye, nor moister
Than a too-long-opened oyster,
Save when at noon his paunch grew mutinous
For a plate of turtle green and glutinous)
"Only a scraping of shoes on the mat?
Anything like the sound of a rat
Makes my heart go pit-a-pat!"

5

"Come in!"—the Mayor cried, looking bigger:
And in did come the strangest figure!
His queer long coat from heel to head
Was half of yellow and half of red,
And he himself was tall and thin,
With sharp blue eyes, each like a pin,
And light loose hair, yet swarthy skin,
No tuft on cheek nor beard on chin,
But lips where smiles went out and in;
There was no guessing his kith and kin:
And nobody could enough admire
The tall man and his quaint attire.
Quoth one: "It 's as my great-grandsire,
Starting up at the Trump of Doom's tone,
Had walked this way from his painted tombstone!"

6

He advanced to the council-table:
And, "Please your honours," said he, "I 'm able,
By means of a secret charm, to draw
   All creatures living beneath the sun,
   That creep or swim or fly or run,
After me so as you never saw!
And I chiefly use my charm
On creatures that do people harm,
The mole and toad and newt and viper;
And people call me the Pied Piper."
(And here they noticed round his neck
   A scarf of red and yellow stripe,
To match with his coat of the self-same cheque;
   And at the scarf's end hung a pipe;
And his fingers, they noticed, were ever straying
As if impatient to be playing
Upon this pipe, as low it dangled

Over his vesture so old-fangled.)
"Yet," said he, "poor piper as I am,
In Tartary I freed the Cham,
  Last June, from his huge swarms of gnats;
I eased in Asia the Nizam
  Of a monstrous brood of vampire-bats:
And as for what your brain bewilders,
  If I can rid your town of rats
Will you give me a thousand guilders?"
"One? fifty thousand!"—was the exclamation
Of the astonished Mayor and Corporation.

7

Into the street the Piper stept,
  Smiling first a little smile,
As if he knew what magic slept
  In his quiet pipe the while;
Then, like a musical adept,
To blow the pipe his lips he wrinkled,
And green and blue his sharp eyes twinkled,
Like a candle-flame where salt is sprinkled;
And ere three shrill notes the pipe uttered,
You heard as if an army muttered;
And the muttering grew to a grumbling;
And the grumbling grew to a mighty rumbling;
And out of the houses the rats came tumbling.
Great rats, small rats, lean rats, brawny rats,
Brown rats, black rats, grey rats, tawny rats,
Grave old plodders, gay young friskers,
  Fathers, mothers, uncles, cousins,
Cocking tails and pricking whiskers,
  Families by tens and dozens,
Brothers, sisters, husbands, wives—
Followed the Piper for their lives.
From street to street he piped advancing,
And step for step they followed dancing,

Until they came to the river Weser,
  Wherein all plunged and perished!
—Save one who, stout as Julius Cæsar,
Swam across and lived to carry
  (As he, the manuscript he cherished)
To Rat-land home his commentary:
Which was, "At the first shrill notes of the pipe,
I heard a sound as of scraping tripe,
And putting apples, wondrous ripe,
Into a cider-press's gripe:
And a moving away of pickle-tub-boards,
And a leaving ajar of conserve-cupboards,
And a drawing the corks of train-oil-flasks,
And a breaking the hoops of butter-casks:
And it seemed as if a voice
  (Sweeter far than by harp or by psaltery
Is breathed) called out, 'Oh rats, rejoice!
  The world is grown to one vast drysaltery!
So munch on, crunch on, take your nuncheon,
Breakfast, supper, dinner, luncheon!'
And just as a bulky sugar-puncheon,
All ready staved, like a great sun shone
Glorious scarce an inch before me,
Just as methought it said, 'Come, bore me!'
—I found the Weser rolling o'er me."

8

You should have heard the Hamelin people
Ringing the bells till they rocked the steeple.
"Go," cried the Mayor, "and get long poles,
Poke out the nests and block up the holes!
Consult with carpenters and builders,
And leave in our town not even a trace
Of the rats!"—when suddenly, up the face
Of the Piper perked in the market-place,
With a, "First, if you please, my thousand guilders!"

9

A thousand guilders! The Mayor looked blue;
So did the Corporation too.
For council dinners made rare havoc
With Claret, Moselle, Vin-de-Grave, Hock;
And half the money would replenish
Their cellar's biggest butt with Rhenish.
To pay this sum to a wandering fellow
With a gipsy coat of red and yellow!
"Beside," quoth the Mayor with a knowing wink,
"Our business was done at the river's brink;
We saw with our eyes the vermin sink,
And what 's dead can't come to life, I think.
So, friend, we 're not the folks to shrink
From the duty of giving you something for drink,
And a matter of money to put in your poke;
But as for the guilders, what we spoke
Of them, as you very well know, was in joke.
Beside, our losses have made us thrifty.
A thousand guilders! Come, take fifty!"

10

The Piper's face fell, and he cried
"No trifling! I can't wait, beside!
I 've promised to visit by dinnertime
Bagdat, and accept the prime
Of the Head-Cook's pottage, all he 's rich in,
For having left, in the Caliph's kitchen,
Of a nest of scorpions no survivor:
With him I proved no bargain-driver,
With you, don't think I 'll bate a stiver!
And folks who put me in a passion
May find me pipe after another fashion."

11

"How?" cried the Mayor, "d' ye think I brook
Being worse treated than a Cook?
Insulted by a lazy ribald
With idle pipe and vesture piebald?
You threaten us, fellow? Do your worst,
Blow your pipe there till you burst!"

12

Once more he stept into the street;
   And to his lips again
   Laid his long pipe of smooth straight cane;
And ere he blew three notes (such sweet
Soft notes as yet musician's cunning
   Never gave the enraptured air)
There was a rustling that seemed like a bustling
Of merry crowds justling at pitching and hustling,
Small feet were pattering, wooden shoes clattering,
Little hands clapping and little tongues chattering,
And, like fowls in a farm-yard when barley is scattering,
Out came the children running.
All the little boys and girls,
With rosy cheeks and flaxen curls,
And sparkling eyes and teeth like pearls,
Tripping and skipping, ran merrily after
The wonderful music with shouting and laughter.

13

The Mayor was dumb, and the Council stood
As if they were changed into blocks of wood,
Unable to move a step, or cry
To the children merrily skipping by,
—Could only follow with the eye
That joyous crowd at the Piper's back.
But how the Mayor was on the rack,

And the wretched Council's bosoms beat,
As the Piper turned from the High Street
To where the Weser rolled its waters
Right in the way of their sons and daughters!
However he turned from South to West,
And to Koppelberg Hill his steps addressed,
And after him the children pressed;
Great was the joy in every breast.
"He never can cross that mighty top!
He's forced to let the piping drop,
And we shall see our children stop!"
When, lo, as they reached the mountain-side,
A wondrous portal opened wide,
As if a cavern was suddenly hollowed;
And the Piper advanced and the children followed,
And when all were in to the very last,
The door in the mountainside shut fast.
Did I say, all? No! One was lame,
  And could not dance the whole of the way;
And in after years, if you would blame
  His sadness, he was used to say,—
"It 's dull in our town since my playmates left!
I can't forget that I 'm bereft
Of all the pleasant sights they see,
Which the Piper also promised me.
For he led us, he said, to a joyous land,
Joining the town and just at hand,
Where waters gushed and fruit-trees grew
And flowers put forth a fairer hue,
And everything was bright and new;
The sparrows were brighter than peacocks here,
And their dogs outran our fallow deer,
And honey-bees had lost their stings,
And horses were born with eagles' wings:
And just as I became assured
My lame foot would be speedily cured,
The music stopped and I stood still,

And found myself outside the hill,
Left alone against my will,
To go now limping as before,
And never hear of that country more!"

14

Alas, alas for Hamelin!
  There came into many a burgher's pate
  A text which says that heaven's gate
  Opes to the rich at as easy rate
As the needle's eye takes a camel in!
The mayor sent East, West, North and South,
To offer the Piper, by word of mouth,
  Wherever it was men's lot to find him,
Silver and gold to his heart's content,
If he 'd only return the way he went,
  And bring the children behind him.
But when they saw 't was a lost endeavour,
And Piper and dancers were gone for ever,
They made a decree that lawyers never
  Should think their records dated duly
If, after the day of the month and year,
These words did not as well appear,
"And so long after what happened here
  On the Twenty-second of July,
Thirteen hundred and seventy-six":
And the better in memory to fix
The place of the children's last retreat,
They called it, the Pied Piper's Street—
Where any one playing on pipe or tabor
Was sure for the future to lose his labour.
Nor suffered they hostelry or tavern
  To shock with mirth a street so solemn;
But opposite the place of the cavern
  They wrote the story on a column,
And on the great church-window painted
The same, to make the world acquainted

How their children were stolen away,
And there it stands to this very day.
And I must not omit to say
That in Transylvania there 's a tribe
Of alien people who ascribe
The outlandish ways and dress
On which their neighbours lay such stress,
To their fathers and mothers having risen
Out of some subterraneous prison
Into which they were trepanned
Long time ago in a mighty band
Out of Hamelin town in Brunswick land,
But how or why, they don't understand.

15

So, Willy, let me and you be wipers
Of scores out with all men—especially pipers!
And, whether they pipe us free from rats or from mice,
If we 've promised them aught, let us keep our promise!

Dramatic Romances

1845

HOW THEY BROUGHT THE GOOD NEWS FROM GHENT TO AIX

Browning wrote this poem at sea somewhere "off the African coast." The galloping measure which so vividly suggests the beating of hooves shows his nostalgia for the good hard earth. The poet doesn't tell us, nor do we particularly care, what "the good news" was. Obviously it has something to do with the fortunes of war, and in this as well as in its quick-pounding meter, it is similar to that other children's favorite, The Ride of Paul Revere. *The horse, Roland, is the real hero of the poem, and when at the end of the journey he is given a drink of wine, we are reminded that in the* Iliad *Hector's horses were sometimes rewarded with a mixture of water and wine by Andromache.*

I

I sprang to the stirrup, and Joris, and he;
I galloped, Dirck galloped, we galloped all three;
"Good speed!" cried the watch, as the gate-bolts undrew;
"Speed!" echoed the wall to us galloping through;
Behind shut the postern, the lights sank to rest,
And into the midnight we galloped abreast.

2

Not a word to each other; we kept the great pace
Neck by neck, stride by stride, never changing our place;
I turned in my saddle and made its girths tight,
Then shortened each stirrup, and set the pique right,
Rebuckled the cheek-strap, chained slacker the bit,
Nor galloped less steadily Roland a whit.

3

'T was moonset at starting; but while we drew near
Lokeren, the cocks crew and twilight dawned clear;
At Boom, a great yellow star came out to see;
At Düffeld, 't was morning as plain as could be;
And from Mecheln church-steeple we heard the half-chime,
So, Joris broke silence with, "Yet there is time!"

4

At Aershot, up leaped of a sudden the sun,
And against him the cattle stood black every one,
To stare thro' the mist at us galloping past,
And I saw my stout galloper Roland at last,
With resolute shoulders, each butting away
The haze, as some bluff river headland its spray:

5

And his low head and crest, just one sharp ear bent back
For my voice, and the other pricked out on his track;
And one eye's black intelligence,—ever that glance
O'er its white edge at me, his own master, askance!
And the thick heavy spume-flakes which aye and anon
His fierce lips shook upwards in galloping on.

6

By Hasselt, Dirck groaned; and cried Joris, "Stay spur!
Your Roos galloped bravely, the fault's not in her,
We 'll remember at Aix"—for one heard the quick wheeze
Of her chest, saw the stretched neck and staggering knees,
And sunk tail, and horrible heave of the flank,
As down on her haunches she shuddered and sank.

7

So, we were left galloping, Joris and I,
Past Looz and past Tongres, no cloud in the sky;
The broad sun above laughed a pitiless laugh,
'Neath our feet broke the brittle bright stubble like chaff;
Till over by Dalhem a dome-spire sprang white,
And "Gallop," gasped Joris, "for Aix is in sight!

8

How they 'll greet us!"—and all in a moment his roan
Rolled neck and croup over, lay dead as a stone;
And there was my Roland to bear the whole weight
Of the news which alone could save Aix from her fate,
With his nostrils like pits full of blood to the brim,
And with circles of red for his eye-sockets' rim.

9

Then I cast loose my buffcoat, each holster let fall,
Shook off both my jack-boots, let go belt and all,
Stood up in the stirrup, leaned, patted his ear,

Called my Roland his pet-name, my horse without peer;
Clapped my hands, laughed and sang, any noise, bad or good,
Till at length into Aix Roland galloped and stood.

10

And all I remember is, friends flocking round
As I sat with his head 'twixt my knees on the ground;
And no voice but was praising this Roland of mine,
As I poured down his throat our last measure of wine,
Which (the burgesses voted by common consent)
Was no more than his due who brought good news from Ghent.

PICTOR IGNOTUS

The title means "unknown painter" in Latin. This monologue captures the feeling of the great religious artists of the Middle Ages, who painted under the eye of God, inspired and rewarded by Him alone. During the Renaissance, artists emerged from the monasteries and began to work for the rewards of men with the result that painting became more free in style and secular in subject. The old painter is not reconciled to the change, although he is tempted to paint in the newer, more realistic manner.

I could have painted pictures like that youth's
　Ye praise so. How my soul springs up! No bar
Stayed me—ah, thought which saddens while it soothes!
　—Never did fate forbid me, star by star,
To outburst on your night with all my gift
　Of fires from God: nor would my flesh have shrunk
From seconding my soul, with eyes uplift
　And wide to heaven, or, straight like thunder, sunk
To the centre, of an instant; or around
　Turned calmly and inquisitive, to scan
The licence and the limit, space and bound,
　Allowed to truth made visible in man.

And, like that youth ye praise so, all I saw,
  Over the canvas could my hand have flung,
Each face obedient to its passion's law,
  Each passion clear proclaimed without a tongue;
Whether Hope rose at once in all the blood,
  A-tiptoe for the blessing of embrace,
Or Rapture drooped the eyes, as when her brood
  Pull down the nesting dove's heart to its place;
Or Confidence lit swift the forehead up,
  And locked the mouth fast, like a castle braved,—
O human faces, hath it spilt, my cup?
  What did ye give me that I have not saved?
Nor will I say I have not dreamed (how well!)
  Of going—I, in each new picture,—forth,
As, making new hearts beat and bosoms swell,
  To Pope or Kaiser, East, West, South, or North,
Bound for the calmly-satisfied great State,
  Or glad aspiring little burgh, it went,
Flowers cast upon the car which bore the freight,
  Through old streets named afresh from the event,
Till it reached home, where learned age should greet
  My face, and youth, the star not yet distinct
Above his hair, lie learning at my feet!—
  Oh, thus to live, I and my picture, linked
With love about, and praise, till life should end,
  And then not go to heaven, but linger here,
Here on my earth, earth's every man my friend,—
  The thought grew frightful, 't was so wildly dear!
But a voice changed it! Glimpses of such sights
  Have scared me, like the revels through a door
Of some strange house of idols at its rites!
  This world seemed not the world it was before:
Mixed with my loving trusting ones, there trooped
  . . . Who summoned those cold faces that begun
To press on me and judge me? Though I stooped
  Shrinking, as from the soldiery a nun,
They drew me forth, and spite of me . . . enough!
  These buy and sell our pictures, take and give,

Count them for garniture and household-stuff,
  And where they live needs must our pictures live
And see their faces, listen to their prate,
  Partakers of their daily pettiness,
Discussed of— "This I love, or this I hate,
  This likes me more, and this affects me less!"
Wherefore I chose my portion. If at whiles
  My heart sinks, as monotonous I paint
These endless cloisters and eternal aisles
  With the same series, Virgin, Babe and Saint,
With the same cold calm beautiful regard,—
  At least no merchant traffics in my heart;
The sanctuary's gloom at least shall ward
  Vain tongues from where my pictures stand apart:
Only prayer breaks the silence of the shrine
  While, blackening in the daily candle-smoke,
They moulder on the damp wall's travertine,
  'Mid echoes the light footstep never woke.
So, die my pictures! surely, gently die!
  O youth, men praise so,—holds their praise its worth?
Blown harshly, keeps the trump its golden cry?
  Tastes sweet the water with such specks of earth?

THE ITALIAN IN ENGLAND

Browning was in Naples in 1844 a few months after the uprising against the Austrian oppressors led by the Bandieri brothers, who had been caught and executed. In this poem the scene is changed to Padua, and one of the brothers is allowed to escape to England, helped by a peasant woman. This is one of several poems using the theme of Italian freedom in which both the Brownings were much interested; it was read by Mazzini to his fellow exiles in London to illustrate English sympathy for the movement.

That second time they hunted me
From hill to plain, from shore to sea,

And Austria, hounding far and wide
Her blood-hounds thro' the country-side,
Breathed hot and instant on my trace,—
I made six days a hiding-place
Of that dry green old aqueduct
Where I and Charles, when boys, have plucked
The fire-flies from the roof above,
Bright creeping thro' the moss they love:
—How long it seems since Charles was lost!
Six days the soldiers crossed and crossed
The country in my very sight;
And when that peril ceased at night,
The sky broke out in red dismay
With signal fires; well, there I lay
Close covered o'er in my recess,
Up to the neck in ferns and cress,
Thinking on Metternich our friend,
And Charles's miserable end,
And much beside, two days; the third,
Hunger o'ercame me when I heard
The peasants from the village go
To work among the maize; you know,
With us in Lombardy, they bring
Provisions packed on mules, a string
With little bells that cheer their task,
And casks, and boughs on every cask
To keep the sun's heat from the wine;
These I let pass in jingling line,
And, close on them, dear noisy crew,
The peasants from the village, too;
For at the very rear would troop
Their wives and sisters in a group
To help, I knew. When these had passed,
I threw my glove to strike the last,
Taking the chance: she did not start,
Much less cry out, but stooped apart,
One instant rapidly glanced round,
And saw me beckon from the ground.

A wild bush grows and hides my crypt;
She picked my glove up while she stripped
A branch off, then rejoined the rest
With that; my glove lay in her breast.
Then I drew breath; they disappeared:
It was for Italy I feared.

An hour, and she returned alone
Exactly where my glove was thrown.
Meanwhile came many thoughts: on me
Rested the hopes of Italy.
I had devised a certain tale
Which, when 't was told her, could not fail
Persuade a peasant of its truth;
I meant to call a freak of youth
This hiding, and give hopes of pay,
And no temptation to betray.
But when I saw that woman's face,
Its calm simplicity of grace,
Our Italy's own attitude
In which she walked thus far, and stood,
Planting each naked foot so firm,
To crush the snake and spare the worm—
At first sight of her eyes, I said,
"I am that man upon whose head
They fix the price, because I hate
The Austrians over us: the State
Will give you gold—oh, gold so much!—
If you betray me to their clutch,
And be your death, for aught I know,
If once they find you saved their foe.
Now, you must bring me food and drink,
And also paper, pen and ink,
And carry safe what I shall write
To Padua, which you 'll reach at night
Before the duomo shuts; go in,
And wait till Tenebræ begin;

Walk to the third confessional,
Between the pillar and the wall,
And kneeling whisper, *Whence comes peace?*
Say it a second time, then cease;
And if the voice inside returns,
From Christ and Freedom; what concerns
The cause of Peace?—for answer, slip
My letter where you placed your lip;
Then come back happy we have done
Our mother service—I, the son,
As you the daughter of our land!"

Three mornings more, she took her stand
In the same place, with the same eyes:
I was no surer of sun-rise
Than of her coming. We conferred
Of her own prospects, and I heard
She had a lover—stout and tall,
She said—then let her eyelids fall,
"He could do much"—as if some doubt
Entered her heart,—then, passing out,
"She could not speak for others, who
Had other thoughts; herself she knew":
And so she brought me drink and food.
After four days, the scouts pursued
Another path; at last arrived
The help my Paduan friends contrived
To furnish me: she brought the news.
For the first time I could not choose
But kiss her hand, and lay my own
Upon her head—"This faith was shown
To Italy, our mother; she
Uses my hand and blesses thee."
She followed down to the sea-shore;
I left and never saw her more.

How very long since I have thought
Concerning—much less wished for—aught
Beside the good of Italy,
For which I live and mean to die!
I never was in love; and since
Charles proved false, what shall now convince
My inmost heart I have a friend?
However, if I pleased to spend
Real wishes on myself—say, three—
I know at least what one should be.
I would grasp Metternich until
I felt his red wet throat distil
In blood thro' these two hands. And next,
—Nor much for that am I perplexed—
Charles, perjured traitor, for his part,
Should die slow of a broken heart
Under his new employers. Last
—Ah, there, what should I wish? For fast
Do I grow old and out of strength.
If I resolved to seek at length
My father's house again, how scared
They all would look, and unprepared!
My brothers live in Austria's pay
—Disowned me long ago, men say;
And all my early mates who used
To praise me so—perhaps induced
More than one early step of mine—
Are turning wise: while some opine
"Freedom grows license," some suspect
"Haste breeds delay," and recollect
They always said, such premature
Beginnings never could endure!
So, with a sullen "All 's for best,"
The land seems settling to its rest.
I think then, I should wish to stand
This evening in that dear, lost land,
Over the sea the thousand miles,
And know if yet that woman smiles

With the calm smile; some little farm
She lives in there, no doubt: what harm
If I sat on the door-side bench,
And, while her spindle made a trench
Fantastically in the dust,
Inquired of all her fortunes—just
Her children's ages and their names,
And what may be the husband's aims
For each of them. I 'd talk this out,
And sit there, for an hour about,
Then kiss her hand once more, and lay
Mine on her head, and go my way.

So much for idle wishing—how
It steals the time! To business now.

THE ENGLISHMAN IN ITALY

Piano di Sorrento

The warm and sensuous countryside around Naples is the background for this lyrical poem which sings so happily of the Englishman's delight in Italy. The sea, sun, wind, mountains, vineyards, orchards, fish, and, above all, the people going about their varied tasks, are vividly flashed before us. After describing the religious fiesta that will take place the next day, Browning dramatically contrasts the color, noise, and movement, with what is going on in England at the same time: men solemnly debating the Corn Laws in Parliament.

Fortù, Fortù, my beloved one,
Sit here by my side,
On my knees put up both little feet!
I was sure, if I tried,
I could make you laugh spite of Scirocco.
Now, open your eyes,

Let me keep you amused till he vanish
  In black from the skies,
With telling my memories over
  As you tell your beads;
All the Plain saw me gather, I garland
  —The flowers or the weeds.

Time for rain! for your long hot dry Autumn
  Had net-worked with brown
The white skin of each grape on the bunches,
  Marked like a quail's crown,
Those creatures you make such account of,
  Whose heads,—speckled white
Over brown like a great spider's back,
  As I told you last night,—
Your mother bites off for her supper.
  Red-ripe as could be,
Pomegranates were chapping and splitting
  In halves on the tree:
And betwixt the loose walls of great flintstone,
  Or in the thick dust
On the path, or straight out of the rock-side,
  Wherever could thrust
Some burnt sprig of bold hardy rock-flower
  Its yellow face up,
For the prize were great butterflies fighting,
  Some five for one cup.
So, I guessed, ere I got up this morning,
  What change was in store,
By the quick rustle-down of the quail-nets
  Which woke me before
I could open my shutter, made fast
  With a bough and a stone,
And look thro' the twisted dead vine-twigs,
  Sole lattice that 's known.
Quick and sharp rang the rings down the net-poles,
  While, busy beneath,

Your priest and his brother tugged at them,
  The rain in their teeth.
And out upon all the flat house-roofs
  Where split figs lay drying,
The girls took the frails under cover:
  Nor use seemed in trying
To get out the boats and go fishing,
  For, under the cliff,
Fierce the black water frothed o'er the blind-rock.
  No seeing our skiff
Arrive about noon from Amalfi,
  —Our fisher arrive,
And pitch down his basket before us,
  All trembling alive
With pink and grey jellies, your sea-fruit;
  You touch the strange lumps,
And mouths gape there, eyes open, all manner
  Of horns and of humps,
Which only the fisher looks grave at,
  While round him like imps
Cling screaming the children as naked
  And brown as his shrimps;
Himself too as bare to the middle
  —You see round his neck
The string and its brass coin suspended,
  That saves him from wreck.
But to-day not a boat reached Salerno,
  So back, to a man,
Came our friends, with whose help in the vineyards
  Grape-harvest began.
In the vat, halfway up in our house-side,
  Like blood the juice spins,
While your brother all bare-legged is dancing
  Till breathless he grins
Dead-beaten in effort on effort
  To keep the grapes under,
Since still when he seems all but master,
  In pours the fresh plunder

From girls who keep coming and going
  With basket on shoulder,
And eyes shut against the rain's driving;
  Your girls that are older,—
For under the hedges of aloe,
  And where, on its bed
Of the orchard's black mould, the love-apple
  Lies pulpy and red,
All the young ones are kneeling and filling
  Their laps with the snails
Tempted out by this first rainy weather,—
  Your best of regales,
As to-night will be proved to my sorrow,
  When, supping in state,
We shall feast our grape-gleaners (two dozen,
  Three over one plate)
With lasagne so tempting to swallow
  In slippery ropes,
And gourds fried in great purple slices,
  That colour of popes.
Meantime, see the grape bunch they 've brought you:
  The rain-water slips
O'er the heavy blue bloom on each globe
  Which the wasp to your lips
Still follows with fretful persistence:
  Nay, taste, while awake,
This half of a curd-white smooth cheese-ball
  That peels, flake by flake,
Like an onion, each smoother and whiter;
  Next, sip this weak wine
From the thin green glass flask, with its stopper,
  A leaf of the vine;
And end with the prickly-pear's red flesh
  That leaves thro' its juice
The stony black seeds on your pearl-teeth.
  Scirocco is loose!
Hark, the quick, whistling pelt of the olives
  Which, thick in one's track,

Tempt the stranger to pick up and bite them,
  Tho' not yet half black!
How the old twisted olive trunks shudder,
  The medlars let fall
Their hard fruit, and the brittle great fig-trees
  Snap off, figs and all,
For here comes the whole of the tempest!
  No refuge, but creep
Back again to my side and my shoulder,
  And listen or sleep.

O how will your country show next week,
  When all the vine-boughs
Have been stripped of their foliage to pasture
  The mules and the cows?
Last eve, I rode over the mountains;
  Your brother, my guide,
Soon left me, to feast on the myrtles
  That offered, each side,
Their fruit-balls, black, glossy and luscious,—
  Or strip from the sorbs
A treasure, or, rosy and wondrous,
  Those hairy gold orbs!
But my mule picked his sure sober path out,
  Just stopping to neigh
When he recognized down in the valley
  His mates on their way
With the faggots and barrels of water;
  And soon we emerged
From the plain, where the woods could scarce follow;
  And still as we urged
Our way, the woods wondered, and left us,
  As up still we trudged
Though the wild path grew wilder each instant,
  And place was e'en grudged
'Mid the rock-chasms and piles of loose stones
  Like the loose broken teeth

Of some monster which climbed there to die
 From the ocean beneath—
Place was grudged to the silver-grey fume-weed
 That clung to the path,
And dark rosemary ever a-dying
 That, 'spite the wind's wrath,
So loves the salt rock's face to seaward,
 And lentisks as staunch
To the stone where they root and bear berries,
 And . . . what shows a branch
Coral-coloured, transparent, with circlets
 Of pale seagreen leaves;
Over all trod my mule with the caution
 Of gleaners o'er sheaves,
Still, foot after foot like a lady,
 Till, round after round,
He climbed to the top of Calvano,
 And God's own profound
Was above me, and round me the mountains,
 And under, the sea,
And within me my heart to bear witness
 What was and shall be.
Oh, heaven and the terrible crystal!
 No rampart excludes
Your eye from the life to be lived
 In the blue solitudes.
Oh, those mountains, their infinite movement!
 Still moving with you;
For, ever some new head and breast of them
 Thrust into view
To observe the intruder; you see it
 If quickly you turn
And, before they escape you, surprise them.
 They grudge you should learn
How the soft plains they look on, lean over
 And love (they pretend)
—Cower beneath them, the flat sea-pine crouches,
 The wild fruit-trees bend,

E'en the myrtle-leaves curl, shrink and shut:
  All is silent and grave:
'T is a sensual and timorous beauty,
  How fair! but a slave.
So, I turned to the sea; and there slumbered
  As greenly as ever
Those isles of the siren, your Galli;
  No ages can sever
The Three, nor enable their sister
  To join them,—halfway
On the voyage, she looked at Ulysses—
  No farther to-day,
Tho' the small one, just launched in the wave,
  Watches breast-high and steady
From under the rock, her bold sister
  Swum halfway already.
Fortù, shall we sail there together
  And see from the sides
Quite new rocks show their faces, new haunts
  Where the siren abides?
Shall we sail round and round them, close over
  The rocks, tho' unseen,
That ruffle the grey glassy water
  To glorious green?
Then scramble from splinter to splinter,
  Reach land and explore,
On the largest, the strange square black turret
  With never a door,
Just a loop to admit the quick lizards;
  Then, stand there and hear
The birds' quiet singing, that tells us
  What life is, so clear?
—The secret they sang to Ulysses
  When, ages ago,
He heard and he knew this life's secret
  I hear and I know.
Ah, see! The sun breaks o'er Calvano;
  He strikes the great gloom

And flutters it o'er the mount's summit
  In airy gold fume.
All is over. Look out, see the gipsy,
  Our tinker and smith,
Has arrived, set up bellows and forge,
  And down-squatted forthwith
To his hammering, under the wall there;
  One eye keeps aloof
The urchins that itch to be putting
  His jews'-harps to proof,
While the other, thro' locks of curled wire,
  Is watching how sleek
Shines the hog, come to share in the windfall
  —Chew, abbot's own cheek!
All is over. Wake up and come out now,
  And down let us go,
And see the fine things got in order
  At church for the show
Of the Sacrament, set forth this evening.
  To-morrow's the Feast
Of the Rosary's Virgin, by no means
  Of Virgins the least,
As you 'll hear in the off-hand discourse
  Which (all nature, no art)
The Dominican brother, these three weeks,
  Was getting by heart.
Not a pillar nor post but is dizened
  With red and blue papers;
All the roof waves with ribbons, each altar
  A-blaze with long tapers;
But the great masterpiece is the scaffold
  Rigged glorious to hold
All the fiddlers and fifers and drummers
  And trumpeters bold,
Not afraid of Bellini nor Auber,
  Who, when the priest's hoarse,
Will strike us up something that's brisk
  For the feast's second course.

And then will the flaxen-wigged Image
  Be carried in pomp
Thro' the plain, while in gallant procession
  The priests mean to stomp.
All round the glad church lie old bottles
  With gunpowder stopped,
Which will be, when the Image re-enters,
  Religiously popped;
And at night from the crest of Calvano
  Great bonfires will hang,
On the plain will the trumpets join chorus,
  And more poppers bang.
At all events, come—to the garden
  As far as the wall;
See me tap with a hoe on the plaster
  Till out there shall fall
A scorpion with wide angry nippers!

  —"Such trifles!" you say?
Fortù, in my England at home,
  Men meet gravely to-day
And debate, if abolishing Corn-laws
  Be righteous and wise
—If 't were proper, Scirocco should vanish
  In black from the skies!

THE LOST LEADER

William Wordsworth is unquestionably the "lost leader" scathingly described here. In his youth he was an ardent supporter of the French Revolution, but with the passing of time grew more conservative and even accepted a titular post in the Tory government which gave him an income. In later life Browning, realizing that he had not been altogether fair, regretted this youthful denunciation of a revered literary figure, and stated that the poem was a synthetic portrait, combining features of several of the leading personalities of the day who had forsaken their early principles. It is interesting to note that Browning's republican sympathies also cooled as he advanced in years.

I

Just for a handful of silver he left us,
  Just for a riband to stick in his coat—
Found the one gift of which fortune bereft us,
  Lost all the others she lets us devote;
They, with the gold to give, doled him out silver,
  So much was theirs who so little allowed:
How all our copper had gone for his service!
  Rags—were they purple, his heart had been proud!
We that had loved him so, followed him, honoured him,
  Lived in his mild and magnificent eye,
Learned his great language, caught his clear accents,
  Made him our pattern to live and to die!
Shakespeare was of us, Milton was for us,
  Burns, Shelley, were with us,—they watch from their graves!
He alone breaks from the van and the freemen,
  —He alone sinks to the rear and the slaves!

2

We shall march prospering,—not thro' his presence;
  Songs may inspirit us,—not from his lyre;
Deeds will be done,—while he boasts his quiescence,
Still bidding crouch whom the rest bade aspire:
Blot out his name, then, record one lost soul more,
  One task more declined, one more footpath untrod,
One more devil's-triumph and sorrow for angels,
  One wrong more to man, one more insult to God!
Life's night begins: let him never come back to us!
  There would be doubt, hesitation and pain,
Forced praise on our part—the glimmer of twilight,
  Never glad confident morning again!

Best fight on well, for we taught him—strike gallantly,
  Menace our heart ere we master his own;
Then let him receive the new knowledge and wait us,
  Pardoned in heaven, the first by the throne!

THE LOST MISTRESS

Several of Browning's early poems reveal the feelings of the rejected lover. In this one, written soon after he came to know Elizabeth Barrett, his native optimism shows through beneath the "all is over" plaint.

1

All 's over, then: does truth sound bitter
  As one at first believes?
Hark, 't is the sparrows' good-night twitter
  About your cottage eaves!

2

And the leaf-buds on the vine are woolly,
  I noticed that, to-day;
One day more bursts them open fully
  —You know the red turns grey.

3

To-morrow we meet the same then, dearest?
  May I take your hand in mine?
Mere friends are we,—well, friends the merest
  Keep much that I resign:

4

For each glance of that eye so bright and black,
  Though I keep with heart's endeavour,—
Your voice, when you wish the snowdrops back,
  Though it stay in my soul for ever!—

5

Yet I will but say what mere friends say,
  Or only a thought stronger;
I will hold your hand but as long as all may,
  Or so very little longer!

HOME THOUGHTS, FROM ABROAD

It is not definitely known that this beautiful and often quoted lyric was written abroad, although the tone is nostalgic. The English countryside in spring is magically called up in these few lines.

I

Oh, to be in England
Now that April 's there,
And whoever wakes in England
Sees, some morning, unaware,
That the lowest boughs and the brushwood sheaf
Round the elm-tree bole are in tiny leaf,
While the chaffinch sings on the orchard bough
In England—now!

2

And after April, when May follows,
And the whitethroat builds, and all the swallows!
Hark, where my blossomed pear-tree in the hedge
Leans to the field and scatters on the clover
Blossoms and dewdrops—at the bent spray's edge—
That 's the wise thrush; he sings each song twice over,
Lest you should think he never could recapture
The first fine careless rapture!
And though the fields look rough with hoary dew.
All will be gay when noontide wakes anew
The buttercups, the little children's dower
—Far brighter than this gaudy melon-flower!

HOME-THOUGHTS, FROM THE SEA

Two great battles, Cape St. Vincent and Trafalgar, were fought by Nelson in 1797, the latter engagement costing him his life. The couplet beginning "Here and here did England help me: how can I help England?" has a peculiar poignancy in our own time.

Nobly, nobly Cape Saint Vincent to the North-west died away;
Sunset ran, one glorious blood-red, reeking into Cadiz Bay;
Bluish 'mid the burning water, full in face Trafalgar lay;
In the dimmest North-east distance dawned Gibraltar grand and gray;
"Here and here did England help me: how can I help England?" —say,
Whoso turns as I, this evening, turn to God to praise and pray,
While Jove's planet rises yonder, silent over Africa.

THE BISHOP ORDERS HIS TOMB AT SAINT PRAXED'S CHURCH

This is one of a series of Browning's poems which derive their inspiration from the Italian Renaissance. The worldly bishop who here reveals himself—far more concerned with the quality of marble to be used for his tomb than in his soul's salvation—may be taken to represent the corruption and paganism which existed at this time in upper ecclesiastical circles, and against which reformers, such as Erasmus, were beginning to cry out. Ruskin wrote that these lines told more of the spirit of the Renaissance than any other English poem or prose work—"its worldliness, inconsistency, pride, hypocrisy, ignorance of itself, love of art, of luxury, and of good Latin."

Vanity, saith the preacher, vanity!
Draw round my bed: is Anselm keeping back?

Nephews—sons mine . . . ah God, I know not! Well—
She, men would have to be your mother once,
Old Gandolf envied me, so fair she was!
What 's done is done, and she is dead beside,
Dead long ago, and I am Bishop since,
And as she died so must we die ourselves,
And thence ye may perceive the world 's a dream.
Life, how and what is it? As here I lie
In this state-chamber, dying by degrees,
Hours and long hours in the dead night, I ask
"Do I live, am I dead?" Peace, peace seems all.
Saint Praxed's ever was the church for peace;
And so, about this tomb of mine. I fought
With tooth and nail to save my niche, ye know:
—Old Gandolf cozened me, despite my care;
Shrewd was that snatch from out the corner South
He graced his carrion with, God curse the same!
Yet still my niche is not so cramped but thence
One sees the pulpit o' the epistle-side,
And somewhat of the choir, those silent seats,
And up into the aery dome where live
The angels, and a sunbeam 's sure to lurk:
And I shall fill my slab of basalt there,
And 'neath my tabernacle take my rest,
With those nine columns round me, two and two,
The odd one at my feet where Anselm stands:
Peach-blossom marble all, the rare, the ripe
As fresh-poured red wine of a mighty pulse.
—Old Gandolf with his paltry onion-stone,
Put me where I may look at him! True peach,
Rosy and flawless: how I earned the prize!
Draw close: that conflagration of my church
—What then? So much was saved if aught were missed!
My sons, ye would not be my death? Go dig
The white-grape vineyard where the oil-press stood,
Drop water gently till the surface sink,
And if ye find . . . Ah God, I know not, I! . . .

Bedded in store of rotten fig-leaves soft,
And corded up in a tight olive-frail,
Some lump, ah God, of *lapis lazuli,*
Big as a Jew's head cut off at the nape,
Blue as a vein o'er the Madonna's breast . . .
Sons, all have I bequeathed you, villas, all,
That brave Frascati villa with its bath,
So, let the blue lump poise between my knees,
Like God the Father's globe on both his hands
Ye worship in the Jesu Church so gay,
For Gandolf shall not choose but see and burst!
Swift as a weaver's shuttle fleet our years:
Man goeth to the grave, and where is he?
Did I say basalt for my slab, sons? Black—
'T was ever antique-black I meant! How else
Shall ye contrast my frieze to come beneath?
The bas-relief in bronze ye promised me,
Those Pans and Nymphs ye wot of, and perchance
Some tripod, thyrsus, with a vase or so,
The Saviour at his sermon on the mount,
Saint Praxed in a glory, and one Pan
Ready to twitch the Nymph's last garment off,
And Moses with the tables . . . but I know
Ye mark me not! What do they whisper thee,
Child of my bowels, Anselm? Ah, ye hope
To revel down my villas while I gasp
Bricked o'er with beggar's mouldy travertine
Which Gandolf from his tomb-top chuckles at!
Nay, boys, ye love me—all of jasper, then!
'T is jasper ye stand pledged to, lest I grieve.
My bath must needs be left behind, alas!
One block, pure green as a pistachio-nut,
There 's plenty jasper somewhere in the world—
And have I not Saint Praxed's ear to pray
Horses for ye, and brown Greek manuscripts,
And mistresses with great smooth marbly limbs?
—That 's if ye carve my epitaph aright,

Choice Latin, picked phrase, Tully's every word,
No gaudy ware like Gandolf's second line—
Tully, my masters? Ulpian serves his need!
And then how I shall lie through centuries,
And hear the blessed mutter of the mass,
And see God made and eaten all day long,
And feel the steady candle-flame, and taste
Good strong thick stupefying incense-smoke!
For as I lie here, hours of the dead night,
Dying in state and by such slow degrees,
I fold my arms as if they clasped a crook,
And stretch my feet forth straight as stone can point,
And let the bedclothes, for a mortcloth, drop
Into great laps and folds of sculptor's-work:
And as yon tapers dwindle, and strange thoughts
Grow, with a certain humming in my ears,
About the life before I lived this life,
And this life too, popes, cardinals and priests,
Saint Praxed at his sermon on the mount,
Your tall pale mother with her talking eyes,
And new-found agate urns as fresh as day,
And marble's language, Latin pure, discreet,
—Aha, ELUCESCEBAT quoth our friend?
No Tully, said I, Ulpian at the best!
Evil and brief hath been my pilgrimage.
All *lapis,* all, sons! Else I give the Pope
My villas! Will ye ever eat my heart?
Ever your eyes were as a lizard's quick,
They glitter like your mother's for my soul,
Or ye would heighten my impoverished frieze,
Piece out its starved design, and fill my vase
With grapes, and add a vizor and a Term,
And to the tripod ye would tie a lynx
That in his struggle throws the thyrsus down,
To comfort me on my entablature
Whereon I am to lie till I must ask
"Do I live, am I dead?" There, leave me, there!

For ye have stabbed me with ingratitude
To death—ye wish it—God, ye wish it! Stone—
Gritstone, a-crumble! Clammy squares which sweat
As if the corpse they keep were oozing through—
And no more *lapis* to delight the world!
Well, go! I bless ye. Fewer tapers there,
But in a row: and, going, turn your backs
—Ay, like departing altar-ministrants,
And leave me in my church, the church for peace,
That I may watch at leisure if he leers—
Old Gandolf, at me, from his onion-stone,
As still he envied me, so fair she was!

GARDEN FANCIES

Part I reveals the sunny fragrance of an English garden through the enraptured senses of a young man falling in love. In the second part, the scene is the same, but the mood changes: the poet is disgusted with pedantry, and tosses the ancient scholarly volume he has been reading into a hollow tree trunk, and chooses jolly old Rabelais for his afternoon reading. Memories of Browning's mother's garden at Hatcham are clearly indicated in this poem.

I. The Flower's Name

I

Here's the garden she walked across,
   Arm in my arm, such a short while since:
Hark, now I push its wicket, the moss
   Hinders the hinges and makes them wince!
She must have reached this shrub ere she turned,
   As back with that murmur the wicket swung;
For she laid the poor snail, my chance foot spurned,
   To feed and forget it the leaves among.

2

Down this side of the gravel-walk
  She went while her robe's edge brushed the box:
And here she paused in her gracious talk
  To point me a moth on the milk-white phlox.
Roses, ranged in valiant row,
  I will never think that she passed you by!
She loves you noble roses, I know;
  But yonder, see, where the rock-plants lie!

3

This flower she stopped at, finger on lip,
  Stooped over, in doubt, as settling its claim;
Till she gave me, with pride to make no slip,
  Its soft meandering Spanish name:
What a name! Was it love or praise?
  Speech half-asleep or song half-awake?
I must learn Spanish, one of these days,
  Only for that slow sweet name's sake.

4

Roses, if I live and do well,
  I may bring her, one of these days,
To fix you fast with as fine a spell,
  Fit you each with his Spanish phrase;
But do not detain me now; for she lingers
  There, like sunshine over the ground,
And ever I see her soft white fingers
  Searching after the bud she found.

5

Flower, you Spaniard, look that you grow not,
  Stay as you are and be loved for ever!
But, if I kiss you 't is that you blow not:
  Mind, the shut pink mouth opens never!

For while it pouts, her fingers wrestle,
  Twinkling the audacious leaves between,
Till round they turn and down they nestle—
  Is not the dear mark still to be seen?

6

Where I find her not, beauties vanish;
  Whither I follow her, beauties flee;
Is there no method to tell her in Spanish
  June's twice June since she breathed it with me?
Come, bud, show me the least of her traces,
  Treasure my lady's lightest footfall!
—Ah, you may flout and turn up your faces—
  Roses, you are not so fair after all!

II. Sibrandus Schafnaburgensis

1

Plague take all your pedants, say I!
  He who wrote what I hold in my hand,
Centuries back was so good as to die,
  Leaving this rubbish to cumber the land;
This, that was a book in its time,
  Printed on paper and bound in leather,
Last month in the white of a matin-prime
  Just when the birds sang all together.

2

Into the garden I brought it to read,
  And under the arbute and laurustine
Read it, so help me grace in my need,
  From title-page to closing line.
Chapter on chapter did I count,
  As a curious traveller counts Stonehenge;
Added up the mortal amount;
  And then proceeded to my revenge.

3

Yonder's a plum-tree with a crevice
   An owl would build in, were he but sage;
For a lap of moss, like a fine pont-levis
   In a castle of the Middle Age,
Joins to a lip of gum, pure amber;
   When he 'd be private, there might he spend
Hours alone in his lady's chamber:
   Into this crevice I dropped our friend.

4

Splash, went he, as under he ducked,
   —At the bottom, I knew, rain-drippings stagnate:
Next, a handful of blossoms I plucked
   To bury him with, my bookshelf's magnate;
Then I went in-doors, brought out a loaf,
   Half a cheese, and a bottle of Chablis;
Lay on the grass and forgot the oaf
   Over a jolly chapter of Rabelais.

5

Now, this morning, betwixt the moss
   And gum that locked our friend in limbo,
A spider had spun his web across,
   And sat in the midst with arms akimbo:
So, I took pity, for learning's sake,
   And, *de profundis, accentibus laetis,*
Cantate! quoth I, as I got a rake;
   And up I fished his delectable treatise.

6

Here you have it, dry in the sun,
   With all the binding all of a blister,
And great blue spots where the ink has run,
   And reddish streaks that wink and glister

O'er the page so beautifully yellow:
  Oh, well have the droppings played their tricks!
Did he guess how toadstools grow, this fellow?
  Here's one stuck in his chapter six!

7

How did he like it when the live creatures
  Tickled and toused and browsed him all over,
And worm, slug, eft, with serious features,
  Came in, each one, for his right of trover?
—When the water-beetle with great blind deaf face
  Made of her eggs the stately deposit,
And the newt borrowed just so much of the preface
  As tiled in the top of his black wife's closet?

8

All that life and fun and romping,
  All that frisking and twisting and coupling,
While slowly our poor friend's leaves were swamping
  And clasps were cracking and covers suppling!
As if you had carried sour John Knox
  To the play-house at Paris, Vienna or Munich,
Fastened him into a front-row box,
  And danced off the ballet with trousers and tunic.

9

Come, old martyr! What, torment enough is it?
  Back to my room shall you take your sweet self.
Good-bye, mother-beetle; husband-eft, *sufficit!*
  See the snug niche I have made on my shelf!
A.'s book shall prop you up, B.'s shall cover you,
  Here's C. to be grave with, or D. to be gay,
And with E. on each side, and F. right over you,
  Dry-rot at ease till the Judgment-day!

THE LABORATORY

Ancien Régime

This little vignette of old France shows us a lady procuring a dose of poison—probably the favorite arsenic—with which she plans to do away with her rival. The monologue is a fine example of Browning's ability to compress an intense human drama into brief space.

1

Now that I, tying thy glass mask tightly,
May gaze thro' these faint smokes curling whitely,
As thou pliest thy trade in this devil's-smithy—
Which is the poison to poison her, prithee?

2

He is with her, and they know that I know
Where they are, what they do: they believe my tears flow
While they laugh, laugh at me, at me fled to the drear
Empty church, to pray God in, for them!—I am here.

3

Grind away, moisten and mash up thy paste,
Pound at thy powder,—I am not in haste!
Better sit thus, and observe thy strange things,
Than go where men wait me and dance at the King's.

4

That in the mortar—you call it a gum?
Ah, the brave tree whence such gold oozings come!
And yonder soft phial, the exquisite blue,
Sure to taste sweetly,—is that poison too?

5

Had I but all of them, thee and thy treasures,
What a wild crowd of invisible pleasures!
To carry pure death in an earring, a casket,
A signet, a fan-mount, a filigree basket!

6

Soon, at the King's, a mere lozenge to give,
And Pauline should have just thirty minutes to live!
But to light a pastile, and Elise, with her head
And her breast and her arms and her hands, should drop dead!

7

Quick—is it finished? The colour 's too grim!
Why not soft like the phial's, enticing and dim?
Let it brighten her drink, let her turn it and stir,
And try it and taste, ere she fix and prefer!

8

What a drop! She 's not little, no minion like me!
That 's why she ensnared him: this never will free
The soul from those masculine eyes,—say, "no!"
To that pulse's magnificent come-and-go.

9

For only last night, as they whispered, I brought
My own eyes to bear on her so, that I thought
Could I keep them one half minute fixed, she would fall
Shrivelled; she fell not; yet this does it all!

10

Not that I bid you spare her the pain;
Let death be felt and the proof remain:
Brand, burn up, bite into its grace—
He is sure to remember her dying face!

11

Is it done? Take my mask off! Nay, be not morose;
It kills her, and this prevents seeing it close:
The delicate droplet, my whole fortune's fee!
If it hurts her, beside, can it ever hurt me?

12

Now, take all my jewels, gorge gold to your fill,
You may kiss me, old man, on my mouth if you will!
But brush this dust off me, lest horror it brings
Ere I know it—next moment I dance at the King's!

EARTH'S IMMORTALITIES

Fame

It is thought that Browning refers here to the graves of Keats and Shelley in the Protestant cemetery in Rome.

See, as the prettiest graves will do in time,
Our poet's wants the freshness of its prime;
Spite of the sexton's browsing horse, the sods
Have struggled through its binding osier rods;
Headstone and half-sunk footstone lean awry,
Wanting the brick-work promised by-and-by;
How the minute grey lichens, plate o'er plate,
Have softened down the crisp-cut name and date!

New Cross, Hatcham, Surrey.

I love your verses with all my heart, dear Miss Barrett,—and this is no off-hand complimentary letter that I shall write,—whatever else, no prompt matter-of-course recognition of your genius and there a graceful and natural end of the thing: since the day last week when I first read your poems, I quite laugh to remember how I have been turning and turning again in my mind what I should be able to tell you of their effect upon me—for in the first flush of delight I thought I would this once get out of my habit of purely passive enjoyment, when I do really enjoy, and thoroughly justify my admiration—perhaps even, as a loyal fellow-craftsman should, try and find fault and do you some little good to be proud of hereafter!—but nothing comes of it

Browning's First Letter to Elizabeth Barrett

all — so into me has it gone, and part of
me has it become, this great living poetry
of yours, not a flower of which but
took root and grew .. oh, how different
that is from lying to be dried and pressed
flat and prized highly and put in a book
with a proper account at top and bottom,
and shut up and put away .. and the book
called a "Flora", besides! After all, I
need not give up the thought of
doing that, too, in time; because even
now, talking with whoever is worthy,
I can give a reason for my faith
in one and another excellence,
the fresh strange music, the affluent
language, the exquisite pathos and
true new brave thought — but in
this addressing myself to you, your

own-self, and for the first time,
my feeling rises altogether—
I do, as I say, love these Books
with all my heart—and I love
you too: do you know I was
once not very far from seeing—
—really seeing you? Mr Kenyon
said to me one morning "would
you like to see Miss Barrett?"
—then he went to announce me,
—then he returned .. you were too
unwell—and now it is years
ago—and I feel as at some un=
=toward passage in my travels—
—as if I had been close, so close, to
some world's-wonder in chapel

or crypt, — only a screen to push
and I might have entered — but
there was some slight .. so it now
seems .. slight and just-sufficient
bar to admission, and the half-
-opened door shut, and I went
home my thousands of miles, —
and the sight was never to be!
Well, these Poems were to be —
and this true thankful joy and
pride with which I feel myself
Yours ever faithfully,
Robert Browning.

Courtesy of The Morgan Library

Love

When asked if the refrain "love me for ever" was cynical, sad, or trustful, Browning wrote in reply that it was "A mournful comment on the short duration of the conventional 'for ever.'"

So, the year's done with!
  (*Love me for ever!*)
All March begun with,
  April's endeavour;
May-wreaths that bound me
  June needs must sever;
Now snows fall round me,
  Quenching June's fever—
  (*Love me for ever!*)

SONG

1

Nay but you, who do not love her,
  Is she not pure gold, my mistress?
Holds earth aught—speak truth—above her?
  Aught like this tress, see, and this tress,
And this last fairest tress of all,
So fair, see, ere I let it fall?

2

Because, you spend your lives in praising;
  To praise, you search the wide world over:
Then why not witness, calmly gazing,
  If earth holds aught—speak truth—above her?
Above this tress, and this, I touch
But cannot praise, I love so much!

THE BOY AND THE ANGEL

This simple tale, told in rhymed couplets, has no basis in fact, but was invented by the poet to point his belief that God loves the hymns of the lowly as much as those of his angels.

Morning, evening, noon and night,
"Praise God!" sang Theocrite.

Then to his poor trade he turned,
Whereby the daily meal was earned.

Hard he laboured, long and well;
O'er his work the boy's curls fell.

But ever, at each period,
He stopped and sang, "Praise God!"

Then back again his curls he threw,
And cheerful turned to work anew.

Said Blaise, the listening monk, "Well done;
I doubt not thou art heard, my son:

As well as if thy voice to-day
Were praising God, the Pope's great way.

This Easter Day, the Pope at Rome
Praises God from Peter's dome."

Said Theocrite, "Would God that I
Might praise him, that great way, and die!"

Night passed, day shone,
And Theocrite was gone.

With God a day endures alway,
A thousand years are but a day.

God said in heaven, "Nor day nor night
Now brings the voice of my delight."

Then Gabriel, like a rainbow's birth,
Spread his wings and sank to earth;

Entered, in flesh, the empty cell,
Lived there, and played the craftsman well;

And morning, evening, noon and night,
Praised God in place of Theocrite.

And from a boy, to youth he grew:
The man put off the stripling's hue:

The man matured and fell away
Into the season of decay:

And ever o'er the trade he bent,
And ever lived on earth content.

(He did God's will; to him, all one
If on the earth or in the sun.)

God said, "A praise is in mine ear;
There is no doubt in it, no fear:

So sing old worlds, and so
New worlds that from my footstool go.

Clearer loves sound other ways:
I miss my little human praise."

Then forth sprang Gabriel's wings, off fell
The flesh disguise, remained the cell.

'T was Easter Day: he flew to Rome,
And paused above Saint Peter's dome.

In the tiring-room close by
The great outer gallery,

With his holy vestments dight,
Stood the new Pope, Theocrite:

And all his past career
Came back upon him clear,

Since when, a boy, he plied his trade,
Till on his life the sickness weighed;

And in his cell, when death drew near,
An angel in a dream brought cheer:

And rising from the sickness drear
He grew a priest, and now stood here.

To the East with praise he turned,
And on his sight the angel burned.

"I bore thee from thy craftsman's cell
And set thee here; I did not well.

Vainly I left my angel-sphere,
Vain was thy dream of many a year.

Thy voice's praise seemed weak; it dropped—
Creation's chorus stopped!

Go back and praise again
The early way, while I remain.

With that weak voice of our disdain,
Take up creation's pausing strain.

Back to the cell and poor employ:
Resume the craftsman and the boy!"

Theocrite grew old at home;
A new Pope dwelt in Peter's dome.

One vanished as the other died:
They sought God side by side.

MEETING AT NIGHT

I

The grey sea and the long black land;
And the yellow half-moon large and low;
And the startled little waves that leap
In fiery ringlets from their sleep,
As I gain the cove with pushing prow,
And quench its speed i' the slushy sand.

2

Then a mile of warm sea-scented beach;
Three fields to cross till a farm appears;
A tap at the pane, the quick sharp scratch
And blue spurt of a lighted match,
And a voice less loud, thro' its joys and fears,
Than the two hearts beating each to each!

PARTING AT MORNING

In response to a request for an explanation of what the speaker in this poem meant, Browning wrote: "It is his confession of how fleeting is the belief (implied in the first part) that such raptures are self-sufficient or enduring as for the time they appear."

Round the cape of a sudden came the sea,
And the sun looked over the mountain's rim:
And straight was a path of gold for him,
And the need of a world of men for me.

NATIONALITY IN DRINKS

The first poem, originally entitled Claret, *was a not very successful attempt in serio-comic vein to catch the spirit of France. The second,* Tokay, *celebrates Hungary's famous wine. Suggesting a gaiety and braggadocio inspired by wine,* Tokay *is symbolized by one of those grotesque wine bottles, shaped like a strutting figure.* Beer, *of course, typifies the lusty spirit of Britain. Mrs. Browning did not admire the first two and they were omitted from the collected edition of 1849. In 1863,* Beer, *with its toast to Nelson, was added and the general title,* Nationality in Drinks, *was given to the three poems.*

1

My heart sank with our Claret-flask,
   Just now, beneath the heavy sedges
That serve this pond's black face for mask;
   And still at yonder broken edges
O' the hole, where up the bubbles glisten,
After my heart I look and listen.

Our laughing little flask, compelled
   Thro' depth to depth more bleak and shady;
As when, both arms beside her held,
   Feet straightened out, some gay French lady
Is caught up from life's light and motion,
And dropped into death's silent ocean!

2

Up jumped Tokay on our table,
Like a pygmy castle-warder,
Dwarfish to see, but stout and able,
Arms and accoutrements all in order;
And fierce he looked North, then, wheeling South,
Blew with his bugle a challenge to Drouth,

Cocked his flap-hat with the tosspot-feather,
Twisted his thumb in his red moustache,
Jingled his huge brass spurs together,
Tightened his waist with its Buda sash,
And then, with an impudence nought could abash,
Shrugged his hump-shoulder, to tell the beholder,
For twenty such knaves he should laugh but the bolder:
And so, with his sword-hilt gallantly jutting,
And dexter-hand on his haunch abutting,
Went the little man, Sir Ausbruch, strutting!

3

Here 's to Nelson's memory!
'T is the second time that I, at sea,
Right off Cape Trafalgar here,
Have drunk it deep in British Beer.
Nelson for ever—any time
Am I his to command in prose or rhyme!
Give me of Nelson only a touch,
And I save it, be it little or much:
Here 's one our Captain gives, and so
Down at the word, by George, shall it go!
He says that at Greenwich they point the beholder
To Nelson's coat, "still with tar on the shoulder:
For he used to lean with one shoulder digging,
Jigging, as it were, and zig-zag-zigging
Up against the mizen-rigging!"

THE GLOVE

(Peter Ronsard *loquitur*)

The Glove *is a good example of Browning's originality and love of paradox. Taking a familiar old story—which had been retold in verse by Schiller, Leigh Hunt, and others—he gives it a "new twist" by vindicating the lady's behavior instead of making her a heartless coquette who deserved rebuke. He presents the French poet Ronsard in the role of storyteller.*

"Heigho," yawned one day King Francis,
"Distance all value enhances!
When a man's busy, why, leisure
Strikes him as wonderful pleasure:
'Faith, and at leisure once is he?
Straightway he wants to be busy.
Here we 've got peace; and aghast I 'm
Caught thinking war the true pastime.
Is there a reason in metre?
Give us your speech, master Peter!"
I who, if mortal dare say so,
Ne'er am at loss with my Naso,
"Sire," I replied, "joys prove cloudlets:
Men are the merest Ixions"—
Here the King whistled aloud, "Let 's
—Heigho—go look at our lions!"
Such are the sorrowful chances
If you talk fine to King Francis.

And so, to the courtyard proceeding,
Our company, Francis was leading,
Increased by new followers tenfold
Before he arrived at the penfold;
Lords, ladies, like clouds which bedizen
At sunset the western horizon.
And Sir De Lorge pressed 'mid the foremost
With the dame he professed to adore most.
Oh, what a face! One by fits eyed
Her, and the horrible pitside;
For the penfold surrounded a hollow
Which led where the eye scarce dared follow,
And shelved to the chamber secluded
Where Bluebeard, the great lion, brooded.
The King hailed his keeper, an Arab

As glossy and black as a scarab,
And bade him make sport and at once stir
Up and out of his den the old monster.
They opened a hole in the wire-work
Across it, and dropped there a firework,
And fled: one's heart's beating redoubled;
A pause, while the pit's mouth was troubled,
The blackness and silence so utter,
By the firework's slow sparkling and sputter;
Then earth in a sudden contortion
Gave out to our gaze her abortion!
Such a brute! Were I friend Clement Marot
(Whose experience of nature 's but narrow,
And whose faculties move in no small mist
When he versifies David the Psalmist)
I should study that brute to describe you
Illum Juda Leonem de Tribu.
One's whole blood grew curdling and creepy
To see the black mane, vast and heapy,
The tail in the air stiff and straining,
The wide eyes, nor waxing nor waning,
As over the barrier which bounded
His platform, and us who surrounded
The barrier, they reached and they rested
On space that might stand him in best stead:
For who knew, he thought, what the amazement,
The eruption of clatter and blaze meant,
And if, in this minute of wonder,
No outlet, 'mid lightning and thunder,
Lay broad, and, his shackles all shivered,
The lion at last was delivered?
Ay, that was the open sky o'erhead!
And you saw by the flash on his forehead,
By the hope in those eyes wide and steady,
He was leagues in the desert already,
Driving the flocks up the mountain,
Or catlike couched hard by the fountain
To waylay the date-gathering negress:

So guarded he entrance or egress.
"How he stands!" quoth the King: "we may well swear,
(No novice, we 've won our spurs elsewhere
And so can afford the confession,)
We exercise wholesome discretion
In keeping aloof from his threshold;
Once hold you, those jaws want no fresh hold,
Their first would too pleasantly purloin
The visitor's brisket or surloin:
But who 's he would prove so fool-hardy?
Not the best man of Marignan, pardie!"

The sentence no sooner was uttered,
Than over the rails a glove fluttered,
Fell close to the lion, and rested:
The dame 't was, who flung it and jested
With life so, De Lorge had been wooing
For months past; he sat there pursuing
His suit, weighing out with nonchalance
Fine speeches like gold from a balance.

Sound the trumpet, no true knight 's a tarrier!
De Lorge made one leap at the barrier,
Walked straight to the glove,—while the lion
Ne'er moved, kept his far-reaching eye on
The palm-tree-edged desert-spring's sapphire,
And the musky oiled skin of the Kaffir,—
Picked it up, and as calmly retreated,
Leaped back where the lady was seated,
And full in the face of its owner
Flung the glove.

"Your heart's queen, you dethrone her?
So should I!"—cried the King—" 't was mere vanity,
Not love, set that task to humanity!"
Lords and ladies alike turned with loathing
From such a proved wolf in sheep's clothing.

Not so, I; for I caught an expression
In her brow's undisturbed self-possession
Amid the Court's scoffing and merriment,—
As if from no pleasing experiment
She rose, yet of pain not much heedful
So long as the process was needful,—
As if she had tried in a crucible,
To what "speeches like gold" were reducible,
And, finding the finest prove copper,
Felt the smoke in her face was but proper;
To know what she had *not* to trust to,
Was worth all the ashes and dust too.
She went out 'mid hooting and laughter;
Clement Marot stayed; I followed after,
And asked, as a grace, what it all meant?
If she wished not the rash deed's recalment?
"For I"—so I spoke—"am a poet:
Human nature,—behoves that I know it!"

She told me, "Too long had I heard
Of the deed proved alone by the word:
For my love—what De Lorge would not dare!
With my scorn—what De Lorge could compare!
And the endless descriptions of death
He would brave when my lip formed a breath,
I must reckon as braved, or, of course,
Doubt his word—and moreover, perforce,
For such gifts as no lady could spurn,
Must offer my love in return.
When I looked on your lion, it brought
All the dangers at once to my thought,
Encountered by all sorts of men,
Before he was lodged in his den,—
From the poor slave whose club or bare hands
Dug the trap, set the snare on the sands,
With no King and no Court to applaud,
By no shame, should he shrink, overawed,
Yet to capture the creature made shift,

That his rude boys might laugh at the gift,
—To the page who last leaped o'er the fence
Of the pit, on no greater pretence
Than to get back the bonnet he dropped,
Lest his pay for a week should be stopped.
So, wiser I judged it to make
One trial what 'death for my sake'
Really meant, while the power was yet mine,
Than to wait until time should define
Such a phrase not so simply as I,
Who took it to mean just 'to die.'
The blow a glove gives is but weak:
Does the mark yet discolour my cheek?
But when the heart suffers a blow,
Will the pain pass so soon, do you know?"

I looked, as away she was sweeping,
And saw a youth eagerly keeping
As close as he dared to the doorway.
No doubt that a noble should more weigh
His life than befits a plebeian;
And yet, had our brute been Nemean—
(I judge by a certain calm fervour
The youth stepped with, forward to serve her)
—He 'd have scarce thought you did him the worst turn
If you whispered "Friend, what you 'd get, first earn!"
And when, shortly after, she carried
Her shame from the Court, and they married,
To that marriage some happiness, maugre
The voice of the Court, I dared augur.

For De Lorge, he made women with men vie,
Those in wonder and praise, these in envy;
And in short stood so plain a head taller
That he wooed and won . . . how do you call her?
The beauty, that rose in the sequel
To the King's love, who loved her a week well.
And 't was noticed he never would honour

De Lorge (who looked daggers upon her)
With the easy commission of stretching
His legs in the service, and fetching
His wife, from her chamber, those straying
Sad gloves she was always mislaying,
While the King took the closet to chat in,—
But of course this adventure came pat in.
And never the King told the story,
How bringing a glove brought such glory,
But the wife smiled—"His nerves are grown firmer:
Mine he brings now and utters no murmur."

Venienti occurrite morbo!
With which moral I drop my theorbo.

Men and Women

1855

LOVE IN A LIFE

I

Room after room,
I hunt the house through
We inhabit together.
Heart, fear nothing, for, heart, thou shalt find her,
Next time, herself!—not the trouble behind her
Left in the curtain, the couch's perfume!
As she brushed it, the cornice-wreath blossomed anew:
Yon looking-glass gleamed at the wave of her feather.

2

Yet the day wears,
And door succeeds door;
I try the fresh fortune—
Range the wide house from the wing to the centre.

Still the same chance! she goes out as I enter.
Spend my whole day in the quest,—who cares?
But 'tis twilight, you see,—with such suites to explore,
Such closets to search, such alcoves to importune!

LIFE IN A LOVE

Escape me?
Never—
Beloved!
While I am I, and you are you,
So long as the world contains us both,
Me the loving and you the loth,
While the one eludes, must the other pursue.
My life is a fault at last, I fear:
It seems too much like a fate, indeed
Though I do my best I shall scarce succeed.
But what if I fail of my purpose here?
It is but to keep the nerves at strain,
To dry one's eyes and laugh at a fall,
And baffled, get up and begin again,—
So the chase takes up one's life, that's all.
While, look but once from your farthest bound
At me so deep in the dust and dark,
No sooner the old hope drops to ground
Than a new one, straight to the self-same mark,
I shape me—
Ever
Removed!

A LOVERS' QUARREL

Browning fails to make this imaginary quarrel sound very serious. The meter is gay and rollicking and the mood expresses not bitterness but complete forgiveness and confidence in the loved one's return. It is interesting to note the reference to

Napoleon III in verse 5 and to "table-tipping" in verse 7, for the merits of Louis Napoleon and mesmerism were two subjects on which the Brownings differed.

1

Oh, what a dawn of day!
How the March sun feels like May!
All is blue again
After last night's rain,
And the South dries the hawthorn-spray.
Only, my Love 's away!
I 'd as lief that the blue were grey.

2

Runnels, which rillets swell,
Must be dancing down the dell,
With a foamy head
On the beryl bed
Paven smooth as a hermit's cell;
Each with a tale to tell,
Could my Love but attend as well.

3

Dearest, three months ago!
When we lived blocked-up with snow,—
When the wind would edge
In and in his wedge,
In, as far as the point could go—
Not to our ingle, though,
Where we loved each the other so!

4

Laughs with so little cause!
We devised games out of straws.
We would try and trace
One another's face

In the ash, as an artist draws;
    Free on each other's flaws,
How we chattered like two church daws!

5

What 's in the "Times"?—a scold
At the Emperor deep and cold;
    He has taken a bride
    To his gruesome side,
That 's as fair as himself is bold:
    There they sit ermine-stoled,
And she powders her hair with gold.

6

Fancy the Pampas' sheen!
Miles and miles of gold and green
    Where the sunflowers blow
    In a solid glow,
And—to break now and then the screen—
    Black neck and eyeballs keen,
Up a wild horse leaps between!

7

Try, will our table turn?
Lay your hands there light, and yearn
    Till the yearning slips
    Thro' the finger-tips
In a fire which a few discern,
    And a very few feel burn,
And the rest, they may live and learn!

8

Then we would up and pace,
For a change, about the place,
    Each with arm o'er neck:
    'T is our quarter-deck,

We are seamen in woeful case.
    Help in the ocean-space!
Or, if no help, we 'll embrace.

9

See, how she looks now, dressed
In a sledging-cap and vest!
    'T is a huge fur cloak—
    Like a reindeer's yoke
Falls the lappet along the breast:
    Sleeves for her arms to rest,
Or to hang, as my Love likes best.

10

Teach me to flirt a fan
As the Spanish ladies can,
    Or I tint your lip
    With a burnt stick's tip
And you turn into such a man!
    Just the two spots that span
Half the bill of the young male swan.

11

Dearest, three months ago
When the mesmerizer Snow
    With his hand's first sweep
    Put the earth to sleep:
'T was a time when the heart could show
    All—how was earth to know,
'Neath the mute hand's to-and-fro?

12

Dearest, three months ago
When we loved each other so,
    Lived and loved the same
    Till an evening came

When a shaft from the devil's bow
    Pierced to our ingle-glow,
And the friends were friend and foe!

13

Not from the heart beneath—
'T was a bubble born of breath,
    Neither sneer nor vaunt,
    Nor reproach nor taunt.
See a word, how it severeth!
    Oh, power of life and death
In the tongue, as the Preacher saith!

14

Woman, and will you cast
For a word, quite off at last
    Me, your own, your You,—
    Since, as truth is true,
I was You all the happy past—
    Me do you leave aghast
With the memories We amassed?

15

Love, if you knew the light
That your soul casts in my sight,
    How I look to you
    For the pure and true
And the beauteous and the right,—
    Bear with a moment's spite
When a mere mote threats the white!

16

What of a hasty word?
Is the fleshly heart not stirred
    By a worm's pin-prick
    Where its roots are quick?

See the eye, by a fly's foot blurred—
    Ear, when a straw is heard
Scratch the brain's coat of curd!

17

Foul be the world or fair
More or less, how can I care?
    'T is the world the same
    For my praise or blame,
And endurance is easy there.
    Wrong in the one thing rare—
Oh, it is hard to bear!

18

Here's the spring back or close,
When the almond-blossom blows:
    We shall have the word
    In a minor third
There is none but the cuckoo knows:
    Heaps of the guelder-rose!
I must bear with it, I suppose.

19

Could but November come,
Were the noisy birds struck dumb
    At the warning slash
    Of his driver's-lash—
I would laugh like the valiant Thumb
    Facing the castle glum
And the giant's fee-faw-fum!

20

Then, were the world well stripped
Of the gear wherein equipped
    We can stand apart,
    Heart dispense with heart

In the sun, with the flowers un-nipped,—
    Oh, the world's hangings ripped,
We were both in a bare-walled crypt!

21

Each in the crypt would cry
"But one freezes here! and why?
    When a heart, as chill,
    At my own would thrill
Back to life, and its fires out-fly?
    Heart, shall we live or die?
The rest. . . . settle by-and-by!"

22

So she 'd efface the score,
And forgive me as before.
    It is twelve o'clock:
    I shall hear her knock
In the worst of a storm's uproar,
    I shall pull her through the door,
I shall have her for evermore!

ANY WIFE TO ANY HUSBAND

1

My love, this is the bitterest, that thou—
Who art all truth, and who dost love me now
  As thine eyes say, as thy voice breaks to say—
Shouldst love so truly, and couldst love me still
A whole long life through, had but love its will,
  Would death that leads me from thee brook delay.

2

I have but to be by thee, and thy hand
Will never let mine go, nor heart withstand
  The beating of my heart to reach its place.

When shall I look for thee and feel thee gone?
When cry for the old comfort and find none?
  Never, I know! Thy soul is in thy face.

3

Oh, I should fade—'t is willed so! Might I save,
Gladly I would, whatever beauty gave
  Joy to thy sense, for that was precious too.
It is not to be granted. But the soul
Whence the love comes, all ravage leaves that whole;
  Vainly the flesh fades; soul makes all things new.

4

It would not be because my eye grew dim
Thou couldst not find the love there, thanks to Him
  Who never is dishonoured in the spark
He gave us from his fire of fires, and bade
Remember whence it sprang, nor be afraid
  While that burns on, though all the rest grow dark.

5

So, how thou wouldst be perfect, white and clean
Outside as inside, soul and soul's demesne
  Alike, this body given to show it by!
Oh, three-parts through the worst of life's abyss,
What plaudits from the next world after this,
  Couldst thou repeat a stroke and gain the sky!

6

And is it not the bitterer to think
That, disengage our hands and thou wilt sink
  Although thy love was love in very deed?
I know that nature! Pass a festive day,
Thou dost not throw its relic-flower away
  Nor bid its music's loitering echo speed.

7

Thou let'st the stranger's glove lie where it fell;
If old things remain old things all is well,
  For thou art grateful as becomes man best:
And hadst thou only heard me play one tune,
Or viewed me from a window, not so soon
  With thee would such things fade as with the rest.

8

I seem to see! We meet and part; 't is brief;
The book I opened keeps a folded leaf,
  The very chair I sat on, breaks the rank;
That is a portrait of me on the wall—
Three lines, my face comes at so slight a call:
  And for all this, one little hour to thank!

9

But now, because the hour through years was fixed,
Because our inmost beings met and mixed,
  Because thou once hast loved me—wilt thou dare
Say to thy soul and Who may list beside,
"Therefore she is immortally my bride;
  Chance cannot change my love, nor time impair.

10

So, what if in the dusk of life that 's left,
I, a tired traveller of my sun bereft,
  Look from my path when, mimicking the same,
The fire-fly glimpses past me, come and gone?
—Where was it till the sunset? where anon
  It will be at the sunrise! What 's to blame?"

11

Is it so helpful to thee? Canst thou take
The mimic up, nor, for the true thing's sake,
  Put gently by such efforts at a beam?

Is the remainder of the way so long,
Thou need'st the little solace, thou the strong?
  Watch out thy watch, let weak ones doze and dream!

12

—Ah, but the fresher faces! "Is it true,"
Thou 'lt ask, "some eyes are beautiful and new?
  Some hair,—how can one choose but grasp such wealth?
And if a man would press his lips to lips
Fresh as the wilding hedge-rose-cup there slips
  The dew-drop out of, must it be by stealth?

13

It cannot change the love still kept for Her,
More than if such a picture I prefer
  Passing a day with, to a room's bare side:
The painted form takes nothing she possessed,
Yet, while the Titian's Venus lies at rest,
  A man looks. Once more, what is there to chide?"

14

So must I see, from where I sit and watch,
My own self sell myself, my hand attach
  Its warrant to the very thefts from me—
Thy singleness of soul that made me proud,
Thy purity of heart I loved aloud,
  Thy man's-truth I was bold to bid God see!

15

Love so, then, if thou wilt! Give all thou canst
Away to the new faces—disentranced,
  (Say it and think it) obdurate no more:
Re-issue looks and words from the old mint,
Pass them afresh, no matter whose the print
  Image and superscription once they bore!

16

Re-coin thyself and give it them to spend,—
It all comes to the same thing at the end,
  Since mine thou wast, mine art and mine shalt be,
Faithful or faithless, sealing up the sum
Or lavish of my treasure, thou must come
  Back to the heart's place here I keep for thee!

17

Only, why should it be with stain at all?
Why must I, 'twixt the leaves of coronal,
  Put any kiss of pardon on thy brow?
Why need the other women know so much,
And talk together, "Such the look and such
  The smile he used to love with, then as now!"

18

Might I die last and show thee! Should I find
Such hardship in the few years left behind,
  If free to take and light my lamp, and go
Into thy tomb, and shut the door and sit,
Seeing thy face on those four sides of it
  The better that they are so blank, I know!

19

Why, time was what I wanted, to turn o'er
Within my mind each look, get more and more
  By heart each word, too much to learn at first;
And join thee all the fitter for the pause
'Neath the low doorway's lintel. That were cause
  For lingering, though thou calledst, if I durst!

20

And yet thou art the nobler of us two:
What dare I dream of, that thou canst not do,
  Outstripping my ten small steps with one stride?

I 'll say then, here 's a trial and a task—
Is it to bear?—if easy, I 'll not ask:
  Though love fail, I can trust on in thy pride.

21

Pride?—when those eyes forestall the life behind
The death I have to go through!—when I find,
  Now that I want thy help most, all of thee!
What did I fear? Thy love shall hold me fast
Until the little minute's sleep is past
  And I wake saved.—And yet it will not be!

ONE WAY OF LOVE

1

All June I bound the rose in sheaves.
Now, rose by rose, I strip the leaves
And strew them where Pauline may pass.
She will not turn aside? Alas!
Let them lie. Suppose they die?
The chance was they might take her eye.

2

How many a month I strove to suit
These stubborn fingers to the lute!
To-day I venture all I know.
She will not hear my music? So!
Break the string; fold music's wing:
Suppose Pauline had bade me sing!

3

My whole life long I learned to love.
This hour my utmost art I prove
And speak my passion—heaven or hell?
She will not give me heaven? 'T is well!
Lose who may—I still can say,
Those who win heaven, blest are they!

ANOTHER WAY OF LOVE

1

June was not over,
Though past the full,
And the best of her roses
Had yet to blow,
When a man I know
(But shall not discover,
Since ears are dull,
And time discloses)
Turned him and said with a man's true air,
Half sighing a smile in a yawn, as 't were,—
"If I tire of your June, will she greatly care?"

2

Well, dear, in-doors with you!
True! serene deadness
Tries a man's temper.
What 's in the blossom
June wears on her bosom?
Can it clear scores with you?
Sweetness and redness.
Eadem semper!
Go, let me care for it greatly or slightly!
If June mend her bower now, your hand left unsightly
By plucking the roses,—my June will do rightly.

3

And after, for pastime,
If June be refulgent
With flowers in completeness,
All petals, no prickles,
Delicious as trickles

Of wine poured at mass-time,—
And choose One indulgent
To redness and sweetness:
Or if, with experience of man and of spider,
June use my June-lightning, the strong insect-ridder,
And stop the fresh film-work,—why, June will consider.

A WOMAN'S LAST WORD

1

Let's contend no more, Love,
Strive nor weep:
All be as before, Love,
—Only sleep!

2

What so wild as words are?
I and thou
In debate, as birds are,
Hawk on bough!

3

See the creature stalking
While we speak!
Hush and hide the talking,
Cheek on cheek!

4

What so false as truth is,
False to thee?
Where the serpent's tooth is,
Shun the tree—

5

Where the apple reddens
   Never pry—
Lest we lose our Edens,
   Eve and I!

6

Be a god and hold me
   With a charm!
Be a man and fold me
   With thine arm!

7

Teach me, only teach, Love!
   As I ought
I will speak thy speech, Love,
   Think thy thought—

8

Meet, if thou require it,
   Both demands,
Laying flesh and spirit
   In thy hands.

9

That shall be to-morrow
   Not to-night:
I must bury sorrow
   Out of sight:

10

—Must a little weep, Love,
   (Foolish me!)
And so fall asleep, Love,
   Loved by thee.

BEFORE

In Browning's day duelling was still in vogue in certain strata of European society. In Before, *a second to one of the duellists speaks, and in* After, *the victor soliloquizes.*

1

Let them fight it out, friend! things have gone too far.
God must judge the couple: leave them as they are
—Whichever one 's the guiltless, to his glory,
And whichever one the guilt 's with, to my story.

2

Why, you would not bid men, sunk in such a slough,
Strike no arm out further, stick and stink as now,
Leaving right and wrong to settle the embroilment,
Heaven with snaky hell, in torture and entoilment?

3

Who 's the culprit of them? How must he conceive
God—the queen he caps to, laughing in his sleeve,
" 'T is but decent to profess oneself beneath her:
Still, one must not be too much in earnest, either!"

4

Better sin the whole sin, sure that God observes;
Then go live his life out! Life will try his nerves,
When the sky, which noticed all, makes no disclosure,
And the earth keeps up her terrible composure.

5

Let him pace at pleasure, past the walls of rose,
Pluck their fruits when grape-trees graze him as he goes!
For he 'gins to guess the purpose of the garden,
With the sly mute thing, beside there, for a warden.

6

What 's the leopard-dog-thing, constant at his side,
A leer and lie in every eye of its obsequious hide?
When will come an end to all the mock obeisance,
And the price appear that pays for the misfeasance?

7

So much for the culprit. Who 's the martyred man?
Let him bear one stroke more, for be sure he can!
He that strove thus evil's lump with good to leaven,
Let him give his blood at last and get his heaven!

8

All or nothing, stake it! Trusts he God or no?
Thus far and no farther? farther? be it so!
Now, enough of your chicane of prudent pauses,
Sage provisos, sub-intents and saving-clauses!

9

Ah, "forgive" you bid him? While God's champion lives,
Wrong shall be resisted: dead, why, he forgives.
But you must not end my friend ere you begin him;
Evil stands not crowned on earth, while breath is in him.

10

Once more—Will the wronger, at this last of all,
Dare to say, "I did wrong," rising in his fall?
No?—Let go, then! Both the fighters to their places!
While I count three, step you back as many paces!

AFTER

Take the cloak from his face, and at first
  Let the corpse do its worst!

How he lies in his rights of a man!
  Death has done all death can.
And, absorbed in the new life he leads,
  He recks not, he heeds
Nor his wrong nor my vengeance; both strike
  On his senses alike,
And are lost in the solemn and strange
  Surprise of the change.

Ha, what avails death to erase
  His offence, my disgrace?
I would we were boys as of old
  In the field, by the fold:
His outrage, God's patience, man's scorn
  Were so easily borne!

I stand here now, he lies in his place:
  Cover the face!

TWO IN THE CAMPAGNA

A memory of the Roman countryside serves as background for this lovers' rift. The fugitive nature of the moment of perfect understanding is exquisitely suggested.

I

I wonder do you feel to-day
  As I have felt since, hand in hand,
We sat down on the grass, to stray
  In spirit better through the land,
This morn of Rome and May?

2

For me, I touched a thought, I know,
  Has tantalized me many times,
(Like turns of thread the spiders throw
  Mocking across our path) for rhymes
To catch at and let go.

3

Help me to hold it! First it left
  The yellowing fennel, run to seed
There, branching from the brickwork's cleft,
  Some old tomb's ruin: yonder weed
Took up the floating weft,

4

Where one small orange cup amassed
  Five beetles,—blind and green they grope
Among the honey-meal: and last,
  Everywhere on the grassy slope
I traced it. Hold it fast!

5

The champaign with its endless fleece
  Of feathery grasses everywhere!
Silence and passion, joy and peace,
  An everlasting wash of air—
Rome's ghost since her decease.

6

Such life there, through such lengths of hours,
  Such miracles performed in play,
Such primal naked forms of flowers,
  Such letting nature have her way
While heaven looks from its towers!

7

How say you? Let us, O my dove,
  Let us be unashamed of soul,
As earth lies bare to heaven above!
  How is it under our control
To love or not to love?

8

I would that you were all to me,
  You that are just so much, no more.
Nor yours nor mine, nor slave nor free!
  Where does the fault lie? What the core
O' the wound, since wound must be?

9

I would I could adopt your will,
  See with your eyes, and set my heart
Beating by yours, and drink my fill
  At your soul's springs,—your part my part
In life, for good and ill.

10

No. I yearn upward, touch you close,
  Then stand away. I kiss your cheek,
Catch your soul's warmth,—I pluck the rose
  And love it more than tongue can speak—
Then the good minute goes.

11

Already how am I so far
  Out of that minute? Must I go
Still like the thistle-ball, no bar,
  Onward, whenever light winds blow,
Fixed by no friendly star?

12

Just when I seemed about to learn!
  Where is the thread now? Off again!
The old trick! Only I discern—
  Infinite passion, and the pain
Of finite hearts that yearn.

IN THREE DAYS

1

So, I shall see her in three days
And just one night, but nights are short
Then two long hours, and that is morn,
See how I come, unchanged, unworn!
Feel, where my life broke off from thine,
How fresh the splinters keep and fine,—
Only a touch and we combine!

2

Too long, this time of year, the days!
But nights, at least the nights are short.
As night shows where her one moon is,
A hand's-breadth of pure light and bliss,
So life's night gives my lady birth
And my eyes hold her! What is worth
The rest of heaven, the rest of earth?

3

O loaded curls, release your store
Of warmth and scent, as once before
The tingling hair did, lights and darks
Outbreaking into fairy sparks,
When under curl and curl I pried
After the warmth and scent inside,
Thro' lights and darks how manifold—
The dark inspired, the light controlled!
As early Art embrowns the gold.

4

What great fear, should one say, "Three days
That change the world might change as well
Your fortune; and if joy delays,
Be happy that no worse befell!"
What small fear, if another says,
"Three days and one short night beside
May throw no shadow on your ways;
But years must teem with change untried,
With chance not easily defied,
With an end somewhere undescried."
No fear!—or if a fear be born
This minute, it dies out in scorn.
Fear? I shall see her in three days
And one night, now the nights are short,
Then just two hours, and that is morn.

IN A YEAR

I

Never any more
  While I live,
Need I hope to see his face
  As before.
Once his love grown chill,
  Mine may strive—
Bitterly we re-embrace,
  Single still.

2

Was it something said,
  Something done,
Vexed him? was it touch of hand,
  Turn of head?

Strange! that very way
  Love begun:
I as little understand
  Love's decay.

3

When I sewed or drew,
  I recall
How he looked as if I sung,
  —Sweetly too.
If I spoke a word,
  First of all
Up his cheek the colour sprung,
  Then he heard.

4

Sitting by my side,
  At my feet,
So he breathed the air I breathed,
  Satisfied!
I, too, at love's brim
  Touched the sweet:
I would die if death bequeathed
  Sweet to him.

5

"Speak, I love thee best!"
  He exclaimed.
"Let thy love my own foretell,"
  I confessed:
"Clasp my heart on thine
  Now unblamed,
Since upon thy soul as well
  Hangeth mine!"

6

Was it wrong to own,
  Being truth?
Why should all the giving prove
  His alone?
I had wealth and ease,
  Beauty, youth—
Since my lover gave me love,
  I gave these.

7

That was all I meant,
  —To be just,
And the passion I had raised,
  To content.
Since he chose to change
  Gold for dust,
If I gave him what he praised
  Was it strange?

8

Would he love me yet,
  On and on,
While I found some way undreamed
  —Paid my debt!
Gave more life and more,
  Till, all gone,
He should smile "She never seemed
  Mine before.

9

What—she felt the while,
  Must I think?
Love's so different with us men,"
  He should smile.

"Dying for my sake—
  White and pink!
Can't we touch these bubbles then
  But they break?"

10

Dear, the pang is brief,
  Do thy part,
Have thy pleasure. How perplext
  Grows belief!
Well, this cold clay clod
  Was man's heart.
Crumble it—and what comes next?
  Is it God?

LOVE AMONG THE RUINS

This poem was written in Paris, in 1852, the first product of Browning's resolve to write a poem a day. The immediate stimulus may have been some romantic painting depicting the ruins of antiquity which he had recently seen; the theme—that of love outliving glory and fame—is of course a characteristic one.

1

Where the quiet-coloured end of evening smiles
    Miles and miles
On the solitary pastures where our sheep
    Half-asleep
Tinkle homeward thro' the twilight, stray or stop
    As they crop—

2

Was the site once of a city great and gay,
    (So they say)
Of our country's very capital, its prince
    Ages since
Held his court in, gathered councils, wielding far
    Peace or war.

3

Now—the country does not even boast a tree,
 As you see,
To distinguish slopes of verdure, certain rills
 From the hills
Intersect and give a name to, (else they run
 Into one)

4

Where the domed and daring palace shot its spires
 Up like fires
O'er the hundred-gated circuit of a wall
 Bounding all,
Made of marble, men might march on nor be prest
 Twelve abreast.

5

And such plenty and perfection, see, of grass
 Never was!
Such a carpet as, this summer-time, o'erspreads
 And embeds
Every vestige of the city, guessed alone,
 Stock or stone—

6

Where a multitude of men breathed joy and woe
 Long ago;
Lust of glory pricked their hearts up, dread of shame
 Struck them tame;
And that glory and that shame alike, the gold
 Bought and sold.

7

Now,—the single little turret that remains
 On the plains,

By the caper overrooted, by the gourd
    Overscored,
While the patching houseleek's head of blossom winks
    Through the chinks—

8

Marks the basement whence a tower in ancient time
    Sprang sublime,
And a burning ring, all round, the chariots traced
    As they raced,
And the monarch and his minions and his dames
    Viewed the games.

9

And I know, while thus the quiet-coloured eve
    Smiles to leave
To their folding, all our many-tinkling fleece
    In such peace,
And the slopes and rills in undistinguished grey
    Melt away—

10

That a girl with eager eyes and yellow hair
    Waits me there
In the turret whence the charioteers caught soul
    For the goal,
When the king looked, where she looks now, breathless, dumb
    Till I come.

11

But he looked upon the city, every side,
    Far and wide,
All the mountains topped with temples, all the glades'
    Colonnades,
All the causeys, bridges, aqueducts,—and then,
    All the men!

12

When I do come, she will speak not, she will stand,
    Either hand
On my shoulder, give her eyes the first embrace
    Of my face,
Ere we rush, ere we extinguish sight and speech
    Each on each.

13

In one year they sent a million fighters forth
    South and North,
And they built their gods a brazen pillar high
    As the sky,
Yet reserved a thousand chariots in full force—
    Gold, of course.

14

Oh, heart! oh, blood that freezes, blood that burns!
    Earth's returns
For whole centuries of folly, noise and sin!
    Shut them in,
With their triumphs and their glories and the rest.
    Love is best!

BY THE FIRE-SIDE

This poem commemorates a trip the Brownings took up an Italian mountainside to visit a ruined chapel. Usually reluctant to admit profane eyes to his domestic sanctuary, Browning, who never took his wife for granted, here gives intimate, personal testimony of his happiness with and his gratitude to Elizabeth Barrett Browning. Beyond doubt, it is one of the finest poems on marriage in English literature.

1

How well I know what I mean to do
  When the long dark autumn-evenings come:
And where, my soul, is thy pleasant hue?
  With the music of all thy voices, dumb
In life's November too!

2

I shall be found by the fire, suppose,
  O'er a great wise book as beseemeth age,
While the shutters flap as the cross-wind blows
  And I turn the page, and I turn the page,
Not verse now, only prose!

3

Till the young ones whisper, finger on lip,
  "There he is at it, deep in Greek:
Now then, or never, out we slip
  To cut from the hazels by the creek
A mainmast for our ship!"

4

I shall be at it indeed, my friends:
  Greek puts already on either side
Such a branch-work forth as soon extends
  To a vista opening far and wide,
And I pass out where it ends.

5

The outside-frame, like your hazel-trees:
  But the inside-archway widens fast,
And a rarer sort succeeds to these,
  And we slope to Italy at last
And youth, by green degrees.

6

I follow wherever I am led,
   Knowing so well the leader's hand:
Oh woman-country, wooed not wed,
   Loved all the more by earth's male-lands,
Laid to their hearts instead!

7

Look at the ruined chapel again
   Half-way up in the Alpine gorge!
Is that a tower, I point you plain,
   Or is it a mill, or an iron-forge
Breaks solitude in vain?

8

A turn, and we stand in the heart of things;
   The woods are round us, heaped and dim;
From slab to slab how it slips and springs,
   The thread of water single and slim,
Through the ravage some torrent brings!

9

Does it feed the little lake below?
   That speck of white just on its marge
Is Pella; see, in the evening-glow,
   How sharp the silver spear-heads charge
When Alp meets heaven in snow!

10

On our other side is the straight-up rock;
   And a path is kept 'twixt the gorge and it
By boulder-stones where lichens mock
   The marks on a moth, and small ferns fit
Their teeth to the polished block.

11

Oh the sense of the yellow mountain-flowers,
  And thorny balls, each three in one,
The chestnuts throw on our path in showers!
  For the drop of the woodland fruit's begun,
These early November hours,

12

That crimson the creeper's leaf across
  Like a splash of blood, intense, abrupt,
O'er a shield else gold from rim to boss,
  And lay it for show on the fairy-cupped
Elf-needled mat of moss,

13

By the rose-flesh mushrooms, undivulged
  Last evening—nay, in to-day's first dew
Yon sudden coral nipple bulged,
  Where a freaked fawn-coloured flaky crew
Of toadstools peep indulged.

14

And yonder, at foot of the fronting ridge
  That takes the turn to a range beyond,
Is the chapel reached by the one-arched bridge
  Where the water is stopped in a stagnant pond
Danced over by the midge.

15

The chapel and bridge are of stone alike,
  Blackish-grey and mostly wet;
Cut hemp-stalks steep in the narrow dyke.
  See here again, how the lichens fret
And the roots of the ivy strike!

16

Poor little place, where its one priest comes
  On a festa-day, if he comes at all,
To the dozen folk from their scattered homes,
  Gathered within that precinct small
By the dozen ways one roams—

17

To drop from the charcoal-burners' huts,
  Or climb from the hemp-dressers' low shed,
Leave the grange where the woodman stores his nuts,
  Or the wattled cote where the fowlers spread
Their gear on the rock's bare juts.

18

It has some pretension too, this front,
  With its bit of fresco half-moon-wise
Set over the porch, Art's early wont:
  'Tis John in the Desert, I surmise,
But has borne the weather's brunt—

19

Not from the fault of the builder, though,
  For a pent-house properly projects
Where three carved beams make a certain show,
  Dating—good thought of our architect's—
'Five, six, nine, he lets you know.

20

And all day long a bird sings there,
  And a stray sheep drinks at the pond at times;
The place is silent and aware;
  It has had its scenes, its joys and crimes,
But that is its own affair.

21

My perfect wife, my Leonor,
Oh heart, my own, oh eyes, mine too,
Whom else could I dare look backward for,
With whom beside should I dare pursue
The path grey heads abhor?

22

For it leads to a crag's sheer edge with them;
Youth, flowery all the way, there stops—
Not they; age threatens and they contemn,
Till they reach the gulf wherein youth drops,
One inch from life's safe hem!

23

With me, youth led . . . I will speak now,
No longer watch you as you sit
Reading by fire-light, that great brow
And the spirit-small hand propping it,
Mutely, my heart knows how—

24

When, if I think but deep enough,
You are wont to answer, prompt as rhyme;
And you, too, find without rebuff
Response your soul seeks many a time
Piercing its fine flesh-stuff.

25

My own, confirm me! If I tread
This path back, is it not in pride
To think how little I dreamed it led
To an age so blest that, by its side,
Youth seems the waste instead?

26

My own, see where the years conduct!
  At first, 'twas something our two souls
Should mix as mists do; each is sucked
  In each now: on, the new stream rolls,
Whatever rocks obstruct.

27

Think, when our one soul understands
  The great Word which makes all things new,
When earth breaks up and heaven expands,
  How will the change strike me and you
In the house not made with hands?

28

Oh I must feel your brain prompt mine,
  Your heart anticipate my heart,
You must be just before, in fine,
  See and make me see, for your part,
New depths of the divine!

29

But who could have expected this
  When we two drew together first
Just for the obvious human bliss,
  To satisfy life's daily thirst
With a thing men seldom miss?

30

Come back with me to the first of all,
  Let us lean and love it over again,
Let us now forget and now recall,
  Break the rosary in a pearly rain,
And gather what we let fall!

31

What did I say?—that a small bird sings
  All day long, save when a brown pair
Of hawks from the wood float with wide wings
  Strained to a bell: 'gainst noon-day glare
You count the streaks and rings.

32

But at afternoon or almost eve
  'Tis better; then the silence grows
To that degree, you half believe
  It must get rid of what it knows,
Its bosom does so heave.

33

Hither we walked then, side by side,
  Arm in arm and cheek to cheek,
And still I questioned or replied,
  While my heart, convulsed to really speak,
Lay choking in its pride.

34

Silent the crumbling bridge we cross,
  And pity and praise the chapel sweet,
And care about the fresco's loss,
  And wish for our souls a like retreat,
And wonder at the moss.

35

Stoop and kneel on the settle under,
  Look through the window's grated square:
Nothing to see! For fear of plunder,
  The cross is down and the altar bare,
As if thieves don't fear thunder.

36

We stoop and look in through the grate,
  See the little porch and rustic door,
Read duly the dead builder's date;
  Then cross the bridge that we crossed before,
Take the path again—but wait!

37

Oh moment, one and infinite!
  The water slips o'er stock and stone;
The West is tender, hardly bright:
  How grey at once is the evening grown—
One star, its chrysolite!

38

We two stood there with never a third,
  But each by each, as each knew well:
The sights we saw and the sounds we heard,
  The lights and the shades made up a spell
Till the trouble grew and stirred.

39

Oh, the little more, and how much it is!
  And the little less, and what worlds away!
How a sound shall quicken content to bliss,
  Or a breath suspend the blood's best play,
And life be a proof of this!

40

Had she willed it, still had stood the screen
  So slight, so sure, 'twixt my love and her:
I could fix her face with a guard between,
  And find her soul as when friends confer,
Friends—lovers that might have been.

41

For my heart had a touch of the woodland-time,
Wanting to sleep now over its best.
Shake the whole tree in the summer-prime,
But bring to the last leaf no such test!
"Hold the last fast!" runs the rhyme.

42

For a chance to make your little much,
To gain a lover and lose a friend,
Venture the tree and a myriad such,
When nothing you mar but the year can mend:
But a last leaf—fear to touch!

43

Yet should it unfasten itself and fall
Eddying down till it find your face
At some slight wind—best chance of all!
Be your heart henceforth its dwelling-place
You trembled to forestall!

44

Worth how well, those dark grey eyes,
That hair so dark and dear, how worth
That a man should strive and agonise,
And taste a veriest hell on earth
For the hope of such a prize!

45

You might have turned and tried a man,
Set him a space to weary and wear,
And prove which suited more your plan,
His best of hope or his worst despair,
Yet end as he began.

46

But you spared me this, like the heart you are,
  And filled my empty heart at a word.
If two lives join, there is oft a scar,
  They are one and one, with a shadowy third;
One near one is too far.

47

A moment after, and hands unseen
  Were hanging the night around us fast;
But we knew that a bar was broken between
  Life and life: we were mixed at last
In spite of the mortal screen.

48

The forests had done it; there they stood;
  We caught for a moment the powers at play:
They had mingled us so, for once and good,
  Their work was done—we might go or stay,
They relapsed to their ancient mood.

49

How the world is made for each of us!
  How all we perceive and know in it
Tends to some moment's product thus,
  When a soul declares itself—to wit,
By its fruit, the thing it does!

50

Be hate that fruit or love that fruit,
  It forwards the general deed of man,
And each of the Many helps to recruit
  The life of the race by a general plan;
Each living his own, to boot.

51

I am named and known by that moment's feat;
  There took my station and degree;
So grew my own small life complete,
  As nature obtained her best of me—
One born to love you, sweet!

52

And to watch you sink by the fire-side now
  Back again, as you mutely sit
Musing by fire-light, that great brow
  And the spirit-small hand propping it,
Yonder, my heart knows how!

53

So, earth has gained by one man the more,
  And the gain of earth must be heaven's gain too;
And the whole is well worth thinking o'er
When autumn comes: which I mean to do
  One day, as I said before.

A PRETTY WOMAN

I

That fawn-skin-dappled hair of hers,
    And the blue eye
    Dear and dewy,
And that infantine fresh air of hers!

2

To think men cannot take you, Sweet,
    And enfold you,
    Ay, and hold you,
And so keep you what they make you, Sweet!

3

You like us for a glance, you know—
  For a word's sake
  Or a sword's sake,
All 's the same, whate'er the chance, you know.

4

And in turn we make you ours, we say—
  You and youth too,
  Eyes and mouth too,
All the face composed of flowers, we say.

5

All 's our own, to make the most of, Sweet—
  Sing and say for,
  Watch and pray for,
Keep a secret or go boast of, Sweet!

6

But for loving, why, you would not, Sweet,
  Though we prayed you,
  Paid you, brayed you
In a mortar—for you could not, Sweet!

7

So, we leave the sweet face fondly there:
  Be its beauty
  Its sole duty!
Let all hope of grace beyond, lie there!

8

And while the face lies quiet there,
  Who shall wonder
  That I ponder
A conclusion? I will try it there.

9

As,—why must one, for the love forgone,
Scout mere liking?
Thunder-striking
Earth,—the heaven, we looked above for, gone!

10

Why, with beauty, needs there money be,
Love with liking?
Crush the fly-king
In his gauze, because no honey-bee?

11

May not liking be so simple-sweet,
If love grew there
'T would undo there
All that breaks the cheek to dimples sweet?

12

Is the creature too imperfect, say?
Would you mend it
And so end it?
Since not all addition perfects aye!

13

Or is it of its kind, perhaps,
Just perfection—
Whence, rejection
Of a grace not to its mind, perhaps?

14

Shall we burn up, tread that face at once
Into tinder,
And so hinder
Sparks from kindling all the place at once?

15

Or else kiss away one's soul on her?
    Your love-fancies!
    —A sick man sees
Truer, when his hot eyes roll on her!

16

Thus the craftsman thinks to grace the rose,—
    Plucks a mould-flower
    For his gold flower,
Uses fine things that efface the rose:

17

Rosy rubies make its cup more rose,
    Precious metals
    Ape the petals,—
Last, some old king locks it up, morose!

18

Then how grace a rose? I know a way!
    Leave it, rather.
    Must you gather?
Smell, kiss, wear it—at last, throw away!

A LIGHT WOMAN

I

So far as our story approaches the end,
  Which do you pity the most of us three?—
My friend, or the mistress of my friend
  With her wanton eyes, or me?

2

My friend was already too good to lose,
   And seemed in the way of improvement yet,
When she crossed his path with her hunting-noose
   And over him drew her net.

3

When I saw him tangled in her toils,
   A shame, said I, if she adds just him
To her nine-and-ninety other spoils,
   The hundredth for a whim!

4

And before my friend be wholly hers,
   How easy to prove to him, I said,
An eagle 's the game her pride prefers,
   Though she snaps at a wren instead!

5

So, I gave her eyes my own eyes to take,
   My hand sought hers as in earnest need,
And round she turned for my noble sake,
   And gave me herself indeed.

6

The eagle am I, with my fame in the world,
   The wren is he, with his maiden face.
—You look away and your lip is curled?
   Patience, a moment's space!

7

For see—my friend goes shaking and white;
   He eyes me as the basilisk:
I have turned, it appears, his day to night,
   Eclipsing his sun's disk.

8

And I did it, he thinks, as a very thief:
  "Though I love her—that, he comprehends—
One should master one's passion, (love, in chief)
  And be loyal to one's friends!"

9

And she,—she lies in my hand as tame
  As a pear late basking over a wall;
Just a touch to try and off it came;
  'T is mine,—can I let it fall?

10

With no mind to eat it, that 's the worst!
  Were it thrown in the road, would the case assist?
'T was quenching a dozen blue-flies' thirst
  When I gave its stalk a twist.

11

And I,—what I seem to my friend, you see:
  What I soon shall seem to his love, you guess:
What I seem to myself, do you ask of me?
  No hero, I confess.

12

'T is an awkward thing to play with souls,
  And matter enough to save one's own:
Yet think of my friend, and the burning coals
  He played with for bits of stone!

13

One likes to show the truth for the truth;
  That the woman was light is very true:
But suppose she says,—Never mind that youth!
  What wrong have I done to you?

14

Well, any how, here the story stays,
So far at least as I understand;
And, Robert Browning, you writer of plays,
Here 's a subject made to your hand!

INSTANS TYRANNUS

To the tyrant it is always a matter for surprise that the spirit of man cannot be extinguished in spite of his devious and diabolic schemes to crush it to earth. Here the hand of God comes to save the victim and smite the tyrant. It is an inspiring poem for these times. The title may be translated "The Tyrant of the Hour."

1

Of the million or two, more or less,
I rule and possess,
One man, for some cause undefined,
Was least to my mind.

2

I struck him, he grovelled of course—
For, what was his force?
I pinned him to earth with my weight
And persistence of hate:
And he lay, would not moan, would not curse,
As his lot might be worse.

3

"Were the object less mean, would he stand
At the swing of my hand!
For obscurity helps him and blots
The hole where he squats."
So, I set my five wits on the stretch

To inveigle the wretch.
All in vain! Gold and jewels I threw,
Still he couched there perdue;
I tempted his blood and his flesh,
Hid in roses my mesh,
Choicest cates and the flagon's best spilth.
Still he kept to his filth.

4

Had he kith now or kin, were access
To his heart, did I press:
Just a son or a mother to seize!
No such booty as these.
Were it simply a friend to pursue
'Mid my million or two,
Who could pay me in person or pelf
What he owes me himself!
No: I could not but smile through my chafe:
For the fellow lay safe
As his mates do, the midge and the nit,
—Through minuteness, to wit.

5

Then a humour more great took its place
At the thought of his face,
The droop, the low cares of the mouth,
The trouble uncouth
'Twixt the brows, all that air one is fain
To put out of its pain.
And, "no!" I admonished myself,
"Is one mocked by an elf,
Is one baffled by toad or by rat?
The gravamen's in that!
How the lion, who crouches to suit
His back to my foot,
Would admire that I stand in debate!

But the small turns the great
If it vexes you,—that is the thing!
Toad or rat vex the king?
Though I waste half my realm to unearth
Toad or rat, 'tis well worth!"

6

So, I soberly laid my last plan
To extinguish the man.
Round his creep-hole, with never a break
Ran my fires for his sake;
Over-head, did my thunder combine
With my underground mine:
Till I looked from my labour content
To enjoy the event.

7

When sudden . . . how think ye, the end?
Did I say "without friend"?
Say rather, from marge to blue marge
The whole sky grew his targe
With the sun's self for visible boss,
While an Arm ran across
Which the earth heaved beneath like a breast
Where the wretch was safe prest!
Did you see? Just my vengeance complete.
The man sprang to his feet,
Stood erect, caught at God's skirts, and prayed!
—So, *I* was afraid!

MY STAR

This beautiful lyric was dedicated to the poet's dead wife. He frequently wrote it out for persons who asked for his autograph.

All that I know
  Of a certain star
Is, it can throw
  (Like the angled spar)
Now a dart of red,
  Now a dart of blue,
Till my friends have said
  They would fain see, too,
My star that dartles the red and the blue!
Then it stops like a bird; like a flower, hangs furled:
  They must solace themselves with the Saturn above it.
What matter to me if their star is a world?
  Mine has opened its soul to me; therefore I love it.

"CHILDE ROLAND TO THE DARK TOWER CAME"

The title of this famous poem comes from Edgar's line in King Lear. *The poem is pure fantasy, or pure creative imagination. We don't know why Childe Roland sought the Tower, but we accept and believe in this quest which irresistibly drew him onward. The entire poem has a vivid but unreal and dream-like quality—the mystery of the quest itself, the sinister nature of the landscape—and we are therefore not surprised to learn that the idea of the poem came to Browning in a dream. It seems to be a forerunner of surrealism.*

My first thought was, he lied in every word,
  That hoary cripple, with malicious eye
  Askance to watch the working of his lie
On mine, and mouth scarce able to afford
Suppression of the glee that pursed and scored
  Its edge at one more victim gained thereby.

What else should he be set for, with his staff?
  What, save to waylay with his lies, ensnare
  All travellers that might find him posted there,
And ask the road? I guessed what skull-like laugh
Would break, what crutch 'gin write my epitaph
  For pastime in the dusty thoroughfare,

If at his counsel I should turn aside
  Into that ominous tract which, all agree,
  Hides the Dark Tower. Yet acquiescingly
I did turn as he pointed; neither pride
Nor hope rekindling at the end descried,
  So much as gladness that some end might be.

For, what with my whole world-wide wandering,
  What with my search drawn out thro' years, my hope
  Dwindled into a ghost not fit to cope
With that obstreperous joy success would bring,—
I hardly tried now to rebuke the spring
  My heart made, finding failure in its scope.

As when a sick man very near to death
  Seems dead indeed, and feels begin and end
  The tears and takes the farewell of each friend,
And hears one bid the other go, draw breath
Freelier outside, ("since all is o'er," he saith,
  "And the blow fallen no grieving can amend;")

While some discuss if near the other graves
  Be room enough for this, and when a day
  Suits best for carrying the corpse away,
With care about the banners, scarves and staves,—
And still the man hears all, and only craves
  He may not shame such tender love and stay.

Thus, I had so long suffered in this quest,
  Heard failure prophesied so oft, been writ
  So many times among "The Band"—to wit,

The knights who to the Dark Tower's search addressed
Their steps—that just to fail as they, seemed best,
  And all the doubt was now—should I be fit.

So, quiet as despair, I turned from him,
  That hateful cripple, out of his highway
  Into the path he pointed. All the day
Had been a dreary one at best, and dim
Was settling to its close, yet shot one grim
  Red leer to see the plain catch its estray.

For mark! no sooner was I fairly found
  Pledged to the plain, after a pace or two,
  Than, pausing to throw backward a last view
To the safe road, 'twas gone; grey plain all round:
Nothing but plain to the horizon's bound.
  I might go on; nought else remained to do.

So, on I went. I think I never saw
  Such starved ignoble nature; nothing throve:
  For flowers—as well expect a cedar grove!
But cockle, spurge, according to their law
Might propagate their kind, with none to awe,
  You'd think; a burr had been a treasure-trove.

No! penury, inertness and grimace,
  In some strange sort, were the land's portion. "See
  Or shut your eyes," said Nature peevishly,
"It nothing skills: I cannot help my case:
'Tis the Last Judgment's fire must cure this place,
  Calcine its clods and set my prisoners free."

If there pushed any ragged thistle-stalk
  Above its mates, the head was chopped—the bents
  Were jealous else. What made those holes and rents
In the dock's harsh swarth leaves—bruised as to balk
All hope of greenness? 'tis a brute must walk
  Pashing their life out, with a brute's intents.

As for the grass, it grew as scant as hair
  In leprosy; thin dry blades pricked the mud
  Which underneath looked kneaded up with blood.
One stiff blind horse, his every bone a-stare,
Stood stupefied, however he came there:
  Thrust out past service from the devil's stud!

Alive? he might be dead for aught I know,
  With that red, gaunt and colloped neck a-strain,
  And shut eyes underneath the rusty mane;
Seldom went such grotesqueness with such woe;
I never saw a brute I hated so;
  He must be wicked to deserve such pain.

I shut my eyes and turned them on my heart.
  As a man calls for wine before he fights,
  I asked one draught of earlier, happier sights,
Ere fitly I could hope to play my part.
Think first, fight afterwards—the soldier's art:
  One taste of the old time sets all to rights!

Not it! I fancied Cuthbert's reddening face
  Beneath its garniture of curly gold,
  Dear fellow, till I almost felt him fold
An arm in mine to fix me to the place,
That way he used. Alas, one night's disgrace!
  Out went my heart's new fire and left it cold.

Giles, then, the soul of honour—there he stands
  Frank as ten years ago when knighted first.
  What honest men should dare (he said) he durst.
Good—but the scene shifts—faugh! what hangman's hands
Pin to his breast a parchment? his own bands
  Read it. Poor traitor, spit upon and curst!

Better this present than a past like that;
  Back therefore to my darkening path again.
  No sound, no sight as far as eye could strain.

Will the night send a howlet or a bat?
I asked: when something on the dismal flat
  Came to arrest my thoughts and change their train.

A sudden little river crossed my path
  As unexpected as a serpent comes.
  No sluggish tide congenial to the glooms—
This, as it frothed by, might have been a bath
For the fiend's glowing hoof—to see the wrath
  Of its black eddy bespate with flakes and spumes.

So petty yet so spiteful! all along,
  Low scrubby alders kneeled down over it;
  Drenched willows flung them headlong in a fit
Of mute despair, a suicidal throng:
The river which had done them all the wrong,
  Whate'er that was, rolled by, deterred no whit.

Which, while I forded,—good saints, how I feared
  To set my foot upon a dead man's cheek,
  Each step, or feel the spear I thrust to seek
For hollows, tangled in his hair or beard!
—It may have been a water-rat I speared,
  But, ugh! it sounded like a baby's shriek.

Glad was I when I reached the other bank.
  Now for a better country. Vain presage!
  Who were the strugglers, what war did they wage
Whose savage trample thus could pad the dank
Soil to a plash? toads in a poisoned tank,
  Or wild cats in a red-hot iron cage—

The fight must so have seemed in that fell cirque.
  What penned them there, with all the plain to choose?
  No foot-print leading to that horrid mews,
None out of it. Mad brewage set to work
Their brains, no doubt, like galley-slaves the Turk
  Pits for his pastime, Christians against Jews.

And more than that—a furlong on—why, there!
What bad use was that engine for, that wheel,
Or brake, not wheel—that harrow fit to reel
Men's bodies out like silk? with all the air
Of Tophet's tool, on earth left unaware,
Or brought to sharpen its rusty teeth of steel.

Then came a bit of stubbed ground, once a wood,
Next a marsh, it would seem, and now mere earth
Desperate and done with; (so a fool finds mirth,
Makes a thing and then mars it, till his mood
Changes and off he goes!) within a rood—
Bog, clay and rubble, sand and stark black dearth.

Now blotches rankling, coloured gay and grim,
Now patches where some leanness of the soil's
Broke into moss or substances like boils;
Then came some palsied oak, a cleft in him
Like a distorted mouth that splits its rim
Gaping at death, and dies while it recoils.

And just as far as ever from the end!
Nought in the distance but the evening, nought
To point my footstep further! At the thought,
A great black bird, Apollyon's bosom-friend,
Sailed past, nor beat his wide wing dragon-penned
That brushed my cap—perchance the guide I sought.

For, looking up, aware I somehow grew,
'Spite of the dusk, the plain had given place
All round to mountains—with such name to grace
Mere ugly heights and heaps now stolen in view.
How thus they had surprised me,—solve it, you!
How to get from them was no clearer case.

Yet half I seemed to recognise some trick
Of mischief happened to me, God knows when—
In a bad dream perhaps. Here ended, then,

Progress this way. When, in the very nick
Of giving up, one time more, came a click
  As when a trap shuts—you're inside the den!

Burningly it came on me all at once,
  This was the place! those two hills on the right,
  Crouched like two bulls locked horn in horn in fight;
While to the left, a tall scalped mountain . . . Dunce,
Fool, to be dozing at the very nonce,
  After a life spent training for the sight!

What in the midst lay but the Tower itself?
  The round squat turret, blind as the fool's heart,
  Built of brown stone, without a counterpart
In the whole world. The tempest's mocking elf
Points to the shipman thus the unseen shelf
  He strikes on, only when the timbers start.

Not see? because of night perhaps?—Why, day
  Came back again for that! before it left,
  The dying sunset kindled through a cleft:
The hills, like giants at a hunting, lay,
Chin upon hand, to see the game at bay,—
  "Now stab and end the creature—to the heft!"

Not hear? when noise was everywhere! it tolled
  Increasing like a bell. Names in my ears,
  Of all the lost adventurers my peers,—
How such a one was strong, and such was bold,
And such was fortunate, yet each of old
  Lost, lost! one moment knelled the woe of years.

There they stood, ranged along the hillsides, met
  To view the last of me, a living frame
  For one more picture! in a sheet of flame
I saw them and I knew them all. And yet
Dauntless the slug-horn to my lips I set,
  And blew, "*Childe Roland to the Dark Tower came.*"

EVELYN HOPE

The poignancy of the theme—the death of a beautiful young girl—has made this exquisite poem much loved. The conception that love does not die but lives and grows through other worlds is one which Browning often expressed.

1

Beautiful Evelyn Hope is dead!
  Sit and watch by her side an hour.
That is her book-shelf, this her bed;
  She plucked that piece of geranium-flower,
Beginning to die too, in the glass;
  Little has yet been changed, I think:
The shutters are shut, no light may pass
  Save two long rays thro' the hinge's chink.

2

Sixteen years old when she died!
  Perhaps she had scarcely heard my name;
It was not her time to love; besides,
  Her life had many a hope and aim,
Duties enough and little cares,
  And now was quiet, now astir,
Till God's hand beckoned unawares,—
  And the sweet white brow is all of her.

3

Is it too late then, Evelyn Hope?
  What, your soul was pure and true,
The good stars met in your horoscope,
  Made you of spirit, fire and dew—
And, just because I was thrice as old
  And our paths in the world diverged so wide,
Each was nought to each, must I be told?
  We were fellow mortals, nought beside?

4

No, indeed! for God above
  Is great to grant, as mighty to make,
And creates the love to reward the love:
  I claim you still, for my own love's sake!
Delayed it may be for more lives yet,
  Through worlds I shall traverse, not a few:
Much is to learn, much to forget
  Ere the time be come for taking you.

5

But the time will come,—at last it will,
  When, Evelyn Hope, what meant (I shall say)
In the lower earth, in the years long still,
  That body and soul so pure and gay?
Why your hair was amber, I shall divine,
  And your mouth of your own geranium's red—
And what you would do with me, in fine,
  In the new life come in the old one's stead.

6

I have lived (I shall say) so much since then,
  Given up myself so many times,
Gained me the gains of various men,
  Ransacked the ages, spoiled the climes;
Yet one thing, one, in my soul's full scope,
  Either I missed or itself missed me:
And I want and find you, Evelyn Hope!
  What is the issue? let us see!

7

I loved you, Evelyn, all the while.
  My heart seemed full as it could hold?
There was place and to spare for the frank young smile,
  And the red young mouth, and the hair's young gold.

So, hush,—I will give you this leaf to keep:
  See, I shut it inside the sweet cold hand!
There that is our secret: go to sleep!
  You will wake, and remember, and understand.

THE LAST RIDE TOGETHER

1

I said—Then, Dearest, since 'tis so,
Since now at length my fate I know,
Since nothing all my love avails,
Since all, my life seemed meant for, fails,
  Since this was written and needs must be—
My whole heart rises up to bless
Your name in pride and thankfulness!
Take back the hope you gave,—I claim
Only a memory of the same,
—And this beside, if you will not blame,
  Your leave for one more last ride with me.

2

My mistress bent that brow of hers;
Those deep dark eyes where pride demurs
When pity would be softening through,
Fixed me a breathing-while or two
  With life or death in the balance: right!
The blood replenished me again;
My last thought was at least not vain:
I and my mistress, side by side
Shall be together, breathe and ride,
So one day more am I deified—
  Who knows but the world may end to-night.

3

Hush! if you saw some western cloud
All billowy-bosomed, over-bowed

By many benedictions—sun's
And moon's and evening-star's at once—
   And so, you, looking and loving best,
Conscious grew, your passion drew
Cloud, sunset, moonrise, star-shine too,
Down on you, near and yet more near,
Till flesh must fade for heaven was here!—
Thus leant she and lingered—joy and fear!
   Thus lay she a moment on my breast.

4

Then we began to ride. My soul
Smoothed itself out—a long-cramped scroll
Freshening and fluttering in the wind.
Past hopes already lay behind.
   What need to strive with a life awry?
Had I said that, had I done this,
So might I gain, so might I miss.
Might she have loved me? just as well
She might have hated,—who can tell?
Where had I been now if the worst befell?
   And here we are riding, she and I.

5

Fail I alone, in words and deeds?
Why, all men strive and who succeeds?
We rode it; it seemed my spirit flew,
Saw other regions, cities new,
   As the world rushed by on either side.
I thought,—All labour, yet no less
Bear up beneath their unsuccess.
Look at the end of work, contrast
The petty Done, the Undone vast,
This Present of theirs with the hopeful Past!
   I hoped she would love me: here we ride.

6

What hand and brain went ever paired?
What heart alike conceived and dared?
What act proved all its thought had been?
What will but felt the fleshly screen?
We ride and I see her bosom heave.
There's many a crown for who can reach.
Ten lines, a statesman's life in each!
The flag struck on a heap of bones,
A soldier's doing! what atones?
They scratch his name on the Abbey-stones.
My riding is better, by their leave.

7

What does it all mean, poet? well,
Your brains beat into rhythm—you tell
What we felt only; you expressed
You hold things beautiful the best,
And pace them in rhyme so, side by side.
'Tis something, nay 'tis much—but then,
Have you yourself what's best for men?
Are you—poor, sick, old ere your time—
Nearer one whit your own sublime
Than we who never have turned a rhyme?
Sing, riding's a joy! For me, I ride.

8

And you, great sculptor—so, you gave
A score of years to Art, her slave,
And that's your Venus—whence we turn
To yonder girl that fords the burn!
You acquiesce, and shall I repine?
What, man of music, you, grown grey
With notes and nothing else to say,
Is this your sole praise from a friend,
"Greatly his opera's strains intend,

But in music we know how fashions end!"
  I gave my youth—but we ride, in fine.

9

Who knows what's fit for us? Had fate
Proposed bliss here should sublimate
My being; had I signed the bond—
Still one must lead some life beyond,
  —Have a bliss to die with, dim-descried.
This foot once planted on the goal,
This glory-garland round my soul,
Could I descry such? Try and test!
I sink back shuddering from the quest—
Earth being so good, would Heaven seem best?
  Now, Heaven and she are beyond this ride.

10

And yet—she has not spoke so long!
What if Heaven be that, fair and strong
At life's best, with our eyes upturned
Whither life's flower is first discerned,
  We, fixed so, ever should so abide?
What if we still ride on, we two,
With life for ever old yet new,
Changed not in kind but in degree,
The instant made eternity,—
And Heaven just prove that I and she
  Ride, ride together, for ever ride?

HOW IT STRIKES A CONTEMPORARY

This poem describes the ways of a Spanish poet as seen by a fellow citizen. The poet of Valladolid has in common with his creator a passionate curiosity about life and people and an intuitive knowledge of them. The poet's function, according to Browning, is to be "God's eye" (the expression is taken from the king's speech at the opening of the third scene of Act V of King Lear*), a divinely-endowed observer of life.*

I only knew one poet in my life:
And this, or something like it, was his way.

You saw go up and down Valladolid,
A man of mark, to know next time you saw.
His very serviceable suit of black
Was courtly once and conscientious still,
And many might have worn it, though none did:
The cloak, that somewhat shone and showed the threads,
Had purpose, and the ruff, significance.
He walked and tapped the pavement with his cane,
Scenting the world, looking it full in face,
An old dog, bald and blindish, at his heels.
They turned up, now, the alley by the church,
That leads nowhither; now, they breathed themselves
On the main promenade just at the wrong time:
You 'd come upon his scrutinizing hat,
Making a peaked shade blacker than itself
Against the single window spared some house
Intact yet with its mouldered Moorish work,—
Or else surprise the ferrel of his stick
Trying the mortar's temper 'tween the chinks
Of some new shop a-building, French and fine.
He stood and watched the cobbler at his trade,
The man who slices lemons into drink,
The coffee-roaster's brazier, and the boys
That volunteer to help him turn its winch.
He glanced o'er books on stalls with half an eye,
And fly-leaf ballads on the vendor's string,
And broad-edge bold-print posters by the wall.
He took such cognizance of men and things,
If any beat a horse, you felt he saw;
If any cursed a woman, he took note;
Yet stared at nobody,—you stared at him,
And found, less to your pleasure than surprise,

He seemed to know you and expect as much.
So, next time that a neighbour's tongue was loosed,
It marked the shameful and notorious fact,
We had among us, not so much a spy,
As a recording chief-inquisitor,
The town's true master if the town but knew!
We merely kept a governor for form,
While this man walked about and took account
Of all thought, said and acted, then went home,
And wrote fully to our Lord the King
Who has an itch to know things, he knows why,
And reads them in his bedroom of a night.
Oh, you might smile! there wanted not a touch,
A tang of . . . well, it was not wholly ease
As back into your mind the man's look came.
Stricken in years a little,—such a brow
His eyes had to live under!—clear as flint
On either side the formidable nose
Curved, cut and coloured like an eagle's claw.
Had he to do with A.'s surprising fate?
When altogether old B. disappeared
And young C. got his mistress,—was 't our friend,
His letter to the King, that did it all?
What paid the bloodless man for so much pains?
Our Lord the King has favourites manifold,
And shifts his ministry some once a month;
Our city gets new governors at whiles,—
But never word or sign, that I could hear,
Notified to this man about the streets
The King's approval of those letters conned
The last thing duly at the dead of night.
Did the man love his office? Frowned our Lord,
Exhorting when none heard—"Beseech me not!
Too far above my people,—beneath me!
I set the watch,—how should the people know?
Forget them, keep me all the more in mind!"
Was some such understanding 'twixt the two?

I found no truth in one report at least—
That if you tracked him to his home, down lanes
Beyond the Jewry, and as clean to pace,
You found he ate his supper in a room
Blazing with lights, four Titians on the wall,
And twenty naked girls to change his plate!
Poor man, he lived another kind of life
In that new stuccoed third house by the bridge,
Fresh-painted, rather smart than otherwise!
The whole street might o'erlook him as he sat,
Leg crossing leg, one foot on the dog's back,
Playing a decent cribbage with his maid
(Jacynth, you 're sure her name was) o'er the cheese
And fruit, three red halves of starved winter-pears,
Or treat of radishes in April. Nine,
Ten, struck the church clock, straight to bed went he.

My father, like the man of sense he was,
Would point him out to me a dozen times;
" 'St—'St," he 'd whisper, "the Corregidor!"
I had been used to think that personage
Was one with lacquered breeches, lustrous belt,
And feathers like a forest in his hat,
Who blew a trumpet and proclaimed the news,
Announced the bull-fights, gave each church its turn,
And memorized the miracle in vogue!
He had a great observance from us boys;
We were in error; that was not the man.

I 'd like now, yet had haply been afraid,
To have just looked, when this man came to die,
And seen who lined the clean gay garret-sides
And stood about the neat low truckle-bed,
With the heavenly manner of relieving guard.
Here had been, mark, the general-in-chief,
Thro' a whole campaign of the world's life and death,
Doing the King's work all the dim day long,
In his old coat and up to knees in mud,

Smoked like a herring, dining on a crust,—
And, now the day was won, relieved at once!
No further show or need for that old coat,
You are sure, for one thing! Bless us, all the while
How sprucely we are dressed out, you and I!
A second, and the angels alter that.
Well, I could never write a verse,—could you?
Let 's to the Prado and make the most of time.

UP AT A VILLA—DOWN IN THE CITY

(As distinguished by an Italian person of quality)

Browning's pleasure in the busy and colorful life of an Italian town, his love for people and movement, is couched in a happy, conversational strain. To him the city meant people with their passions and problems and conflicts—all grist for his mill. He particularly loved the Italian towns where so much of life goes on in the market place and streets.

1

Had I but plenty of money, money enough and to spare,
The house for me, no doubt, were a house in the city-square;
Ah, such a life, such a life, as one leads at the window there!

2

Something to see, by Bacchus, something to hear, at least!
There, the whole day long, one's life is a perfect feast;
While up at a villa one lives, I maintain it, no more than a beast.

3

Well now, look at our villa! stuck like the horn of a bull
Just on a mountain-edge as bare as the creature's skull,
Save a mere shag of a bush with hardly a leaf to pull!
—I scratch my own, sometimes, to see if the hair 's turned wool.

4

But the city, oh the city—the square with the houses! Why?
They are stone-faced, white as a curd, there 's something to take the eye!
Houses in four straight lines, not a single front awry;
You watch who crosses and gossips, who saunters, who hurries by;
Green blinds, as a matter of course, to draw when the sun gets high;
And the shops with fanciful signs which are painted properly.

5

What of a villa? Though winter be over in March by rights,
'T is May perhaps ere the snow shall have withered well off the heights:
You 've the brown ploughed land before, where the oxen steam and wheeze,
And the hills over-smoked behind by the faint grey olive-trees,

6

Is it better in May, I ask you? You 've summer all at once;
In a day he leaps complete with a few strong April suns.
'Mid the sharp short emerald wheat, scarce risen three fingers well,
The wild tulip, at end of its tube, blows out its great red bell
Like a thin clear bubble of blood, for the children to pick and sell.

7

Is it ever hot in the square? There 's a fountain to spout and splash!
In the shade it sings and springs; in the shine such foam-bows flash
On the horses with curling fish-tails, that prance and paddle and pash

Round the lady atop in her conch—fifty gazers do not abash,
Though all that she wears is some weeds round her waist in a sort of sash.

8

All the year long at the villa, nothing to see though you linger,
Except yon cypress that points like death's lean lifted forefinger.
Some think fireflies pretty, when they mix i' the corn and mingle,
Or thrid the stinking hemp till the stalks of it seem a-tingle.
Late August or early September, the stunning cicala is shrill,
And the bees keep their tiresome whine round the resinous firs on the hill.
Enough of the seasons,—I spare you the months of the fever and chill.

9

Ere you open your eyes in the city, the blessed church-bells begin:
No sooner the bells leave off than the diligence rattles in:
You get the pick of the news, and it costs you never a pin.
By-and-by there 's the travelling doctor gives pills, lets blood, draws teeth;
Or the Pulcinello-trumpet breaks up the market beneath.
At the post-office such a scene-picture—the new play, piping hot!
And a notice how, only this morning, three liberal thieves were shot.
Above it, behold the Archbishop's most fatherly of rebukes,
And beneath, with his crown and his lion, some little new law of the Duke's!
Or a sonnet with flowery marge, to the Reverend Don So-and-so
Who is Dante, Boccaccio, Petrarca, Saint Jerome and Cicero,
"And moreover," (the sonnet goes rhyming) "the skirts of Saint Paul has reached,
Having preached us those six Lent-lectures more unctuous than ever he preached."

Noon strikes,—here sweeps the procession! our Lady borne smiling and smart
With a pink gauze gown all spangles, and seven swords stuck in her heart!
Bang-whang-whang goes the drum, *tootle-te-tootle* the fife;
No keeping one's haunches still: it 's the greatest pleasure in life.

10

But bless you, it 's dear—it 's dear! fowls, wine, at double the rate.
They have clapped a new tax upon salt, and what oil pays passing the gate
It 's a horror to think of. And so, the villa for me, not the city!
Beggars can scarcely be choosers: but still—ah, the pity, the pity!
Look, two and two go the priests, then the monks with cowls and sandals,
And the penitents dressed in white shirts, a-holding the yellow candles;
One, he carries a flag up straight, and another a cross with handles,
And the Duke's guard brings up the rear, for the better prevention of scandals:
Bang-whang-whang goes the drum, *tootle-te-tootle* the fife.
Oh, a day in the city-square, there is no such pleasure in life!

THE PATRIOT

Inspired by the Italian struggle for independence, The Patriot *is a generalized statement of what happens to a leader when the loyalties of a people change.*

I

It was roses, roses, all the way,
With myrtle mixed in my path like mad:
The house-roofs seemed to heave and sway,
The church-spires flamed, such flags they had,
A year ago on this very day.

2

The air broke into a mist with bells,
  The old walls rocked with the crowd and cries.
Had I said, "Good folk, mere noise repels—
  "But give me your sun from yonder skies!"
They had answered, "And afterward, what else?"

3

Alack, it was I who leaped at the sun
  To give it my loving friends to keep!
Nought man could do, have I left undone:
  And you see my harvest, what I reap
This very day, now a year is run.

4

There 's nobody on the house-tops now—
  Just a palsied few at the windows set;
For the best of the sight is, all allow,
  At the Shambles' Gate—or, better yet,
By the very scaffold's foot, I trow.

5

I go in the rain, and, more than needs,
  A rope cuts both my wrists behind;
And I think, by the feel, my forehead bleeds,
  For they fling, whoever has a mind,
Stones at me for my year's misdeeds.

6

Thus I entered, and thus I go!
  In triumphs, people have dropped down dead.
"Paid by the world, what dost thou owe
  Me?"—God might question; now instead,
'Tis God shall repay: I am safer so.

Browning Explains His Indifference to Popularity

I can have little doubt but that my writing has been, in the main, too hard for many I should have been pleased to communicate with: but I never designedly tried to puzzle people, as some of my critics have supposed. On the other hand, I never pretended to offer such literature as should be a substitute for a cigar, or game at dominoes to an idle man. So perhaps on the whole I get my deserts and something over,—not a crowd but a few I value more. Let me see:

-member gratefully that I may keep you, and the friends you mention, among these: while you, in turn, must remember me as

Yours, my dear sir, very faithfully

Robert Browning

"I can have little doubt but that my writing has been, in the main, too hard for many I should have been pleased to communicate with; but I never designedly tried to puzzle people, as some of my critics have supposed. On the other hand, I never pretended to offer such literature as should be a substitute for a cigar or game of dominos to an idle man. So, perhaps on the whole I get my deserts and something over,—not a crowd but a few I value more. Let me remember gratefully that I may keep you, and the friends you mention, among these: while you, in turn, must remember me as

"Yours, my dear sir, very faithfully

"Robert Browning"

Letter to William Kingsland, London, November, 1868.

Courtesy of the New York Public Library

RESPECTABILITY

This poem was probably written in Paris during the winter of 1852. It reflects the French spirit of good form: do as you please as long as you adhere to custom and convention. In tune with this spirit, a lover speaks to his lady as they stroll along the Seine. As they pass the Institute he is reminded that politicians and men of letters must conform, too. Only recently had the famous statesman and historian, Guizot, made the speech that welcomed his worst enemy, Montalembert, into the Academie Française.

1

Dear, had the world in its caprice
  Deigned to proclaim "I know you both,
  Have recognised your plighted troth,
Am sponsor for you: live in peace!"—
How many precious months and years
  Of youth had passed, that speed so fast,
  Before we found it out at last,
The world, and what it fears?

2

How much of priceless life were spent
  With men that every virtue decks,
  And women models of their sex,
Society's true ornament,—
Ere we dared wander, nights like this
  Thro' wind and rain, and watch the Seine,
  And feel the Boulevard break again
To warmth and light and bliss?

3

I know! the world proscribes not love;
  Allows my finger to caress
  Your lips' contour and downiness,
Provided it supply a glove.

The world's good word!—the Institute!
  Guizot receives Montalembert!
  Eh? Down the court three lampions flare:
Put forward your best foot!

MASTER HUGUES OF SAXE-GOTHA

Obviously Browning is writing about the great master of the fugue, Johann Sebastian Bach; he invented Hugues merely to rhyme with fugues. With the dexterity of a virtuoso he here captures the spirit of a complex musical form in verse, a feat which would not have been possible without a profound knowledge of music. Browning had a habit, while in Italy, of straying into churches and asking permission of the sacristan to play the organ, and the last verse which describes the organist stumbling down "rat-riddled stairs" was doubtless a personal reminiscence.

1

Hist, but a word, fair and soft!
  Forth and be judged, Master Hugues!
Answer the question I 've put you so oft:
  What do you mean by your mountainous fugues?
See, we 're alone in the loft,—

2

I, the poor organist here,
  Hugues, the composer of note,
Dead though, and done with, this many a year:
  Let 's have a colloquy, something to quote,
Make the world prick up its ear!

3

See, the church empties apace:
  Fast they extinguish the lights.
Hallo there, sacristan! Five minutes' grace!
  Here 's a crank pedal wants setting to rights,
Balks one of holding the base.

4

See, our huge house of the sounds,
  Hushing its hundreds at once,
Bids the last loiterer back to his bounds!
  —O you may challenge them, not a response
Get the church-saints on their rounds!

5

(Saints go their rounds, who shall doubt?
  —March, with the moon to admire,
Up nave, down chancel, turn transept about,
  Supervise all betwixt pavement and spire,
Put rats and mice to the rout—

6

Aloys and Jurien and Just—
  Order things back to their place,
Have a sharp eye lest the candlesticks rust,
  Rub the church-plate, darn the sacrament-lace,
Clear the desk-velvet of dust.)

7

Here 's your book, younger folks shelve!
  Played I not off-hand and runningly,
Just now, your masterpiece, hard number twelve?
  Here 's what should strike, could one handle it cunningly:
Help the axe, give it a helve!

8

Page after page as I played,
  Every bar's rest, where one wipes
Sweat from one's brow, I looked up and surveyed,
  O'er my three claviers, yon forest of pipes
Whence you still peeped in the shade.

9

Sure you were wishful to speak?
  You, with brow ruled like a score,
Yes, and eyes buried in pits on each cheek,
  Like two great breves, as they wrote them of yore,
Each side that bar, your straight beak!

10

Sure you said—"Good, the mere notes!
  Still, couldst thou take my intent,
Know what procured me our Company's votes—
  A master were lauded and sciolists shent,
Parted the sheep from the goats!"

11

Well then, speak up, never flinch!
  Quick, ere my candle 's a snuff
—Burnt, do you see? to its uttermost inch—
  I believe in you, but that 's not enough:
Give my conviction a clinch!

12

First you deliver your phrase
  —Nothing propound, that I see,
Fit in itself for much blame or much praise—
  Answered no less, where no answer needs be:
Off start the Two on their ways.

13

Straight must a Third interpose,
   Volunteer needlessly help;
In strikes a Fourth, a Fifth thrusts in his nose,
   So the cry 's open, the kennel 's a-yelp,
Argument 's hot to the close.

14

One dissertates, he is candid;
   Two must discept,—has distinguished;
Three helps the couple, if ever yet man did;
   Four protests; Five makes a dart at the thing wished:
Back to One, goes the case bandied.

15

One says his say with a difference;
   More of expounding, explaining!
All now is wrangle, abuse, and vociferance;
   Now there 's a truce, all 's subdued, self-restraining:
Five, though, stands out all the stiffer hence.

16

One is incisive, corrosive;
   Two retorts, nettled, curt, crepitant;
Three makes rejoinder, expansive, explosive;
   Four overbears them all, strident and strepitant:
Five . . . O Danaides, O Sieve!

17

Now, they ply axes and crowbars;
   Now, they prick pins at a tissue
Fine as a skein of the casuist Escobar's
   Worked on the bone of a lie. To what issue?
Where is our gain at the Two-bars?

18

Est fuga, volvitur rota.
On we drift: where looms the dim port?
One, Two, Three, Four, Five, contribute their quota;
Something is gained, if one caught but the import—
Show it us, Hugues of Saxe-Gotha!

19

What with affirming, denying,
Holding, risposting, subjoining,
All 's like . . . it 's like . . . for an instance I 'm trying . . .
There! See our roof, its gilt moulding and groining
Under those spider-webs lying!

20

So your fugue broadens and thickens,
Greatens and deepens and lengthens,
Till we exclaim—"But where 's music, the dickens?
Blot ye the gold, while your spider-web strengthens
—Blacked to the stoutest of tickens?"

21

I for man's effort am zealous:
Prove me such censure unfounded!
Seems it surprising a lover grows jealous—
Hopes 't was for something, his organ-pipes sounded,
Tiring three boys at the bellows?

22

Is it your moral of Life?
Such a web, simple and subtle,
Weave we on earth here in impotent strife,
Backward and forward each throwing his shuttle,
Death ending all with a knife?

23

Over our heads truth and nature—
  Still our life's zigzags and dodges,
Ins and outs, weaving a new legislature—
  God's gold just shining its last where that lodges,
Palled beneath man's usurpature.

24

So we o'ershroud stars and roses,
  Cherub and trophy and garland;
Nothings grow something which quietly closes
  Heaven's earnest eye: not a glimpse of the far land
Gets through our comments and glozes.

25

Ah but traditions, inventions,
  (Say we and make up a visage)
So many men with such various intentions,
  Down the past ages, must know more than this age!
Leave we the web its dimensions!

26

Who thinks Hugues wrote for the deaf,
  Proved a mere mountain in labour?
Better submit; try again; what 's the clef?
  'Faith, 't is no trifle for pipe and for tabor—
Four flats, the minor in F.

27

Friend, your fugue taxes the finger:
  Learning it once, who would lose it?
Yet all the while a misgiving will linger,
  Truth 's golden o'er us although we refuse it—
Nature, thro' cobwebs we string her.

28

Hugues! I advise *meâ pœnâ*
(Counterpoint glares like a Gorgon)
Bid One, Two, Three, Four, Five, clear the arena!
Say the word, straight I unstop the full-organ,
Blare out the *mode Palestrina.*

29

While in the roof, if I'm right there,
. . . Lo you, the wick in the socket!
Hallo, you sacristan, show us a light there!
Down it dips, gone like a rocket.
What, you want, do you, to come unawares,
Sweeping the church up for first morning-prayers,
And find a poor devil has ended his cares
At the foot of your rotten-runged rat-riddled stairs?
Do I carry the moon in my pocket?

MEMORABILIA

Browning's youthful rapture, recollected in maturity, at meeting someone who had known and spoken with Shelley is dramatized in this lovely lyric. As a young man, Browning's adoration of Shelley led to his adoption—for a brief period—of Shelley's vegetarianism and his atheism.

1

Ah, did you once see Shelley plain,
And did he stop and speak to you
And did you speak to him again?
How strange it seems and new!

2

But you were living before that,
And also you are living after;
And the memory I started at—
My starting moves your laughter.

3

I crossed a moor, with a name of its own
    And a certain use in the world no doubt,
Yet a hand's-breadth of it shines alone
    'Mid the blank miles round about:

4

For there I picked up on the heather
    And there I put inside my breast
A moulted feather, an eagle-feather!
    Well, I forget the rest.

ANDREA DEL SARTO
(Called "the Faultless Painter")

Andrea del Sarto, known as "the faultless painter," because of the perfection of his technique, flourished in the early sixteenth century. He was the son of a tailor. The painting which might have inspired this poem represents Andrea and his wife Lucrezia, who was also his model, discussing a letter which she holds. Vasari wrote of del Sarto that he lacked the integrity and elevation of spirit without which there is no true greatness. Browning gives us his interpretation of this fatal weakness of character in the painter's own revealing monologue.

But do not let us quarrel any more,
No, my Lucrezia; bear with me for once:
Sit down and all shall happen as you wish.
You turn your face, but does it bring your heart?
I 'll work then for your friend's friend, never fear,
Treat his own subject after his own way,
Fix his own time, accept too his own price,
And shut the money into this small hand
When next it takes mine. Will it? tenderly?
Oh, I 'll content him,—but to-morrow, Love!

I often am much wearier than you think,
This evening more than usual, and it seems
As if—forgive now—should you let me sit
Here by the window with your hand in mine
And look a half-hour forth on Fiesole,
Both of one mind, as married people use,
Quietly, quietly the evening through,
I might get up to-morrow to my work
Cheerful and fresh as ever. Let us try.
To-morrow, how you shall be glad for this!
Your soft hand is a woman of itself,
And mine the man's bared breast she curls inside.
Don't count the time lost, neither; you must serve
For each of the five pictures we require:
It saves a model. So! keep looking so—
My serpentining beauty, rounds on rounds!
—How could you ever prick those perfect ears,
Even to put the pearl there! oh, so sweet—
My face, my moon, my everybody's moon,
Which everybody looks on and calls his,
And, I suppose, is looked on by in turn,
While she looks—no one's: very dear, no less.
You smile? why, there 's my picture ready made,
There 's what we painters call our harmony!
A common greyness silvers everything,—
All in a twilight, you and I alike
—You, at the point of your first pride in me
(That 's gone you know),—but I, at every point;
My youth, my hope, my art, being all toned down
To yonder sober pleasant Fiesole.
There 's the bell clinking from the chapel-top;
That length of convent-wall across the way
Holds the trees safer, huddled more inside;
The last monk leaves the garden; days decrease,
And autumn grows, autumn in everything.
Eh? the whole seems to fall into a shape
As if I saw alike my work and self
And all that I was born to be and do,

A twilight-piece. Love, we are in God's hand.
How strange now, looks the life he makes us lead;
So free we seem, so fettered fast we are!
I feel he laid the fetter: let it lie!
This chamber for example—turn your head—
All that 's behind us! You don't understand
Nor care to understand about my art,
But you can hear at least when people speak:
And that cartoon, the second from the door
—It is the thing, Love! so such things should be—
Behold Madonna!—I am bold to say.
I can do with my pencil what I know,
What I see, what at bottom of my heart
I wish for, if I ever wish so deep—
Do easily, too—when I say, perfectly,
I do not boast, perhaps: yourself are judge,
Who listened to the Legate's talk last week,
And just as much they used to say in France.
At any rate 't is easy, all of it!
No sketches first, no studies, that 's long past:
I do what many dream of, all their lives,
—Dream? strive to do, and agonize to do,
And fail in doing. I could count twenty such
On twice your fingers, and not leave this town,
Who strive—you don't know how the others strive
To paint a little thing like that you smeared
Carelessly passing with your robes afloat,—
Yet do much less, so much less, Someone says,
(I know his name, no matter)—so much less!
Well, less is more, Lucrezia: I am judged.
There burns a truer light of God in them,
In their vexed beating stuffed and stopped-up brain,
Heart, or whate'er else, than goes on to prompt
This low-pulsed forthright craftsman's hand of mine.
Their works drop groundward, but themselves, I know,
Reach many a time a heaven that 's shut to me,
Enter and take their place there sure enough,
Though they come back and cannot tell the world.

My works are nearer heaven, but I sit here.
The sudden blood of these men! at a word—
Praise them, it boils, or blame them, it boils too.
I, painting from myself and to myself,
Know what I do, am unmoved by men's blame
Or their praise either. Somebody remarks
Morello's outline there is wrongly traced,
His hue mistaken; what of that? or else,
Rightly traced and well ordered; what of that?
Speak as they please, what does the mountain care?
Ah, but a man's reach should exceed his grasp,
Or what 's a heaven for? All is silver-grey
Placid and perfect with my art: the worse!
I know both what I want and what might gain,
And yet how profitless to know, to sigh
"Had I been two, another and myself,
Our head would have o'erlooked the world!" No doubt.
Yonder 's a work now, of that famous youth
The Urbinate who died five years ago.
('T is copied, George Vasari sent it me.)
Well, I can fancy how he did it all,
Pouring his soul, with kings and popes to see,
Reaching, that heaven might so replenish him,
Above and through his art—for it gives way;
That arm is wrongly put—and there again—
A fault to pardon in the drawing's lines,
Its body, so to speak: its soul is right,
He means right—that, a child may understand.
Still, what an arm! and I could alter it:
But all the play, the insight and the stretch—
Out of me, out of me! And wherefore out?
Had you enjoined them on me, given me soul,
We might have risen to Rafael, I and you!
Nay, Love, you did give all I asked, I think—
More than I merit, yes, by many times.
But had you—oh, with the same perfect brow,
And perfect eyes, and more than perfect mouth,
And the low voice my soul hears, as a bird

The fowler's pipe, and follows to the snare—
Had you, with these the same, but brought a mind!
Some women do so. Had the mouth there urged
"God and the glory! never care for gain.
The present by the future, what is that?
Live for fame, side by side with Agnolo!
Rafael is waiting: up to God, all three!"
I might have done it for you. So it seems:
Perhaps not. All is as God over-rules.
Beside, incentives come from the soul's self;
The rest avail not. Why do I need you?
What wife had Rafael, or has Agnolo?
In this world, who can do a thing, will not;
And who would do it, cannot, I perceive:
Yet the will 's somewhat—somewhat, too, the power—
And thus we half-men struggle. At the end,
God, I conclude, compensates, punishes.
'T is safer for me, if the award be strict,
That I am something underrated here,
Poor this long while, despised, to speak the truth.
I dared not, do you know, leave home all day,
For fear of chancing on the Paris lords.
The best is when they pass and look aside;
But they speak sometimes; I must bear it all.
Well may they speak! That Francis, that first time,
And that long festal year at Fontainebleau!
I surely then could sometimes leave the ground,
Put on the glory, Rafael's daily wear,
In that humane great monarch's golden look,—
One finger in his beard or twisted curl
Over his mouth's good mark that made the smile,
One arm about my shoulder, round my neck,
The jingle of his gold chain in my ear,
I painting proudly with his breath on me,
All his court round him, seeing with his eyes,
Such frank French eyes, and such a fire of souls
Profuse, my hand kept plying by those hearts,—
And, best of all, this, this, this face beyond,

This in the background, waiting on my work,
To crown the issue with a last reward!
A good time, was it not, my kingly days?
And had you not grown restless . . . but I know—
'T is done and past; 't was right, my instinct said;
Too live the life grew, golden and not grey,
And I 'm the weak-eyed bat no sun should tempt
Out of the grange whose four walls make his world.
How could it end in any other way?
You called me, and I came home to your heart.
The triumph was—to reach and stay there; since
I reached it ere the triumph, what is lost?
Let my hands frame your face in your hair's gold,
You beautiful Lucrezia that are mine!
"Rafael did this, Andrea painted that;
The Roman's is the better when you pray,
But still the other's Virgin was his wife—"
Men will excuse me. I am glad to judge
Both pictures in your presence; clearer grows
My better fortune, I resolve to think.
For, do you know, Lucrezia, as God lives,
Said one day Agnolo, his very self,
To Rafael . . . I have known it all these years . . .
(When the young man was flaming out his thoughts
Upon a palace-wall for Rome to see,
Too lifted up in heart because of it)
"Friend, there 's a certain sorry little scrub
Goes up and down our Florence, none cares how,
Who, were he set to plan and execute
As you are, pricked on by your popes and kings,
Would bring the sweat into that brow of yours!"
To Rafael's!—And indeed the arm is wrong.
I hardly dare . . . yet, only you to see,
Give the chalk here—quick, thus the line should go!
Ay, but the soul! he 's Rafael! rub it out!
Still, all I care for, if he spoke the truth,
(What he? why, who but Michel Agnolo?
Do you forget already words like those?)

If really there was such a chance, so lost,—
Is, whether you 're—not grateful—but more pleased.
Well, let me think so. And you smile indeed!
This hour has been an hour! Another smile?
If you would sit thus by me every night
I should work better, do you comprehend?
I mean that I should earn more, give you more.
See, it is settled dusk now; there 's a star;
Morello 's gone, the watch-lights show the wall,
The cue-owls speak the name we call them by.
Come from the window, love,—come in, at last,
Inside the melancholy little house
We built to be so gay with. God is just.
King Francis may forgive me: oft at nights
When I look up from painting, eyes tired out,
The walls become illumined, brick from brick
Distinct, instead of mortar, fierce bright gold,
That gold of his I did cement them with!
Let us but love each other. Must you go?
That Cousin here again? he waits outside?
Must see you—you, and not with me? Those loans?
More gaming debts to pay? you smiled for that?
Well, let smiles buy me! have you more to spend?
While hand and eye and something of a heart
Are left me, work 's my ware, and what 's it worth?
I 'll pay my fancy. Only let me sit
The grey remainder of the evening out,
Idle, you call it, and muse perfectly
How I could paint, were I but back in France,
One picture, just one more—the Virgin's face,
Not yours this time! I want you at my side
To hear them—that is, Michel Agnolo—
Judge all I do and tell you of its worth.
Will you? To-morrow, satisfy your friend.
I take the subjects for his corridor,
Finish the portrait out of hand—there, there,
And throw him in another thing or two
If he demurs; the whole should prove enough

To pay for this same Cousin's freak. Beside,
What 's better and what 's all I care about,
Get you the thirteen scudi for the ruff!
Love, does that please you? Ah, but what does he,
The Cousin! what does he to please you more?

I am grown peaceful as old age to-night.
I regret little, I would change still less.
Since there my past life lies, why alter it?
The very wrong to Francis!—it is true
I took his coin, was tempted and complied,
And built this house and sinned, and all is said.
My father and my mother died of want.
Well, had I riches of my own? you see
How one gets rich! Let each one bear his lot.
They were born poor, lived poor, and poor they died:
And I have laboured somewhat in my time
And not been paid profusely. Some good son
Paint my two hundred pictures—let him try!
No doubt, there 's something strikes a balance. Yes,
You loved me quite enough, it seems to-night.
This must suffice me here. What would one have?
In heaven, perhaps, new chances, one more chance—
Four great walls in the New Jerusalem,
Meted on each side by the angel's reed,
For Leonard, Rafael, Agnolo and me
To cover—the three first without a wife,
While I have mine! So—still they overcome
Because there 's still Lucrezia,—as I choose.

Again the Cousin's whistle! Go, my Love.

FRA LIPPO LIPPI

Browning's love of contrast made him relish the idea of a rough and rowdy fellow like Lippi becoming a famous painter of religious pictures. Left an orphan, Lippi was reared by an aunt who placed him in the hands of the Carmelite Friars. His talent was quickly discovered. Cosimo de Medici became his patron, and it was from Cosimo's palace where he had been locked up to finish a picture that he escaped to enjoy the pleasures of the streets. In "The Coronation of the Virgin," mentioned in the poem, Lippi had painted himself into the picture.

I am poor brother Lippo, by your leave!
You need not clap your torches to my face.
Zooks, what's to blame? you think you see a monk!
What, it's past midnight, and you go the rounds,
And here you catch me at an alley's end
Where sportive ladies leave their doors ajar?
The Carmine's my cloister: hunt it up,
Do,—harry out, if you must show your zeal,
Whatever rat, there, haps on his wrong hole,
And nip each softling of a wee white mouse,
Weke, weke, that's crept to keep him company!
Aha, you know your betters? Then, you'll take
Your hand away that's fiddling on my throat,
And please to know me likewise. Who am I?
Why, one, sir, who is lodging with a friend
Three streets off—he's a certain . . . how d'ye call?
Master—a . . . Cosimo of the Medici,
In the house that caps the corner. Boh! you were best!
Remember and tell me, the day you're hanged,
How you affected such a gullet's-gripe!
But you, sir, it concerns you that your knaves
Pick up a manner nor discredit you.
Zooks, are we pilchards, that they sweep the streets
And count fair prize what comes into their net?
He's Judas to a tittle, that man is!
Just such a face! why, sir, you make amends.
Lord, I'm not angry! Bid your hangdogs go
Drink out this quarter-florin to the health
Of the munificent House that harbours me
(And many more beside, lads! more beside!)
And all's come square again. I'd like his face—
His, elbowing on his comrade in the door

With the pike and lantern,—for the slave that holds
John Baptist's head a-dangle by the hair
With one hand ('look you, now,' as who should say)
And his weapon in the other, yet unwiped!
It's not your chance to have a bit of chalk,
A wood-coal or the like? or you should see!
Yes, I'm the painter, since you style me so.
What, brother Lippo's doings, up and down,
You know them and they take you? like enough!
I saw the proper twinkle in your eye—
'Tell you, I liked your looks at very first.
Let's sit and set things straight now, hip to haunch.
Here's spring come, and the nights one makes up bands
To roam the town and sing out carnival,
And I've been three weeks shut within my mew,
A-painting for the great man, saints and saints
And saints again. I could not paint all night—
Ouf! I leaned out of window for fresh air.
There came a hurry of feet and little feet,
A sweep of lute-strings, laughs, and whifts of song,—
Flower o' the broom,
Take away love, and our earth is a tomb!
Flower o' the quince,
I let Lisa go, and what good's in life since?
Flower o' the thyme—and so on. Round they went.
Scarce had they turned the corner when a titter
Like the skipping of rabbits by moonlight,—three slim shapes—
And a face that looked up . . . zooks, sir, flesh and blood,
That's all I'm made of! Into shreds it went,
Curtain and counterpane and coverlet,
All the bed-furniture—a dozen knots,
There was a ladder! down I let myself,
Hands and feet, scrambling somehow, and so dropped,
And after them. I came up with the fun
Hard by Saint Laurence, hail fellow, well met,—
Flower o' the rose,
If I've been merry, what matter who knows?
And so as I was stealing back again

To get to bed and have a bit of sleep
Ere I rise up to-morrow and go work
On Jerome knocking at his poor old breast
With his great round stone to subdue the flesh,
You snap me of the sudden. Ah, I see!
Though your eye twinkles still, you shake your head—
Mine's shaved,—a monk, you say—the sting's in that!
If Master Cosimo announced himself,
Mum's the word naturally; but a monk!
Come, what am I a beast for? tell us, now!
I was a baby when my mother died
And father died and left me in the street.
I starved there, God knows how, a year or two
On fig skins, melon-parings, rinds and shucks,
Refuse and rubbish. One fine frosty day
My stomach being empty as your hat,
The wind doubled me up and down I went.
Old Aunt Lapaccia trussed me with one hand,
(Its fellow was a stinger as I knew)
And so along the wall, over the bridge,
By the straight cut to the convent. Six words, there,
While I stood munching my first bread that month:
"So, boy, you're minded," quoth the good fat father
Wiping his own mouth, 'twas refection-time,—
"To quit this very miserable world?
Will you renounce?" . . . The mouthful of bread? thought I;
By no means! Brief, they made a monk of me;
I did renounce the world, its pride and greed,
Palace, farm, villa, shop and banking-house,
Trash, such as these poor devils of Medici
Have given their hearts to—all at eight years old.
Well, sir, I found in time, you may be sure,
'Twas not for nothing—the good bellyful,
The warm serge and the rope that goes all round,
And day-long blessed idleness beside!
"Let's see what the urchin's fit for"—that came next.
Not overmuch their way, I must confess.
Such a to-do! they tried me with their books.

Lord, they'd have taught me Latin in pure waste!
Flower o' the clove,
All the Latin I construe is, 'amo' I love!
But, mind you, when a boy starves in the streets
Eight years together, as my fortune was,
Watching folk's faces to know who will fling
The bit of half-stripped grape-bunch he desires,
And who will curse or kick him for his pains—
Which gentleman processional and fine,
Holding a candle to the Sacrament
Will wink and let him lift a plate and catch
The droppings of the wax to sell again,
Or holla for the Eight and have him whipped,—
How say I?—nay, which dog bites, which lets drop
His bone from the heap of offal in the street,—
Why, soul and sense of him grow sharp alike,
He learns the look of things, and none the less
For admonitions from the hunger-pinch.
I had a store of such remarks, be sure,
Which, after I found leisure, turned to use:
I drew men's faces on my copy-books,
Scrawled them within the antiphonary's marge,
Joined legs and arms to the long music-notes,
Found nose and eyes and chin for A.s and B.s,
And made a string of pictures of the world
Betwixt the ins and outs of verb and noun,
On the wall, the bench, the door. The monks looked black.
"Nay," quoth the Prior, "turn him out, d'ye say?
In no wise. Lose a crow and catch a lark.
What if at last we get our man of parts,
We Carmelites, like those Camaldolese
And Preaching Friars, to do our church up fine
And put the front on it that ought to be!"
And hereupon they bade me daub away.
Thank you! my head being crammed, their walls a blank,
Never was such prompt disemburdening.
First, every sort of monk, the black and white,
I drew them, fat and lean: then, folks at church,

From good old gossips waiting to confess
Their cribs of barrel-droppings, candle-ends,—
To the breathless fellow at the altar-foot,
Fresh from his murder, safe and sitting there
With the little children round him in a row
Of admiration, half for his beard and half
For that white anger of his victim's son
Shaking a fist at him with one fierce arm,
Signing himself with the other because of Christ
(Whose sad face on the cross sees only this
After the passion of a thousand years)
Till some poor girl, her apron o'er her head
Which the intense eyes looked through, came at eve
On tip-toe, said a word, dropped in a loaf,
Her pair of earrings and a bunch of flowers
The brute took growling, prayed, and then was gone.
I painted all, then cried " 'T is ask and have—
Choose, for more's ready!"—laid the ladder flat,
And showed my covered bit of cloister-wall.
The monks closed in a circle and praised loud
Till checked,—taught what to see and not to see,
Being simple bodies,—"That's the very man!
Look at the boy who stoops to pat the dog!
That woman's like the Prior's niece who comes
To care about his asthma: it's the life!"
But there my triumph's straw-fire flared and funked—
Their betters took their turn to see and say:
The Prior and the learned pulled a face
And stopped all that in no time. "How? what's here?
Quite from the mark of painting, bless us all!
Faces, arms, legs and bodies like the true
As much as pea and pea! it's devil's-game!
Your business is not to catch men with show,
With homage to the perishable clay,
But lift them over it, ignore it all,
Make them forget there's such a thing as flesh.
Your business is to paint the souls of men—
Man's soul, and it's a fire, smoke . . . no it's not . . .

It's vapour done up like a new-born babe—
(In that shape when you die it leaves your mouth)
It's . . . well, what matters talking, it's the soul!
Give us no more of body than shows soul!
Here's Giotto, with his Saint a-praising God,
That sets you praising,—why not stop with him?
Why put all thoughts of praise out of our heads
With wonder at lines, colours, and what not?
Paint the soul, never mind the legs and arms!
Rub all out, try at it a second time.
Oh, that white smallish female with the breasts,
She's just my niece . . . Herodias, I would say,—
Who went and danced and got men's heads cut off—
Have it all out!" Now, is this sense, I ask?
A fine way to paint soul, by painting body
So ill, the eye can't stop there, must go further
And can't fare worse! Thus, yellow does for white
When what you put for yellow's simply black,
And any sort of meaning looks intense
When all beside itself means and looks nought.
Why can't a painter lift each foot in turn,
Left foot and right foot, go a double step,
Make his flesh liker and his soul more like,
Both in their order? Take the prettiest face,
The Prior's niece . . . patron-saint—is it so pretty
You can't discover if it means hope, fear,
Sorrow or joy? won't beauty go with these?
Suppose I've made her eyes all right and blue,
Can't I take breath and try to add life's flash,
And then add soul and heighten them threefold?
Or say there's beauty with no soul at all—
(I never saw it—put the case the same—)
If you get simple beauty and nought else,
You get about the best thing God invents,—
That's somewhat. And you'll find the soul you have missed,
Within yourself when you return Him thanks,
"Rub all out!" Well, well, there's my life, in short.
And so the thing has gone on ever since.

I'm grown a man no doubt, I've broken bounds—
You should not take a fellow eight years old
And make him swear to never kiss the girls.
I'm my own master, paint now as I please—
Having a friend, you see, in the Corner-house!
Lord, it's fast holding by the rings in front—
Those great rings serve more purposes than just
To plant a flag in, or tie up a horse!
And yet the old schooling sticks, the old grave eyes
Are peeping o'er my shoulder as I work,
The heads shake still—"It's Art's decline, my son!
You're not of the true painters, great and old;
Brother Angelico's the man, you'll find;
Brother Lorenzo stands his single peer:
Fag on at flesh, you'll never make the third!"
Flower o' the pine,
You keep your mistr . . . manners, and I'll stick to mine!
I'm not the third, then: bless us, they must know!
Don't you think they're the likeliest to know,
They with their Latin? so, I swallow my rage,
Clench my teeth, suck my lips in tight, and paint
To please them—sometimes do, and sometimes don't,
For, doing most, there's pretty sure to come
A turn, some warm eve finds me at my saints—
A laugh, a cry, the business of the world—
(*Flower o' the peach,*
Death for us all, and his own life for each!)
And my whole soul revolves, the cup runs over,
The world and life's too big to pass for a dream,
And I do these wild things in sheer despite,
And play the fooleries you catch me at,
In pure rage! the old mill-horse, out at grass
After hard years, throws up his stiff heels so,
Although the miller does not preach to him
The only good of grass is to make chaff.
What would men have? Do they like grass or no—
May they or mayn't they? all I want's the thing
Settled for ever one way: as it is,

You tell too many lies and hurt yourself.
You don't like what you only like too much,
You do like what, if given you at your word,
You find abundantly detestable.
For me, I think I speak as I was taught—
I always see the Garden and God there
A-making man's wife—and, my lesson learned,
The value and significance of flesh,
I can't unlearn ten minutes afterwards.

You understand me: I'm a beast, I know.
But see, now—why, I see as certainly
As that the morning-star's about to shine,
What will hap some day. We've a youngster here
Comes to our convent, studies what I do,
Slouches and stares and lets no atom drop—
His name is Guidi—he'll not mind the monks—
They call him Hulking Tom, he lets them talk—
He picks my practice up—he'll paint apace,
I hope so—though I never live so long,
I know what's sure to follow. You be judge!
You speak no Latin more than I, belike—
However, you're my man, you've seen the world
—The beauty and the wonder and the power,
The shapes of things, their colours, lights and shades,
Changes, surprises,—and God made it all!
—For what? do you feel thankful, ay or no,
For this fair town's face, yonder river's line,
The mountain round it and the sky above,
Much more the figures of man, woman, child,
These are the frame to? What's it all about?
To be passed over, despised? or dwelt upon,
Wondered at? oh, this last of course!—you say.
But why not do as well as say,—paint these
Just as they are, careless what comes of it?
God's works—paint anyone, and count it crime
To let a truth slip. Don't object, "His works
Are here already—nature is complete:

Suppose you reproduce her—(which you can't)
There's no advantage! you must beat her, then."
For, don't you mark, we're made so that we love
First when we see them painted, things we have passed
Perhaps a hundred times nor cared to see;
And so they are better, painted—better to us,
Which is the same thing. Art was given for that—
God uses us to help each other so,
Lending our minds out. Have you noticed, now,
Your cullion's hanging face? A bit of chalk,
And trust me but you should, though! How much more,
If I drew higher things with the same truth!
That were to take the Prior's pulpit-place,
Interpret God to all of you! oh, oh,
It makes me mad to see what men shall do
And we in our graves! This world's no blot for us,
Nor blank—it means intensely, and means good:
To find its meaning is my meat and drink.
"Ay, but you don't so instigate to prayer!"
Strikes in the Prior: "when your meaning's plain
It does not say to folks—remember matins,
Or, mind you fast next Friday." Why, for this
What need of art at all? A skull and bones,
Two bits of stick nailed cross-wise, or, what's best,
A bell to chime the hour with, does as well.
I painted a Saint Laurence six months since
At Prato, splashed the fresco in fine style:
"How looks my painting, now the scaffold's down?"
I ask a brother: "Hugely," he returns—
"Already not one phiz of your three slaves
That turn the Deacon off his toasted side,
But's scratched and prodded to our heart's content,
The pious people have so eased their own
When coming to say prayers there in a rage:
We get on fast to see the bricks beneath.
Expect another job this time next year,
For pity and religion grow i' the crowd—
Your painting serves its purpose!" Hang the fools!

—That is—you'll not mistake an idle word
Spoke in a huff by a poor monk, God wot,
Tasting the air this spicy night which turns
The unaccustomed head like Chianti wine!
Oh, the church knows! don't misreport me, now!
It's natural a poor monk out of bounds
Should have his apt word to excuse himself:
And hearken how I plot to make amends.
I have bethought me: I shall paint a piece
. . . There's for you! Give me six months, then go, see
Something in Sant' Ambrogio's! Bless the nuns!
They want a cast o' my office. I shall paint
God in the midst, Madonna and her babe,
Ringed by a bowery flowery angel-brood,
Lilies and vestments and white faces, sweet
As puff on puff of grated orris-root
When ladies crowd to Church at midsummer.
And then i' the front, of course, a saint or two—
Saint John, because he saves the Florentines,
Saint Ambrose, who puts down in black and white
The convent's friends and gives them a long day,
And Job, I must have him there past mistake,
The man of Uz (and Us without the z,
Painters who need his patience). Well, all these
Secured at their devotion, up shall come
Out of a corner when you least expect,
As one by a dark stair into a great light,
Music and talking, who but Lippo! I!—
Mazed, motionless and moonstruck—I'm the man!
Back I shrink—what is this I see and hear?
I, caught up with my monk's-things by mistake,
My old serge gown and rope that goes all round,
I, in this presence, this pure company!
Where's a hole, where's a corner for escape?
Then steps a sweet angelic slip of a thing
Forward, puts out a soft palm—"Not so fast!"
—Addresses the celestial presence, "nay—
He made you and devised you, after all,

Though he's none of you! Could Saint John there draw—
His camel-hair make up a painting-brush?
We come to brother Lippo for all that,
Iste perfecit opus!" So, all smile—
I shuffle sideways with my blushing face
Under the cover of a hundred wings
Thrown like a spread of kirtles when you're gay
And play hot cockles, all the doors being shut,
Till, wholly unexpected, in there pops
The hothead husband! Thus I scuttle off
To some safe bench behind, not letting go
The palm of her, the little lily thing
That spoke the good word for me in the nick,
Like the Prior's niece . . . Saint Lucy, I would say.
And so all's saved for me, and for the church
A pretty picture gained. Go, six months hence!
Your hand, sir, and good-bye: no lights, no lights!
The street's hushed, and I know my own way back,
Don't fear me! There's the grey beginning. Zooks!

"DE GUSTIBUS—"

I

Your ghost will walk, you lover of trees,
(If our loves remain)
In an English lane,
By a cornfield-side a-flutter with poppies.
Hark, those two in the hazel coppice—
A boy and a girl, if the good fates please,
Making love, say,—
The happier they!
Draw yourself up from the light of the moon,
And let them pass, as they will too soon,
With the beanflowers' boon,
And the blackbird's tune,
And May, and June!

2

What I love best in all the world,
Is, a castle, precipice-encurled,
In a gash of the wind-grieved Apennine.
Or look for me, old fellow of mine,
(If I get my head from out the mouth
O' the grave, and loose my spirit's bands,
And come again to the land of lands)—
In a sea-side house to the farther South,
Where the baked cicalas die of drouth,
And one sharp tree—'tis a cypress—stands,
By the many hundred years red-rusted,
Rough iron-spiked, ripe fruit-o'er-crusted,
My sentinel to guard the sands
To the water's edge. For, what expands
Before the house, but the great opaque
Blue breadth of sea without a break?
While, in the house, for ever crumbles
Some fragment of the frescoed walls,
From blisters where a scorpion sprawls.
A girl bare-footed brings, and tumbles
Down on the pavement, green-flesh melons,
And says there's news to-day—the king
Was shot at, touched in the liver-wing,
Goes with his Bourbon arm in a sling:
—She hopes they have not caught the felons.
    Italy, my Italy!
Queen Mary's saying serves for me—
    (When fortune's malice
    Lost her, Calais)
Open my heart and you will see
Graved inside of it, 'Italy.'
Such lovers old are I and she;
So it always was, so shall ever be!

POPULARITY

Keats' line, "Blue! 'Tis the life of heaven," gave Browning the key word "blue" which runs through the poem. And his theme —that the true creator or inventor is less likely to be rewarded than his imitators—is pointed at the end by the direct reference to Keats. The final two lines of the poem are often quoted: they illustrate Browning's genius for combining seemingly unrelated facts or ideas (called catachresis by Coleridge), which has been described as the prime function of the poetic imagination.

1

Stand still, true poet that you are!
  I know you; let me try and draw you.
Some night you 'll fail us: when afar
  You rise, remember one man saw you,
Knew you, and named a star!

2

My star, God's glow-worm! Why extend
  That loving hand of his which leads you,
Yet locks you safe from end to end
  Of this dark world, unless he needs you,
Just saves your light to spend?

3

His clenched hand shall unclose at last,
  I know, and let out all the beauty:
My poet holds the future fast,
  Accepts the coming ages' duty,
Their present for this past.

4

That day, the earth's feast-master's brow
  Shall clear, to God the chalice raising;
"Others give best at first, but thou
  Forever set'st our table praising,
Keep'st the good wine till now!"

5

Meantime, I 'll draw you as you stand,
  With few or none to watch and wonder:
I 'll say—a fisher, on the sand
  By Tyre the old, with ocean-plunder,
A netful, brought to land.

6

Who has not heard how Tyrian shells
  Enclosed the blue, that dye of dyes
Whereof one drop worked miracles,
  And coloured like Astarte's eyes
Raw silk the merchant sells?

7

And each bystander of them all
  Could criticize, and quote tradition
How depths of blue sublimed some pall
  —To get which, pricked a king's ambition;
Worth sceptre, crown and ball.

8

Yet there 's the dye, in that rough mesh,
  The sea has only just o'er-whispered!
Live whelks, each lip's beard dripping fresh,
  As if they still the water's lisp heard
Through foam the rock-weeds thresh.

9

Enough to furnish Solomon
  Such hangings for his cedar-house,
That, when gold-robed he took the throne
  In that abyss of blue, the Spouse
Might swear his presence shone

10

Most like the centre-spike of gold
  Which burns deep in the bluebell's womb,
What time, with ardours manifold,
  The bee goes singing to her groom,
Drunken and overbold.

11

Mere conchs! not fit for warp or woof!
  Till cunning comes to pound and squeeze
And clarify,—refine to proof
  The liquor filtered by degrees,
While the world stands aloof.

12

And there 's the extract, flasked and fine,
  And priced and saleable at last!
And Hobbs, Nobbs, Stokes and Nokes combine
  To paint the future from the past,
Put blue into their line.

13

Hobbs hints blue,—straight he turtle eats:
  Nobbs prints blue,—claret crowns his cup:
Nokes outdares Stokes in azure feats,—
  Both gorge. Who fished the murex up?
What porridge had John Keats?

SAUL

This Messianic poem has a distinctly modern theme: the power of music to heal those who are mentally sick. David comes to Saul when he is in utter despair. He plays tunes which he believes will cure the King's disorder: first, simple birdlike melodies, then shepherds' and reapers' songs; then hymns for the honored dead; then the marriage chant; the comradeship of men and the worship of God; the values of friendship and the joys of living, of kingship and high ambition; lastly, a prophetic chant about the coming of Christ. In a revelation born of his compassion for Saul, David sees that, as he is willing to suffer for the King he loves so well, God is also willing to suffer for man, the faulty, straying creature He loves.

1

Said Abner, "At last thou art come! Ere I tell, ere thou speak,
Kiss my cheek, wish me well!" Then I wished it, and did kiss
his cheek.
And he, "Since the King, O my friend, for thy countenance
sent,
Neither drunken nor eaten have we; nor until from his tent
Thou return with the joyful assurance the King liveth yet,
Shall our lip with the honey be bright, with the water be wet.
For out of the black mid-tent's silence, a space of three days,
Not a sound hath escaped to thy servants, of prayer nor of praise,
To betoken that Saul and the Spirit have ended their strife,
And, that, faint in his triumph, the monarch sinks back upon life.

2

"Yet now my heart leaps, O beloved! God's child with his dew
On thy gracious gold hair, and those lilies still living and blue
Just broken to twine round thy harp-strings, as if no wild heat
Were now raging to torture the desert!"

3

Then I, as was meet,
Knelt down to the God of my fathers, and rose on my feet,
And ran o'er the sand burnt to powder. The tent was unlooped;
I pulled up the spear that obstructed, and under I stooped;
Hands and knees on the slippery grass-patch, all withered and
gone,
That extends to the second enclosure, I groped my way on

Till I felt where the foldskirts fly open. Then once more I prayed,
And opened the foldskirts and entered, and was not afraid,
But spoke, "Here is David, thy servant!" And no voice replied.
At the first I saw nought but the blackness; but soon I descried
A something more black than the blackness—the vast, the upright
Main prop which sustains the pavilion: and slow into sight
Grew a figure against it, gigantic and blackest of all:
Then a sunbeam, that burst thro' the tent-roof, showed Saul.

4

He stood as erect as that tent-prop; both arms stretched out wide
On the great cross-support in the centre, that goes to each side;
He relaxed not a muscle, but hung there, as, caught in his pangs
And waiting his change, the king-serpent all heavily hangs,
Far away from his kind, in the pine, till deliverance come
With the spring-time,—so agonized Saul, drear and stark, blind and dumb.

5

Then I tuned my harp,—took off the lilies we twine round its chords
Lest they snap 'neath the stress of the noontide—those sunbeams like swords!
And I first played the tune all our sheep know, as, one after one,
So docile they come to the pen-door, till folding be done.
They are white and untorn by the bushes, for lo, they have fed
Where the long grasses stifle the water within the stream's bed;
And now one after one seeks its lodging, as star follows star
Into eve and the blue far above us,—so blue and so far!

6

—Then the tune, for which quails on the cornland will each leave his mate
To fly after the player; then, what makes the crickets elate,

Till for boldness they fight one another: and then, what has weight
To set the quick jerboa a-musing outside his sand house—
There are none such as he for a wonder, half bird and half mouse!
God made all the creatures and gave them our love and our fear,
To give sign, we and they are His children, one family here.

7

Then I played the help-tune of our reapers, their wine-song, when hand
Grasps at hand, eye lights eye in good friendship, and great hearts expand
And grow one in the sense of this world's life.—And then, the last song
When the dead man is praised on his journey—"Bear, bear him along
With his few faults shut up like dead flowerets! are balm-seeds not here
To console us? The land has none left such as he on the bier.
Oh, would we might keep thee, my brother!"—And then, the glad chaunt
Of the marriage,—first go the young maidens, next, she whom we vaunt
As the beauty, the pride of our dwelling.—And then, the great march
Wherein man runs to man to assist him and buttress an arch
Nought can break; who shall harm them, our friends?—Then, the chorus intoned
As the Levites go up to the altar in glory enthroned.
But I stopped here—for here in the darkness, Saul groaned.

8

And I paused, held my breath in such silence, and listened apart;
And the tent shook, for mighty Saul shuddered—and sparkles 'gan dart
From the jewels that woke in his turban at once with a start—

All its lordly male-sapphires, and rubies courageous at heart.
So the head—but the body still moved not, still clung there erect.
And I bent once again to my playing, pursued it unchecked,
As I sang,—

9

"Oh, our manhood's prime vigour! no spirit feels waste,
Not a muscle is stopped in its playing, nor sinew unbraced.
Oh, the wild joys of living! the leaping from rock up to rock—
The strong rending of boughs from the fir-tree,—the cool silver shock
Of the plunge in a pool's living water,—the hunt of the bear,
And the sultriness showing the lion is couched in his lair.
And the meal—the rich dates yellowed over with gold dust divine,
And the locust's-flesh steeped in the pitcher! the full draught of wine,
And the sleep in the dried river-channel where bulrushes tell
That the water was wont to go warbling so softly and well.
How good is man's life, the mere living! how fit to employ
All the heart and the soul and the senses, for ever in joy!
Hast thou loved the white locks of thy father, whose sword thou didst guard
When he trusted thee forth with the armies, for glorious reward?
Didst thou see the thin hands of thy mother, held up as men sung
The low song of the nearly-departed, and heard her faint tongue
Joining in while it could to the witness, 'Let one more attest,
I have lived, seen God's hand thro' a lifetime, and all was for best!'
Then they sung thro' their tears in strong triumph, not much—but the rest.
And thy brothers, the help and the contest, the working whence grew
Such result as, from seething grape-bundles, the spirit strained true!
And the friends of thy boyhood—that boyhood of wonder and hope,

Present promise, and wealth of the future beyond the eye's scope,—
Till lo, thou art grown to a monarch; a people is thine;
And all gifts, which the world offers singly, on one head combine!
On one head, all the beauty and strength, love and rage (like the throe
That, a-work in the rock, helps its labour and lets the gold go)
High ambition and deeds which surpass it, fame crowning it,—all
Brought to blaze on the head of one creature—King Saul!"

10

And lo, with that leap of my spirit,—heart, hand, harp and voice,
Each lifting Saul's name out of sorrow, each bidding rejoice
Saul's fame in the light it was made for—as when, dare I say,
The Lord's army, in rapture of service, strains through its array,
And upsoareth the cherubim-chariot—"Saul!" cried I, and stopped,
And waited the thing that should follow. Then Saul, who hung propped
By the tent's cross-support in the centre, was struck by his name.
Have ye seen when Spring's arrowy summons goes right to the aim,
And some mountain, the last to withstand her, that held (he alone,
While the vale laughed in freedom and flowers) on a broad bust of stone
A year's snow bound about for a breast-plate,—leaves grasp of the sheet?
Fold on fold all at once it crowds thunderously down to his feet,
And there fronts you, stark, black, but alive yet, your mountain of old,
With his rents, the successive bequeathings of ages untold—
Yea, each harm got in fighting your battles, each furrow and scar
Of his head thrust 'twixt you and the tempest—all hail, there they are!

Now again to be softened with verdure, again hold the nest
Of the dove, tempt the goat and its young to the green on its
crest
For their food in the ardours of summer! One long shudder
thrilled
All the tent till the very air tingled, then sank and was stilled
At the King's self left standing before me, released and aware.
What was gone, what remained? all to traverse 'twixt hope and
despair;
Death was past, life not come: so he waited. Awhile his right
hand
Held the brow, helped the eyes left too vacant forthwith to
remand
To their place what new objects should enter: 'twas Saul as
before.
I looked up and dared gaze at those eyes, nor was hurt any more
Than by slow pallid sunsets in autumn, ye watch from the shore,
At their sad level gaze o'er the ocean—a sun's slow decline
Over hills which, resolved in stern silence, o'erlap and entwine
Base with base to knit strength more intense: so, arm folded in
arm
O'er the chest whose slow heavings subsided.

II

What spell or what charm,
(For, awhile there was trouble within me) what next should
I urge
To sustain him where song had restored him?—Song filled to
the verge
His cup with the wine of this life, pressing all that it yields
Of mere fruitage, the strength and the beauty! Beyond, on what
fields,
Glean a vintage more potent and perfect to brighten the eye
And bring blood to the lip, and commend them the cup they
put by?
He saith, "It is good"; still he drinks not: he lets me praise life,
Gives assent, yet would die for his own part.

12

Then fancies grew rife
Which had come long ago on the pastures, when round me the sheep
Fed in silence—above, the one eagle wheeled slow as in sleep;
And I lay in my hollow, and mused on the world that might lie
'Neath his ken, though I saw but the strip 'twixt the hill and the sky:
And I laughed—"Since my days are ordained to be passed with my flocks,
Let me people at least, with my fancies, the plains and the rocks,
Dream the life I am never to mix with, and image the show
Of mankind as they live in those fashions I hardly shall know!
Schemes of life, its best rules and right uses, the courage that gains,
And the prudence that keeps what men strive for." And now these old trains
Of vague thought came again; I grew surer; so, once more the string
Of my harp made response to my spirit, as thus—

13

"Yea, my king,"
I began—"thou dost well in rejecting mere comforts that spring
From the mere mortal life held in common by man and by brute:
In our flesh grows the branch of this life, in our soul it bears fruit.
Thou hast marked the slow rise of the tree,—how its stem trembled first
Till it passed the kid's lip, the stag's antler; then safely outburst
The fan-branches all round; and thou mindedst when these too, in turn
Broke a-bloom and the palm-tree seemed perfect: yet more was to learn,
Ev'n the good that comes in with the palm-fruit. Our dates shall we slight,

When their juice brings a cure for all sorrow? or care for the plight
Of the palm's self whose slow growth produced them? Not so! stem and branch
Shall decay, nor be known in their place, while the palm-wine shall staunch
Every wound of man's spirit in winter. I pour thee such wine.
Leave the flesh to the fate it was fit for! the spirit be thine!
By the spirit, when age shall o'ercome thee, thou still shalt enjoy
More indeed, than at first when inconscious, the life of a boy.
Crush that life, and behold its wine running! each deed thou hast done
Dies, revives, goes to work in the world; until e'en as the sun
Looking down on the earth, though clouds spoil him, though tempests efface,
Can find nothing his own deed produced not, must everywhere trace
The results of his past summer-prime,—so, each ray of thy will,
Every flash of thy passion and prowess, long over, shall thrill
Thy whole people the countless, with ardour, till they too give forth
Alike cheer to their sons, who in turn, fill the South and the North
With the radiance thy deed was the germ of. Carouse in the Past!
But the license of age has its limit; thou diest at last:
As the lion when age dims his eyeball, the rose at her height,
So with man—so his power and his beauty for ever take flight.
No! again a long draught of my soul-wine! look forth o'er the years—
Thou hast done now with eyes for the actual; begin with the seer's!
Is Saul dead? in the depth of the vale make his tomb—bid arise
A grey mountain of marble heaped four-square, till, built to the skies,
Let it mark where the great First King slumbers; whose fame would ye know
Up above see the rock's naked face, where the record shall go
In great characters cut by the scribe.—Such was Saul, so he did;

With the sages directing the work, by the populace chid,—
For not half, they'll affirm, is comprised there! Which fault to amend,
In the grove with his kind grows the cedar, whereon they shall spend
(See, in tablets 'tis level before them) their praise, and record
With the gold of the graver, Saul's story,—the statesman's great word
Side by side with the poet's sweet comment. The river's a-wave
With smooth paper-reeds grazing each other when prophet winds rave:
So the pen gives unborn generations their due and their part
In thy being! Then, first of the mighty, thank God that thou art!"

14

And behold while I sang . . . But O Thou who didst grant me that day,
And before it not seldom hast granted Thy help to essay,
Carry on and complete an adventure,—my Shield and my Sword
In that act where my soul was Thy servant, Thy word was my word,—
Still be with me, who then at the summit of human endeavour
And scaling the highest, man's thought could, gazed hopeless as ever
On the new stretch of Heaven above me—till, mighty to save,
Just one lift of Thy hand cleared that distance—God's throne from man's grave!
Let me tell out my tale to its ending—my voice to my heart
Which can scarce dare believe in what marvels last night I took part,
As this morning I gather the fragments, alone with my sheep,
And still fear lest the terrible glory evanish like sleep!
For I wake in the grey dewy covert, while Hebron upheaves
The dawn struggling with night on his shoulder, and Kidron retrieves
Slow the damage of yesterday's sunshine.

15

I say then,—my song
While I sang thus, assuring the monarch, and ever more strong
Made a proffer of good to console him—he slowly resumed
His old motions and habitudes kingly. The right hand replumed
His black locks to their wonted composure, adjusted the swathes
Of his turban, and see—the huge sweat that his countenance bathes,
He wipes off with the robe; and he girds now his loins as of yore,
And feels slow for the armlets of price, with the clasp set before.
He is Saul, ye remember in glory,—ere error had bent
The broad brow from the daily communion; and still, though much spent
Be the life and the bearing that front you, the same, God did choose,
To receive what a man may waste, desecrate, never quite lose.
So sank he along by the tent-prop till, stayed by the pile
Of his armour and war-cloak and garments, he leaned there awhile,
And so sat out my singing,—one arm round the tent-prop, to raise
His bent head, and the other hung slack—till I touched on the praise
I foresaw from all men in all times, to the man patient there;
And thus ended, the harp falling forward. Then first I was 'ware
That he sat, as I say, with my head just above his vast knees
Which were thrust out on each side around me, like oak roots which please
To encircle a lamb when it slumbers. I looked up to know
If the best I could do had brought solace: he spoke not, but slow
Lifted up the hand slack at his side, till he laid it with care
Soft and grave, but in mild settled will, on my brow: thro' my hair
The large fingers were pushed, and he bent back my head, with kind power—
All my face back, intent to peruse it, as men do a flower.
Thus held he me there with his great eyes that scrutinized mine—

And oh, all my heart how it loved him! but where was the sign?
I yearned—"Could I help thee, my father, inventing a bliss,
I would add to that life of the Past, both the Future and this;
I would give thee new life altogether, as good, ages hence,
As this moment,—had love but the warrant, love's heart to dispense!"

16

Then the truth came upon me. No harp more—no song more! outbroke—

17

"I have gone the whole round of Creation: I saw and I spoke!
I, a work of God's hand for that purpose, received in my brain
And pronounced on the rest of His handwork—returned Him again
His creation's approval or censure: I spoke as I saw.
I report, as a man may of God's work—all's love, yet all's law!
Now I lay down the judgeship He lent me. Each faculty tasked
To perceive Him, has gained an abyss, where a dewdrop was asked.
Have I knowledge? confounded it shrivels at Wisdom laid bare.
Have I forethought? how purblind, how blank, to the Infinite Care!
Do I task any faculty highest, to image success?
I but open my eyes,—and perfection, no more and no less,
In the kind I imagined, full-fronts me, and God is seen God
In the star, in the stone, in the flesh, in the soul and the clod.
And thus looking within and around me, I ever renew
(With that stoop of the soul which in bending upraises it too)
The submission of Man's nothing-perfect to God's All-Complete,
As by each new obeisance in spirit, I climb to His feet!
Yet with all this abounding experience, this Deity known,
I shall dare to discover some province, some gift of my own.
There's a faculty pleasant to exercise, hard to hoodwink,
I am fain to keep still in abeyance, (I laugh as I think)
Lest, insisting to claim and parade in it, wot ye, I worst
E'en the Giver in one gift.—Behold! I could love if I durst!

But I sink the pretension as fearing a man may o'ertake
God's own speed in the one way of love: I abstain for love's sake.
—What, my soul? see thus far and no farther? when doors great
and small,
Nine-and-ninety flew ope at our touch, should the hundredth
appal?
In the least things, have faith, yet distrust in the greatest of all?
Do I find love so full in my nature, God's ultimate gift,
That I doubt His own love can compete with it? here, the parts
shift?
Here, the creature surpass the Creator, the end, what Began?—
Would I fain in my impotent yearning do all for this man,
And dare doubt He alone shall not help him, who yet alone can?
Would it ever have entered my mind, the bare will, much less
power,
To bestow on this Saul what I sang of, the marvellous dower
Of the life he was gifted and filled with? to make such a soul,
Such a body, and then such an earth for insphering the whole?
And doth it not enter my mind (as my warm tears attest)
These good things being given, to go on, and give one more,
the best?
Ay, to save and redeem and restore him, maintain at the height
This perfection,—succeed with life's dayspring, death's minute
of night?
Interpose at the difficult minute, snatch Saul, the mistake,
Saul, the failure, the ruin he seems now,—and bid him awake
From the dream, the probation, the prelude, to find himself set
Clear and safe in new light and new life,—a new harmony yet
To be run, and continued, and ended—who knows?—or endure!
The man taught enough by life's dream, of the rest to make
sure;
By the pain-throb, triumphantly winning intensified bliss,
And the next world's reward and repose, by the struggles in this.

18

"I believe it! 'tis Thou, God, that givest, 'tis I who receive:
In the first is the last, in Thy will is my power to believe.

All's one gift: Thou canst grant it moreover, as prompt to my prayer
As I breathe out this breath, as I open these arms to the air.
From Thy will, stream the worlds, life and nature, thy dread Sabaoth:
I will?—the mere atoms despise me! why am I not loth
To look that, even that in the face too? why is it I dare
Think but lightly of such impuissance? what stops my despair?
This;—'tis not what man Does which exalts him, but what man Would do!
See the King—I would help him but cannot, the wishes fall through.
Could I wrestle to raise him from sorrow, grow poor to enrich,
To fill up his life, starve my own out, I would—knowing which,
I know that my service is perfect. Oh, speak through me now!
Would I suffer for him that I love? So wouldst Thou—so wilt Thou!
So shall crown Thee the topmost, ineffablest, uttermost crown—
And Thy love fill infinitude wholly, nor leave up nor down
One spot for the creature to stand in! It is by no breath,
Turn of eye, wave of hand, that salvation joins issue with death!
As Thy Love is discovered almighty, almighty be proved
Thy power, that exists with and for it, of being Beloved!
He who did most, shall bear most; the strongest shall stand the most weak.
'Tis the weakness in strength, that I cry for! my flesh, that I seek
In the Godhead! I seek and I find it. O Saul, it shall be
A Face like my face that receives thee; a Man like to me,
Thou shalt love and be loved by, for ever: a Hand like this hand
Shall throw open the gates of new life to thee! See the Christ stand!"

19

I know not too well how I found my way home in the night.
There were witnesses, cohorts about me, to left and to right,
Angels, powers, the unuttered, unseen, the alive, the aware—
I repressed. I got through them as hardly, as strugglingly there,
As a runner beset by the populace famished for news—

Life or death. The whole earth was awakened, hell loosed with
her crews;
And the stars of night beat with emotion, and tingled and shot
Out in fire the strong pain of pent knowledge: but I fainted not,
For the Hand still impelled me at once and supported, suppressed
All the tumult, and quenched it with quiet, and holy behest,
Till the rapture was shut in itself, and the earth sank to rest.
Anon at the dawn, all that trouble had withered from earth—
Not so much, but I saw it die out in the day's tender birth;
In the gathered intensity brought to the grey of the hills;
In the shuddering forests' new awe; in the sudden wind-thrills;
In the startled wild beasts that bore off, each with eye sidling
still
Though averted with wonder and dread; in the birds stiff and
chill
That rose heavily, as I approached them, made stupid with awe!
E'en the serpent that slid away silent,—he felt the new Law.
The same stared in the white humid faces upturned by the
flowers;
The same worked in the heart of the cedar, and moved the vine-
bowers:
And the little brooks witnessing murmured, persistent and low,
With their obstinate, all but hushed voices—"E'en so, it is so!"

A GRAMMARIAN'S FUNERAL

In the person of the Greek grammarian, Browning glorifies the early Renaissance hunger for knowledge. The humble scholar becomes a hero, a man of courage and steadfast purpose, successful in his failures. In another poem, Sibrandus Schafnaburgensis, *pedantry is ridiculed, but here the scholarship whose aim was to disinter the language and culture of Greece becomes a lofty and exciting pursuit.*

Let us begin and carry up this corpse,
Singing together.
Leave we the common crofts, the vulgar thorpes,
Each in its tether

Sleeping safe on the bosom of the plain,
    Cared-for till cock-crow:
Look out if yonder be not day again
    Rimming the rock-row!
That's the appropriate country; there, man's thought,
    Rarer, intenser,
Self-gathered for an outbreak, as it ought,
    Chafes in the censer!
Leave we the unlettered plain its herd and crop;
    Seek we sepulture
On a tall mountain, citied to the top,
    Crowded with culture!
All the peaks soar, but one the rest excels;
    Clouds overcome it;
No, yonder sparkle is the citadel's
    Circling its summit!
Thither our path lies; wind we up the heights:
    Wait ye the warning?
Our low life was the level's and the night's;
    He's for the morning!
Step to a tune, square chests, erect the head,
    'Ware the beholders!
This is our master, famous, calm, and dead,
    Borne on our shoulders.

Sleep, crop and herd! sleep, darkling thorpe and croft,
    Safe from the weather!
He, whom we convoy to his grave aloft,
    Singing together,
He was a man born with thy face and throat,
    Lyric Apollo!
Long he lived nameless: how should spring take note
    Winter would follow?
Till lo, the little touch, and youth was gone!
    Cramped and diminished,
Moaned he, "New measures, other feet anon!
    My dance is finished?"

No, that's the world's way! (keep the mountain-side,
Make for the city,)
He knew the signal, and stepped on with pride
Over men's pity;
Left play for work, and grappled with the world
Bent on escaping:
"What's in the scroll," quoth he, "thou keepest furled?
Show me their shaping,
Theirs, who most studied man, the bard and sage,—
Give!"—So he gowned him,
Straight got by heart that book to its last page:
Learned, we found him!
Yea, but we found him bald too—eyes like lead,
Accents uncertain:
"Time to taste life," another would have said,
"Up with the curtain!"—
This man said rather, "Actual life comes next?
Patience a moment!
Grant I have mastered learning's crabbed text,
Still, there's the comment.
Let me know all! Prate not of most or least,
Painful or easy:
Even to the crumbs I'd fain eat up the feast,
Ay, nor feel queasy!"
Oh, such a life as he resolved to live,
When he had learned it,
When he had gathered all books had to give!
Sooner, he spurned it.
Image the whole, then execute the parts—
Fancy the fabric
Quite, ere you build, ere steel strike fire from quartz,
Ere mortar dab brick!

(Here's the town-gate reached: there's the market-place
Gaping before us.)
Yea, this in him was the peculiar grace
(Hearten our chorus)

That before living he'd learn how to live—
    No end to learning:
Earn the means first—God surely will contrive
    Use for our earning.
Others mistrust and say—'But time escapes!
    Live now or never!'
He said, "What's time? leave Now for dogs and apes!
    Man has Forever."
Back to his book then: deeper drooped his head:
    Calculus racked him:
Leaden before, his eyes grew dross of lead:
    Tussis attacked him.
"Now, Master, take a little rest!"—not he!
    (Caution redoubled!
Step two a-breast, the way winds narrowly)
    Not a whit troubled,
Back to his studies, fresher than at first,
    Fierce as a dragon
He (soul-hydroptic with a sacred thirst)
    Sucked at the flagon.
Oh, if we draw a circle premature,
    Heedless of far gain,
Greedy for quick returns of profit, sure,
    Bad is our bargain!
Was it not great? did not he throw on God,
    (He loves the burthen)—
God's task to make the heavenly period
    Perfect the earthen?
Did not he magnify the mind, show clear
    Just what it all meant?
He would not discount life, as fools do here,
    Paid by instalment!
He ventured neck or nothing—Heaven's success
    Found, or earth's failure:
"Wilt thou trust death or not?" He answered "Yes!
    Hence with life's pale lure!"
That low man seeks a little thing to do,
    Sees it and does it:

This high man, with a great thing to pursue,
Dies ere he knows it.
That low man goes on adding one to one,
His hundred's soon hit:
This high man, aiming at a million,
Misses an unit.
That, has the world here—should he need the next,
Let the world mind him!
This, throws himself on God, and unperplext
Seeking shall find Him.
So, with the throttling hands of Death at strife,
Ground he at grammar;
Still, thro' the rattle, parts of speech were rife:
While he could stammer
He settled *Hoti's* business—let it be!—
Properly based *Oun*—
Gave us the doctrine of the enclitic *De,*
Dead from the waist down.
Well, here's the platform, here's the proper place.
Hail to your purlieus,
All ye highfliers of the feathered race,
Swallows and curlews!
Here's the top-peak! the multitude below
Live, for they can, there.
This man decided not to Live but Know—
Bury this man there?
Here—here's his place, where meteors shoot, clouds form,
Lightnings are loosened,
Stars come and go! let joy break with the storm,
Peace let the dew send!
Lofty designs must close in like effects:
Loftily lying,
Leave him—still loftier than the world suspects,
Living and dying.

A TOCCATA OF GALUPPI'S

Baldassare Galuppi was a famous eighteenth century Venetian composer. The toccata is a "touch-piece," light and free, highly developed by Bach. Browning's genius in reproducing the feeling of a musical form is well exemplified in this mannered and sharply accented poem. It celebrates the spirit of Venice, as does the sonnet Goldoni.

1

Oh, Galuppi, Baldassaro, this is very sad to find!
I can hardly misconceive you; it would prove me deaf and blind;
But although I take your meaning, 'tis with such a heavy mind!

2

Here you come with your old music, and here's all the good it brings.
What, they lived once thus at Venice where the merchants were the kings,
Where St. Mark's is, where the Doges used to wed the sea with rings?

3

Ay, because the sea's the street there; and 'tis arched by . . . what you call
. . . Shylock's bridge with houses on it, where they kept the carnival:
I was never out of England—it's as if I saw it all!

4

Did young people take their pleasure when the sea was warm in May?
Balls and masks begun at midnight, burning ever to mid-day
When they made up fresh adventures for the morrow, do you say?

5

Was a lady such a lady, cheeks so round and lips so red,—
On her neck the small face buoyant, like a bell-flower on its bed,
O'er the breast's superb abundance where a man might base his
head?

6

Well, (and it was graceful of them) they'd break talk off and
afford
—She, to bite her mask's black velvet, he, to finger on his sword,
While you sat and played Toccatas, stately at the clavichord?

7

What? Those lesser thirds so plaintive, sixths diminished, sigh
on sigh,
Told them something? Those suspensions, those solutions—
"Must we die?"
Those commiserating sevenths—"Life might last! we can but
try!"

8

"Were you happy?"—"Yes."—"And are you still as happy?"
—"Yes. And you?"
—"Then, more kisses!"—"Did *I* stop them, when a million
seemed so few?"
Hark! the dominant's persistence, till it must be answered to!

9

So an octave struck the answer. Oh, they praised you, I dare say!
"Brave Galuppi! that was music! good alike at grave and gay!
I can always leave off talking, when I hear a master play."

10

Then they left you for their pleasure: till in due time, one by one,
Some with lives that came to nothing, some with deeds as well
undone,
Death came tacitly and took them where they never see the sun.

11

But when I sit down to reason, think to take my stand nor swerve,
While I trumph o'er a secret wrung from nature's close reserve,
In you come with your cold music, till I creep thro' every nerve.

12

Yes, you, like a ghostly cricket, creaking where a house was
burned—
"Dust and ashes, dead and done with, Venice spent what Venice
earned!
The soul, doubtless, is immortal—where a soul can be discerned.

13

"Yours for instance: you know physics, something of geology,
Mathematics are your pastime; souls shall rise in their degree;
Butterflies may dread extinction,—you'll not die, it cannot be!

14

"As for Venice and its people merely born to bloom and drop,
Here on earth they bore their fruitage, mirth and folly were the
crop:
What of soul was left, I wonder, when the kissing had to stop?

15

"Dust and ashes!" So you creak it, and I want the heart to scold.
Dear dead women, with such hair, too—what's become of all
the gold
Used to hang and brush their bosoms? I feel chilly and grown
old.

HOLY-CROSS DAY

This is one of several poems, including Rabbi Ben Ezra, *which reflect Browning's sympathy and respect for the Jews. Ben Ezra's "death song" forms the last part of this poem. Forcing the Jews of Rome to attend the Bishop's sermon on Holy Cross*

Day (commemorating Constantine's vision of a cross in the sky at midday) was not given up until the nineteenth century. The extract from the diary of the Bishop's secretary prefacing the poem was invented by Browning.

["Now was come about Holy-Cross Day, and now must my lord preach his first sermon to the Jews: as it was of old cared for in the merciful bowels of the Church, that, so to speak, a crumb at least from her conspicuous table here in Rome, should be, though but once yearly, cast to the famishing dogs, under-trampled and bespitten-upon beneath the feet of the guests. And a moving sight in truth, this, of so many of the besotted, blind, restive and ready-to-perish Hebrews! now maternally brought—nay, (for He saith, 'Compel them to come in') haled, as it were, by the head and hair, and against their obstinate hearts, to partake of the heavenly grace. What awakening, what striving with tears, what working of a yeasty conscience! Nor was my lord wanting to himself on so apt an occasion; witness the abundance of conversions which did incontinently reward him: though not to my lord be altogether the glory."—*Diary by the Bishop's Secretary,* 1600.]

Though what the Jews really said, on thus being driven to church, was rather to this effect:—

Fee, faw, fum! bubble and squeak!
Blessedest Thursday's the fat of the week.
Rumble and tumble, sleek and rough,
Stinking and savoury, smug and gruff,
Take the church-road, for the bell's due chime
Gives us the summons—'tis sermon-time.

Boh, here's Barnabas! Job, that's you?
Up stumps Solomon—bustling too?
Shame, man! greedy beyond your years
To handsel the bishop's shaving-shears?
Fair play's a jewel! leave friends in the lurch?
Stand on a line ere you start for the church.

Higgledy piggledy, packed we lie,
Rats in a hamper, swine in a stye,
Wasps in a bottle, frogs in a sieve,
Worms in a carcase, fleas in a sleeve.
Hist! square shoulders, settle your thumbs
And buzz for the bishop—here he comes.

Bow, wow, wow—a bone for the dog!
I liken his Grace to an acorned hog.
What, a boy at his side, with the bloom of a lass,
To help and handle my lord's hour-glass!
Didst ever behold so lithe a chine?
His cheek hath laps like a fresh-singed swine.

Aaron's asleep—shove hip to haunch,
Or somebody deal him a dig in the paunch!
Look at the purse with the tassel and knob,
And the gown with the angel and thingumbob,
What's he at, quotha? reading his text!
Now you've his curtsey—and what comes next?

See to our converts—you doomed black dozen—
No stealing away—nor coz nor cozen!
You five that were thieves, deserve it fairly;
You seven that were beggars, will live less sparely;
You took your turn and dipped in the hat,
Got fortune—and fortune gets you; mind that!

Give your first groan—compunction's at work;
And soft! from a Jew you mount to a Turk.
Lo, Micah,—the selfsame beard on chin
He was four times already converted in!
Here's a knife, clip quick—it's a sign of grace—
Or he ruins us all with his hanging-face.

Whom now is the bishop a-leering at?
I know a point where his text falls pat.
I'll tell him to-morrow, a word just now
Went to my heart and made me vow
I meddle no more with the worst of trades—
Let somebody else pay his serenades.

Groan all together now, whee—hee—hee!
It's a-work, it's a-work, ah, woe is me!
It began, when a herd of us, picked and placed,
Were spurred through the Corso, stripped to the waist;
Jew-brutes, with sweat and blood well spent
To usher in worthily Christian Lent.

It grew, when the hangman entered our bounds,
Yelled, pricked us out to his church like hounds.
It got to a pitch, when the hand indeed
Which gutted my purse, would throttle my creed.
And it overflows, when, to even the odd,
Men I helped to their sins, help me to their God.

But now, while the scapegoats leave our flock,
And the rest sit silent and count the clock,
Since forced to muse the appointed time
On these precious facts and truths sublime,—
Let us fitly employ it, under our breath,
In saying Ben Ezra's Song of Death.

For Rabbi Ben Ezra, the night he died,
Called sons and sons' sons to his side,
And spoke, "This world has been harsh and strange;
Something is wrong: there needeth a change.
But what, or where? at the last, or first?
In one point only we sinned, at worst.

"The Lord will have mercy on Jacob yet,
And again in his border see Israel set.
When Judah beholds Jerusalem,

The stranger-seed shall be joined to them:
To Jacob's House shall the Gentiles cleave.
So the Prophet saith and his sons believe.

"Ay, the children of the chosen race
Shall carry and bring them to their place:
In the land of the Lord shall lead the same,
Bondsmen and handmaids. Who shall blame,
When the slaves enslave, the oppressed ones o'er
The oppressor triumph for evermore?

"God spoke, and gave us the word to keep:
Bade never fold the hands nor sleep
'Mid a faithless world,—at watch and ward,
Till Christ at the end relieve our guard.
By His servant Moses the watch was set:
Though near upon cock-crow, we kept it yet.

"Thou! if Thou wast He, who at mid-watch came,
By the starlight, naming a dubious Name!
And if, too heavy with sleep—too rash
With fear—O Thou, if that martyr-gash
Fell on Thee coming to take Thine own,
And we gave the Cross, when we owed the Throne—

"Thou art the Judge. We are bruised thus.
But, the judgment over, join sides with us!
Thine too is the cause! and not more Thine
Than ours, is the work of these dogs and swine,
Whose life laughs through the spits at their creed,
Who maintain Thee in word, and defy Thee in deed!

"We withstood Christ then? be mindful how
At least we withstand Barabbas now!
Was our outrage sore? but the worst we spared,
To have called these—Christians, had we dared!
Let defiance to them pay mistrust of Thee,
And Rome make amends for Calvary!

"By the torture, prolonged from age to age,
By the infamy, Israel's heritage,
By the Ghetto's plague, by the garb's disgrace,
By the badge of shame, by the felon's place,
By the branding-tool, the bloody whip,
And the summons to Christian fellowship,—

"We boast our proof that at least the Jew
Would wrest Christ's name from the Devil's crew.
Thy face took never so deep a shade
But we fought them in it, God our aid!
A trophy to bear, as we march, Thy band
South, East, and on to the Pleasant Land!"

The present Pope abolished this bad business of the sermon.—*R. B.*

MISCONCEPTIONS

1

This is a spray the Bird clung to,
    Making it blossom with pleasure,
Ere the high tree-top she sprung to,
    Fit for her nest and her treasure.
    Oh, what a hope beyond measure
Was the poor spray's, which the flying feet hung to,—
So to be singled out, built in, and sung to!

2

This is a heart the Queen leant on,
    Thrilled in a minute erratic,
Ere the true bosom she bent on,
    Meet for love's regal dalmatic.
    Oh, what a fancy ecstatic
Was the poor heart's ere the wanderer went on—
Love to be saved for it, proffered to, spent on!

6

You and I would rather see that angel,
Painted by the tenderness of Dante,
Would we not?—than read a fresh Inferno.

7

You and I will never see that picture.
While he mused on love and Beatrice,
While he softened o'er his outlined angel,
In they broke, those "people of importance":
We and Bice bear the loss for ever.

8

What of Rafael's sonnets, Dante's picture?
This: no artist lives and loves, that longs not
Once, and only once, and for one only,
(Ah, the prize!) to find his love a language
Fit and fair and simple and sufficient—
Using nature that 's an art to others,
Not, this one time, art that 's turned his nature.
Ay, of all the artists living, loving,
None but would forego his proper dowry,—
Does he paint? he fain would write a poem,—
Does he write? he fain would paint a picture,
Put to proof art alien to the artist's,
Once, and only once, and for one only,
So to be the man and leave the artist,
Gain the man's joy, miss the artist's sorrow.

9

Wherefore? Heaven's gift takes earth's abatement!
He who smites the rock and spreads the water,
Bidding drink and live a crowd beneath him,
Even he, the minute makes immortal,

Proves, perchance, but mortal in the minute,
Desecrates, belike, the deed in doing.
While he smites, how can he but remember,
So he smote before, in such a peril,
When they stood and mocked—"Shall smiting help us?"
When they drank and sneered—"A stroke is easy!"
When they wiped their mouths and went their journey,
Throwing him for thanks—"But drought was pleasant."
Thus old memories mar the actual triumph;
Thus the doing savours of disrelish;
Thus achievement lacks a gracious somewhat;
O'er-importuned brows becloud the mandate,
Carelessness or consciousness, the gesture.
For he bears an ancient wrong about him,
Sees and knows again those phalanxed faces,
Hears, yet one time more, the 'customed prelude—
"How shouldst thou, of all men, smite, and save us?"
Guesses what is like to prove the sequel—
"Egypt's flesh-pots—nay, the drought was better."

10

Oh, the crowd must have emphatic warrant!
Theirs, the Sinai-forehead's cloven brilliance,
Right-arm's rod-sweep, tongue's imperial fiat.
Never dares the man put off the prophet.

11

Did he love one face from out the thousands,
(Were she Jethro's daughter, white and wifely,
Were she but the Æthiopian bondslave,)
He would envy yon dumb patient camel,
Keeping a reserve of scanty water
Meant to save his own life in the desert;
Ready in the desert to deliver
(Kneeling down to let his breast be opened)
Hoard and life together for his mistress.

12

I shall never, in the years remaining,
Paint you pictures, no, nor carve you statues,
Make you music that should all-express me;
So it seems: I stand on my attainment.
This of verse alone, one life allows me;
Verse and nothing else have I to give you.
Other heights in other lives, God willing:
All the gifts from all the heights, your own, Love!

13

Yet a semblance of resource avails us—
Shade so finely touched, love's sense must seize it.
Take these lines, look lovingly and nearly,
Lines I write the first time and the last time.
He who works in fresco, steals a hair-brush,
Curbs the liberal hand, subservient proudly,
Cramps his spirit, crowds its all in little,
Makes a strange art of an art familiar,
Fills his lady's missal-marge with flowerets.
He who blows thro' bronze, may breathe thro' silver,
Fitly serenade a slumbrous princess.
He who writes, may write for once as I do.

14

Love, you saw me gather men and women,
Live or dead or fashioned by my fancy,
Enter each and all, and use their service,
Speak from every mouth,—the speech, a poem.
Hardly shall I tell my joys and sorrows,
Hopes and fears, belief and disbelieving:
I am mine and yours—the rest be all men's,
Karshish, Cleon, Norbert and the fifty.
Let me speak this once in my true person,
Not as Lippo, Roland or Andrea,
Though the fruit of speech be just this sentence:

Pray you, look on these my men and women,
Take and keep my fifty poems finished;
Where my heart lies, let my brain lie also!
Poor the speech; be how I speak, for all things.

15

Not but that you know me! Lo, the moon's self!
Here in London, yonder late in Florence,
Still we find her face, the thrice-transfigured.
Curving on a sky imbrued with colour,
Drifted over Fiesole by twilight,
Came she, our new crescent of a hair's-breadth.
Full she flared it, lamping Samminiato,
Rounder 'twixt the cypresses and rounder,
Perfect till the nightingales applauded.
Now, a piece of her old self, impoverished,
Hard to greet, she traverses the houseroofs,
Hurries with unhandsome thrift of silver,
Goes dispiritedly, glad to finish.

16

What, there 's nothing in the moon noteworthy?
Nay: for if that moon could love a mortal,
Use, to charm him (so to fit a fancy),
All her magic ('t is the old sweet mythos)
She would turn a new side to her mortal,
Side unseen of herdsman, huntsman, steersman—
Blank to Zoroaster on his terrace,
Blind to Galileo on his turret,
Dumb to Homer, dumb to Keats—him, even!
Think, the wonder of the moonstruck mortal—
When she turns round, comes again in heaven,
Opens out anew for worse or better!
Proves she like some portent of an iceberg
Swimming full upon the ship it founders,
Hungry with huge teeth of splintered crystals?

Proves she as the paved work of a sapphire
Seen by Moses when he climbed the mountain?
Moses, Aaron, Nadab and Abihu
Climbed and saw the very God, the Highest,
Stand upon the paved work of a sapphire.
Like the bodied heaven in his clearness
Shone the stone, the sapphire of that paved work,
When they ate and drank and saw God also!

17

What were seen? None knows, none ever shall know.
Only this is sure—the sight were other,
Not the moon's same side, born late in Florence,
Dying now impoverished here in London.
God be thanked, the meanest of his creatures
Boasts two soul-sides, one to face the world with,
One to show a woman when he loves her!

18

This I say of me, but think of you, Love!
This to you—yourself my moon of poets!
Ah, but that 's the world's side, there 's the wonder,
Thus they see you, praise you, think they know you!
There, in turn I stand with them and praise you—
Out of my own self, I dare to phrase it.
But the best is when I glide from out them,
Cross a step or two of dubious twilight,
Come out on the other side, the novel
Silent silver lights and darks undreamed of,
Where I hush and bless myself with silence.

19

Oh, their Rafael of the dear Madonnas,
Oh, their Dante of the dread Inferno,
Wrote one song—and in my brain I sing it,
Drew one angel—borne, see, on my bosom!

Dramatis Personae

1864

JAMES LEE'S WIFE

This is really a little novel, and in its understanding of feminine psychology reminds one of the work of both George Meredith and Virginia Woolf. In brief, it is the record of the dissolution of an unhappy marriage, beginning with the woman's first realization that all is not well, and progressing steadily through various stages of disillusion up to final separation and resignation. It was written near Pornic, on the Brittany coast, and the rather gloomy landscape forms a fitting background for the poem.

I

James Lee's Wife Speaks at the Window

Ah, love, but a day,
  And the world has changed!
The sun's away,
  And the bird's estranged;
The wind has dropped,
  And the sky's deranged:
Summer has stopped.

Look in my eyes!
Wilt thou change too?
Should I fear surprise?
  Shall I find aught new
In the old and dear,
  In the good and true,
With the changing year?

Thou art a man,
  But I am thy love!
For the lake, its swan;
  For the dell, its dove;

And for thee—(oh, haste!)
Me, to bend above,
Me, to hold embraced!

2

By the Fireside

Is all our fire of shipwreck wood,
Oak and pine?
Oh, for the ills half-understood,
The dim, dead woe
Long ago
Befallen this bitter coast of France!
Well, poor sailors took their chance; I take mine.

A ruddy shaft our fire must shoot
O'er the sea:
Do sailors eye the casement—mute,
Drenched and stark,
From their bark—
And envy, gnash their teeth for hate
O' the warm safe house and happy freight
—Thee and me?

God help you, sailors, at your need!
Spare the curse!
For some ships, safe in port indeed,
Rot and rust,
Run to dust,
All through worms i' the wood, which crept,
Gnawed our hearts out while we slept:
That is worse!

Who lived here before us two?
Old-world pairs!
Did a woman ever—would I knew!—
Watch the man
With whom began

Love's voyage full-sail,—(now, gnash your teeth!)
When planks start, open hell beneath
  Unawares?

3

In the Doorway

The swallow has set her six young on the rail,
  And looks sea-ward:
The water 's in stripes like a snake, olive-pale
  To the leeward,—
On the weather-side, black, spotted white with the wind:
"Good fortune departs, and disaster's behind,"—
Hark, the wind with its wants and its infinite wail!

Our fig-tree, that leaned for the saltness, has furled
  Her five fingers,
Each leaf like a hand opened wide to the world
  Where there lingers
No glint of the gold, Summer sent for her sake:
How the vines writhe in rows, each impaled on its stake!
My heart shrivels up, and my spirit shrinks curled.

Yet here are we two; we have love, house enough,
  With the field there,
This house of four rooms, that field red and rough,
  Though it yield there,
For the rabbit that robs, scarce a blade or a bent;
If a magpie alight now, it seems an event;
And they both will be gone at November's rebuff.

But why must cold spread? but wherefore bring change
  To the spirit,
God meant should mate His with an infinite range,
  And inherit
His power to put life in the darkness and cold?
Oh, live and love worthily, bear and be bold!
Whom Summer made friends of, let Winter estrange!

4
Along the Beach

I will be quiet and talk with you,
  And reason why you are wrong:
You wanted my love—is that much true?
And so I did love, so I do:
  What has come of it all along?

I took you—how could I otherwise?
  For a world to me, and more;
For all, love greatens and glorifies
Till God 's a-glow, to the loving eyes,
  In what was mere earth before.

Yes, earth—yes, mere ignoble earth!
  Now do I mis-state, mistake?
Do I wrong your weakness and call it worth?
Expect all harvest, dread no dearth,
  Seal my sense up for your sake?

Oh, love, love, no, love! not so, indeed!
  You were just weak earth, I knew:
With much in you waste, with many a weed,
And plenty of passions run to seed,
  But a little good grain too.

And such as you were, I took you for mine:
  Did not you find me yours,
To watch the olive and wait the vine,
And wonder when rivers of oil and wine
  Would flow, as the Book assures?

Well, and if none of these good things came,
  What did the failure prove?
The man was my whole world, all the same,
With his flowers to praise, or his weeds to blame,
  And, either or both, to love.

Yet this turns now to a fault—there! there!
   That I do love, watch too long,
And wait too well, and weary and wear;
And 'tis all an old story, and my despair
   Fit subject for some new song:

How the light, light love, he has wings to fly
   At suspicion of a bond:
How my wisdom has bidden your pleasure good-bye,
Which will turn up next in a laughing eye,
   And why should you look beyond?

5

On the Cliff

I leaned on the turf,
I looked at a rock
Left dry by the surf;
For the turf, to call it grass were to mock:
Dead to the roots, so deep was done
The work of the summer sun.

And the rock lay flat
As an anvil's face:
No iron like that!
Baked dry; of a weed, of a shell, no trace:
Sunshine outside, but ice at the core,
Death's altar by the lone shore.

On the turf, sprang gay
With his films of blue,
No cricket, I'll say,
But a warhorse, barded and chanfroned too,
The gift of a quixote-mage to his knight,
Real fairy, with wings all right.

On the rock, they scorch
Like a drop of fire
From a brandished torch,
Fell two red fans of a butterfly:
No turf, no rock, in their ugly stead,
See, wonderful blue and red!

Is it not so
With the minds of men?
The level and low,
The burnt and bare, in themselves; but then
With such a blue and red grace, not theirs,
Love settling unawares!

6

Reading a Book, Under the Cliff

"Still ailing, Wind? Wilt be appeased or no?
  Which needs the other's office, thou or I?
Dost want to be disburthened of a woe,
  And can, in truth, my voice untie
Its links, and let it go?

"Art thou a dumb, wronged thing that would be righted,
  Entrusting thus thy cause to me? Forbear.
No tongue can mend such pleadings; faith, requited
  With falsehood,—love, at last aware
Of scorn,—hopes, early blighted,—

"We have them; but I know not any tone
  So fit as thine to falter forth a sorrow:
Dost think men would go mad without a moan,
  If they knew any way to borrow
A pathos like thy own?

"Which sigh wouldst mock, of all the sighs? The one
So long escaping from lips starved and blue,
That lasts while on her pallet-bed the nun
Stretches her length; her foot comes through
The straw she shivers on;

"You had not thought she was so tall: and spent,
Her shrunk lids open, her lean fingers shut
Close, close, their sharp and livid nails indent
The clammy palm; then all is mute:
That way, the spirit went.

"Or wouldst thou rather that I understand
Thy will to help me?—like the dog I found
Once, pacing sad this solitary strand,
Who would not take my food, poor hound,
But whined and licked my hand."

All this, and more, comes from some young man's pride
Of power to see,—in failure and mistake,
Relinquishment, disgrace, on every side,—
Merely examples for his sake,
Helps to his path untried:

Instances he must—simply recognize?
Oh, more than so!—must, with a learner's zeal,
Make doubly prominent, twice emphasize,
By added touches that reveal
The god in babe's disguise.

Oh, he knows what defeat means, and the rest!
Himself the undefeated that shall be:
Failure, disgrace, he flings them you to test,—
His triumph, in eternity
Too plainly manifest!

Whence, judge if he learn forthwith what the wind
Means in its moaning—by the happy, prompt,

Instinctive way of youth, I mean; for kind
  Calm years, exacting their accompt
Of pain, mature the mind:

And some midsummer morning, at the lull
  Just about daybreak, as he looks across
A sparkling foreign country, wonderful
  To the sea's edge for gloom and gloss,
Next minute must annul,—

Then, when the wind begins among the vines,
So low, so low, what shall it mean but this?
"Here is the change beginning, here the lines
  Circumscribe beauty, set to bliss
The limit time assigns."

Nothing can be as it has been before;
  Better, so call it, only not the same.
To draw one beauty into our hearts' core,
  And keep it changeless! such our claim;
So answered,—Never more!

Simple? Why this is the old woe o' the world;
  Tune, to whose rise and fall we live and die.
Rise with it, then! Rejoice that man is hurled
  From change to change unceasingly.
His soul's wings never furled!

That 's a new question; still replies the fact,
  Nothing endures: the wind moans, saying so;
We moan in acquiescence: there 's life's pact,
  Perhaps probation—do *I* know?
God does: endure His act!

Only, for man, how bitter not to grave
  On his soul's hands' palms, one fair, good, wise thing
Just as he grasped it! For himself, death's wave;
  While time first washes—ah, the sting!—
O'er all he'd sink to save.

7

Among the Rocks

Oh, good gigantic smile o' the brown old earth,
  This autumn morning! How he sets his bones
To bask i' the sun, and thrusts out knees and feet
For the ripple to run over in its mirth;
  Listening the while, where on the heap of stones
The white breast of the sea-lark twitters sweet.
That is the doctrine, simple, ancient, true;
  Such is life's trial, as old earth smiles and knows.
If you loved only what were worth your love,
Love were clear gain, and wholly well for you:
  Make the low nature better by your throes!
Give earth yourself, go up for gain above!

8

Beside the Drawing-Board

"As like as a Hand to another Hand!"
  Whoever said that foolish thing,
Could not have studied to understand
  The councils of God in fashioning,
Out of the infinite love of his heart,
This Hand, whose beauty I praise, apart
From the world of wonder left to praise,
If I tried to learn the other ways
Of love in its skill, or love in its power.
  "As like as a Hand to another Hand":
Who said that, never took his stand,
Found and followed, like me, an hour,
The beauty in this,—how free, how fine
To fear, almost,—of the limit-line!
As I looked at this, and learned and drew,
  Drew and learned, and looked again,

While fast the happy minutes flew,
   Its beauty mounted into my brain,
   And a fancy seized me; I was fain
To efface my work, begin anew,
Kiss what before I only drew;
Ay, laying the red chalk 'twixt my lips,
   With soul to help if the mere lips failed,
   I kissed all right where the drawing ailed,
Kissed fast the grace that somehow slips
Still from one's soulless finger-tips.

'Tis a clay cast, the perfect thing,
   From Hand live once, dead long ago:
Princess-like it wears the ring
   To fancy's eye, by which we know
That here at length a master found
   His match, a proud lone soul its mate,
As soaring genius sank to ground,
   And pencil could not emulate
The beauty in this,—how free, how fine
To fear almost!—of the limit-line.
Long ago the god, like me
The worm, learned, each in our degree:
Looked and loved, learned and drew,
   Drew and learned and loved again,
While fast the happy minutes flew,
   Till beauty mounted into his brain
And on the finger which outvied
   His art he placed the ring that 's there,
Still by fancy's eye descried,
   In token of a marriage rare:
For him on earth, his art's despair,
For him in heaven, his soul's fit bride.

Little girl with the poor coarse hand
   I turned from to a cold clay cast—
I have my lesson, understand
   The worth of flesh and blood at last!

Nothing but beauty in a Hand?
  Because he could not change the hue,
  Mend the lines and make them true
To this which met his soul's demand,—
  Would Da Vinci turn from you?
I hear him laugh my woes to scorn—
"The fool forsooth is all forlorn
Because the beauty, she thinks best,
Lived long ago or was never born,—
Because no beauty bears the test
In this rough peasant Hand! Confessed
'Art is null and study void!'
So sayest thou? So said not I,
Who threw the faulty pencil by,
And years instead of hours employed,
Learning the veritable use
Of flesh and bone and nerve beneath
Lines and hue of the outer sheath,
If haply I might reproduce
One motive of the powers profuse,
Flesh and bone and nerve that make
The poorest coarsest human hand
An object worthy to be scanned
A whole life long for their sole sake.
Shall earth and the cramped moment-space
Yield the heavenly crowning grace?
Now the parts and then the whole!
Who art thou, with stinted soul
And stunted body, thus to cry,
'I love,—shall that be life's strait dole?
I must live beloved or die!'
This peasant hand that spins the wool
And bakes the bread, why lives it on,
Poor and coarse with beauty gone,—
What use survives the beauty?" Fool!

Go, little girl with the poor coarse hand!
I have my lesson, shall understand.

9

On Deck

There is nothing to remember in me,
   Nothing I ever said with a grace,
Nothing I did that you cared to see,
   Nothing I was that deserves a place
In your mind, now I leave you, set you free.

Conceded! In turn, concede to me,
   Such things have been as a mutual flame.
Your soul's locked fast; but, love for a key,
   You might let it loose, till I grew the same
In your eyes, as in mine you stand: strange plea!

For then, then, what would it matter to me
   That I was the harsh, ill-favoured one?
We both should be like as pea and pea;
   It was ever so since the world begun:
So, let me proceed with my reverie.

How strange it were if you had all me,
   As I have all you in my heart and brain,
You, whose least word brought gloom or glee,
   Who never lifted the hand in vain
Will hold mine yet, from over the sea!

Strange, if a face, when you thought of me,
   Rose like your own face present now,
With eyes as dear in their due degree,
   Much such a mouth, and as bright a brow,
Till you saw yourself, while you cried " 'Tis She!"

Well, you may, or you must, set down to me
   Love that was life, life that was love;
A tenure of breath at your lips' decree,
   A passion to stand as your thoughts approve,
A rapture to fall where your foot might be.

But did one touch of such love for me
  Come in a word or a look of yours,
Whose words and looks will, circling, flee
  Round me and round while life endures,—
Could I fancy "As I feel, thus feels He";

Why, fade you might to a thing like me,
  And your hair grow these coarse hanks of hair,
And your skin, this bark of a gnarled tree,—
  You might turn myself; should I know or care,
When I should be dead of joy, James Lee?

PROSPICE

This poem, written shortly after Mrs. Browning's death, expresses the poet's belief in personal immortality and is often compared with Tennyson's Ulysses. *It was first published in* The Atlantic Monthly.

Fear death?—to feel the fog in my throat,
  The mist in my face,
When the snows begin, and the blasts denote
  I am nearing the place,
The power of the night, the press of the storm,
  The post of the foe;
Where he stands, the Arch Fear in a visible form,
  Yet the strong man must go:
For the journey is done and the summit attained,
  And the barriers fall,
Though a battle 's to fight ere the guerdon be gained,
  The reward of it all.
I was ever a fighter, so—one fight more,
  The best and the last!
I would hate that death bandaged my eyes, and forebore,
  And bade me creep past.
No! let me taste the whole of it, fare like my peers
  The heroes of old,

Bear the brunt, in a minute pay glad life's arrears
    Of pain, darkness and cold.
For sudden the worst turns the best to the brave,
    The black minute 's at end,
And the elements' rage, the fiend-voices that rave,
    Shall dwindle, shall blend,
Shall change, shall become first a peace out of pain,
    Then a light, then thy breast,
O thou soul of my soul! I shall clasp thee again,
    And with God be the rest!

YOUTH AND ART

This little song about two might-have-been young lovers and what happened to them when they went their separate ways voices a sentimental yearning: one feels, however, that the lady's wistfulness is merely self-indulgence and that she is well content at having married a lord.

I

It once might have been, once only:
  We lodged in a street together,
You, a sparrow on the housetop lonely,
  I, a lone she-bird of his feather.

2

Your trade was with sticks and clay,
  You thumbed, thrust, patted and polished,
Then laughed "They will see some day
  Smith made, and Gibson demolished."

3

My business was song, song, song;
  I chirped, cheeped, trilled and twittered,
"Kate Brown 's on the boards ere long,
  And Grisi's existence embittered!"

4

I earned no more by a warble
  Than you by a sketch in plaster;
You wanted a piece of marble,
  I needed a music-master.

5

We studied hard in our styles,
  Chipped each at a crust like Hindoos,
For air looked out on the tiles,
  For fun watched each other's windows.

6

You lounged, like a boy of the South,
  Cap and blouse—nay, a bit of beard too;
Or you got it, rubbing your mouth
  With fingers the clay adhered to.

7

And I—soon managed to find
  Weak points in the flower-fence facing,
Was forced to put up a blind
  And be safe in my corset-lacing.

8

No harm! It was not my fault
  If you never turned your eye's tail up,
As I shook upon E *in alt,*
  Or ran the chromatic scale up:

9

For spring bade the sparrows pair,
  And the boys and girls gave guesses,
And stalls in our street looked rare
  With bulrush and watercresses.

10

Why did not you pinch a flower
   In a pellet of clay and fling it?
Why did not I put a power
   Of thanks in a look, or sing it?

11

I did look, sharp as a lynx,
   (And yet the memory rankles)
When models arrived, some minx
   Tripped up-stairs, she and her ankles.

12

But I think I gave you as good!
   "That foreign fellow,—who can know
How she pays, in a playful mood,
   For his tuning her that piano?"

13

Could you say so, and never say
   "Suppose we join hands and fortunes,
And I fetch her from over the way,
   Her, piano, and long tunes and short tunes?"

14

No, no: you would not be rash,
   Nor I rasher and something over:
You 've to settle yet Gibson's hash,
   And Grisi yet lives in clover.

15

But you meet the Prince at the Board,
   I 'm queen myself at *bals-paré,*
I 've married a rich old lord,
   And you 're dubbed knight and an R.A.

16

Each life unfulfilled, you see;
  It hangs still, patchy and scrappy:
We have not sighed deep, laughed free,
  Starved, feasted, despaired,—been happy.

17

And nobody calls you a dunce,
  And people suppose me clever:
This could but have happened once,
  And we missed it, lost it for ever.

A LIKENESS

Browning's father, who was an art collector in a modest way, may have served as the inspiration for the whimsical connoisseur who doesn't hang his most prized possession (an etching of a tantalizing face) on the wall for everybody to see, but leaves it in a portfolio, where it will be discovered, if at all, by only the most discriminating of his friends, on whom—in sheer delight that another sees what he sees—he will bestow it with quixotic generosity.

Some people hang portraits up
In a room where they dine or sup:
  And the wife clinks tea-things under,
And her cousin, he stirs his cup,
  Asks, "Who was the lady, I wonder?"
" 'T is a daub John bought at a sale,"
  Quoth the wife,—looks black as thunder:
"What a shade beneath her nose!
Snuff-taking, I suppose,—"
Adds the cousin, while John's corns ail.

Or else there 's no wife in the case,
But the portrait 's queen of the place,
Alone mid the other spoils

Of youth,—masks, gloves and foils,
And pipe-sticks, rose, cherry-tree, jasmine,
  And the long whip, the tandem-lasher,
And the cast from a fist ("not, alas! mine,
  But my master's, the Tipton Slasher"),
And the cards where pistol-balls mark ace,
And a satin shoe used for cigar-case,
And the chamois-horns ("shot in the Chablais")
  And prints—Rarey drumming on Cruiser,
  And Sayers, our champion, the bruiser,
And the little edition of Rabelais:
Where a friend, with both hands in his pockets,
  May saunter up close to examine it,
  And remark a good deal of Jane Lamb in it,
"But the eyes are half out of their sockets;
That hair 's not so bad, where the gloss is,
But they 've made the girl's nose a proboscis:
Jane Lamb, that we danced with at Vichy!
What, is not she Jane? Then, who is she?"

All that I own is a print,
An etching, a mezzotint;
'T is a study, a fancy, a fiction,
Yet a fact (take my conviction)
Because it has more than a hint
  Of a certain face, I never
Saw elsewhere touch or trace of
In women I 've seen the face of:
  Just an etching, and, so far, clever.

I keep my prints, an imbroglio,
Fifty in one portfolio.
When somebody tries my claret,
We turn round chairs to the fire,
Chirp over days in a garret,
  Chuckle o'er increase of salary,
Taste the good fruits of our leisure,

Talk about pencil and lyre,
  And the National Portrait Gallery:
Then I exhibit my treasure.
After we 've turned over twenty,
  And the debt of wonder my crony owes
  Is paid to my Marc Antonios,
He stops me—"*Festina lentè!*
What 's that sweet thing there, the etching?"
How my waistcoat-strings want stretching,
  How my cheeks grow red as tomatoes,
How my heart leaps! But hearts, after leaps, ache.

"By the by, you must take, for a keepsake,
  That other, you praised, of Volpato's."
The fool! would he try a flight further and say—
He never saw, never before to-day,
What was able to take his breath away,
A face to lose youth for, to occupy age
With the dream of, meet death with,—why, I 'll not engage
But that, half in a rapture and half in a rage,
I should toss him the thing's self—" 'T is only a duplicate,
A thing of no value! Take it, I supplicate!"

ABT VOGLER

This is one of Browning's most famous poems on music, illustrating his deep knowledge of the subject as well as his almost mystical belief in its importance in the human scheme of things. The influence of Plato is clearly indicated when he describes its effect and function. Abt or Abbé Georg Joseph Vogler was an eighteenth century concert musician, and teacher of Meyerbeer and Weber. He invented a small portable organ called the orchestrion on which he extemporized.

Would that the structure brave, the manifold music I build,
  Bidding my organ obey, calling its keys to their work,
Claiming each slave of the sound, at a touch, as when Solomon willed

Armies of angels that soar, legions of demons that lurk,
Man, brute, reptile, fly,—alien of end and of aim,
Adverse, each from the other heaven-high, hell-deep removed,—
Should rush into sight at once as he named the ineffable Name,
And pile him a palace straight, to pleasure the princess he loved!

Would it might tarry like his, the beautiful building of mine,
This which my keys in a crowd pressed and importuned to raise!
Ah, one and all, how they helped, would dispart now and now combine,
Zealous to hasten the work, heighten their master his praise!
And one would bury his brow with a blind plunge down to hell,
Burrow awhile and build, broad on the roots of things,
Then up again swim into sight, having based me my palace well,
Founded it, fearless of flame, flat on the nether springs.

And another would mount and march, like the excellent minion he was.
Ay, another and yet another, one crowd but with many a crest,
Raising my rampired walls of gold as transparent as glass,
Eager to do and die, yield each his place to the rest:
For higher still and higher (as a runner tips with fire,
When a great illumination surprises a festal night—
Outlining round and round Rome's dome from space to spire)
Up, the pinnacled glory reached, and the pride of my soul was in sight.

In sight? Not half! for it seemed, it was certain, to match man's birth,
Nature in turn conceived, obeying an impulse as I;

And the emulous heaven yearned down, made effort to reach the earth,
As the earth had done her best, in my passion, to scale the sky:
Novel splendours burst forth, grew familiar and dwelt with mine,
Not a point nor peak but found and fixed its wandering star;
Meteor-moons, balls of blaze: and they did not pale nor pine,
For earth had attained to heaven, there was no more near nor far.

Nay more; for there wanted not who walked in the glare and glow,
Presences plain in the place; or, fresh from Protoplast,
Furnished for ages to come, when a kindlier wind should blow,
Lured now to begin and live, in a house to their liking at last;
Or else the wonderful Dead who have passed through the body and gone,
But were back once more to breathe in an old world worth their new:
What never had been, was now; what was, as it shall be anon;
And what is,—shall I say, matched both? for I was made perfect too.

All through my keys that gave their sounds to a wish of my soul,
All through my soul that praised as its wish flowed visibly forth
All through music and me! For think, had I painted the whole,
Why, there it had stood, to see, nor the process so wonder-worth:
Had I written the same, made verse—still, effect proceeds from cause,
Ye know why the forms are fair, ye hear how the tale is told;
It is all triumphant art, but art in obedience to laws,
Painter and poet are proud in the artist-list enrolled:—

But here is the finger of God, a flash of the will that can,
Existent behind all laws, that made them and, lo, they are!

And I know not if, save in this, such gift be allowed to man,
  That out of three sounds he frame, not a fourth sound, but
      a star.
Consider it well: each tone of our scale in itself is nought;
  It is everywhere in the world—loud, soft, and all is said:
Give it to me to use! I mix it with two in my thought;
  And, there! Ye have heard and seen: consider and bow the
      head!

Well, it is gone at last, the palace of music I reared;
  Gone! and the good tears start, the praises that come too slow;
For one is assured at first, one scarce can say that he feared,
  That he even gave it a thought, the gone thing was to go.
Never to be again! But many more of the kind
  As good, nay, better perchance: is this your comfort to me?
To me, who must be saved because I cling with my mind
  To the same, same self, same love, same God: ay, what was
      shall be.

Therefore to whom turn I but to Thee, the ineffable Name?
  Builder and maker, Thou, of houses not made with hands!
What, have fear of change from Thee who art ever the same?
  Doubt that Thy power can fill the heart that Thy power
      expands?
There shall never be one lost good! What was, shall live as
      before;
  The evil is null, is nought, is silence implying sound;
What was good, shall be good, with, for evil, so much good
      more;
  On the earth the broken arcs; in the heaven, a perfect round.

All we have willed or hoped or dreamed of good, shall exist;
  Not its semblance, but itself; no beauty, nor good, nor power
Whose voice has gone forth, but each survives for the melodist
  When eternity affirms the conception of an hour.
The high that proved too high, the heroic for earth too hard,
  The passion that left the ground to lose itself in the sky,

Are music sent up to God by the lover and the bard;
  Enough that He heard it once: we shall hear it by and by.

And what is our failure here but a triumph's evidence
  For the fullness of the days? Have we withered or agonized?
Why else was the pause prolonged but that singing might issue thence?
  Why rushed the discords in, but that harmony should be prized?
Sorrow is hard to bear, and doubt is slow to clear,
  Each sufferer says his say, his scheme of the weal and woe:
But God has a few of us whom He whispers in the ear;
  The rest may reason and welcome: 'tis we musicians know.

Well, it is earth with me; silence resumes her reign:
  I will be patient and proud, and soberly acquiesce.
Give me the keys. I feel for the common chord again,
  Sliding by semitones, till I sink to the minor,—yes,
And I blunt it into a ninth, and I stand on alien ground,
  Surveying a while the heights I rolled from into the deep;
Which, hark, I have dared and done, for my resting-place is found,
  The C Major of this life: so, now I will try to sleep.

RABBI BEN EZRA

Rabbi Ben Ezra, a Jewish scholar born in Toledo at the end of the eleventh century, had mastered most of the knowledge of his day: he was an astronomer, physician, poet, grammarian, philosopher, and rabbinical commentator. He left Spain during one of the outbreaks against the Jews, and lived in Rome, Mantua, and later in England. Ben Ezra believed that the soul developed as bodily passions were conquered, and Browning here puts into his mouth the noble words which most triumphantly assert his own belief in the power of the human spirit. The poem is by way of answer to the hedonistic philosophy of Omar Khayyám's Rubáiyát, which Edward FitzGerald had re-

cently translated and which was creating a great sensation. Because of the nobility of its mood, its clarity and conviction, Rabbi Ben Ezra *ranks high in popularity.*

Grow old along with me!
The best is yet to be,
The last of life, for which the first was made:
Our times are in His hand
Who saith "A whole I planned,
Youth shows but half; trust God: see all, nor be afraid!"

Not that, amassing flowers,
Youth sighed "Which rose make ours,
Which lily leave and then as best recall?"
Not that, admiring stars,
It yearned "Nor Jove, nor Mars;
Mine be some figured flame which blends, transcends them all!"

Not for such hopes and fears
Annulling youth's brief years,
Do I remonstrate: folly wide the mark!
Rather I prize the doubt
Low kinds exist without
Finished and finite clods, untroubled by a spark.

Poor vaunt of life indeed,
Were man but formed to feed
On joy, to solely seek and find and feast:
Such feasting ended, then
As sure an end to men;
Irks care the crop-full bird? Frets doubt the maw-crammed beast?

Rejoice we are allied
To That which doth provide
And not partake, effect and not receive!
A spark disturbs our clod;
Nearer we hold of God
Who gives, than of His tribes that take, I must believe.

Then, welcome each rebuff
That turns earth's smoothness rough,
Each sting that bids nor sit nor stand but go!
Be our joys three-parts pain!
Strive, and hold cheap the strain;
Learn, nor account the pang; dare, never grudge the throe!

For thence,—a paradox
Which comforts while it mocks,—
Shall life succeed in that it seems to fail:
What I aspired to be,
And was not, comforts me:
A brute I might have been, but would not sink i' the scale.

What is he but a brute
Whose flesh hath soul to suit,
Whose spirit works lest arms and legs want play?
To man, propose this test—
The body at its best,
How far can that project thy soul on its lone way?

Yet gifts should prove their use:
I own the Past profuse
Of power each side, perfection every turn:
Eyes, ears took in their dole,
Brain treasured up the whole;
Should not the heart beat once "How good to live and learn?"

Not once beat "Praise be Thine!
I see the whole design,
I, who saw Power, see now Love perfect too:
Perfect I call Thy plan:
Thanks that I was a man!
Maker, remake, complete,—I trust what Thou shalt do!"

For pleasant is this flesh;
Our soul in its rose-mesh
Pulled ever to the earth, still yearns for rest:

Would we some prize might hold
To match those manifold
Possessions of the brute,—gain most, as we did best!

Let us not always say
"Spite of this flesh to-day
I strove, made head, gained ground upon the whole!"
As the bird wings and sings,
Let us cry "All good things
Are ours, nor soul helps flesh more, now, than flesh helps soul!"

Therefore I summon age
To grant youth's heritage,
Life's struggle having so far reached its term:
Thence shall I pass, approved
A man, for aye removed
From the developed brute; a God though in the germ.

And I shall thereupon
Take rest, ere I be gone
Once more on my adventure brave and new:
Fearless and unperplexed,
When I wage battle next,
What weapons to select, what armour to indue.

Youth ended, I shall try
My gain or loss thereby;
Be the fire ashes, what survives is gold:
And I shall weigh the same,
Give life its praise or blame:
Young, all lay in dispute; I shall know, being old.

For note, when evening shuts,
A certain moment cuts
The deed off, calls the glory from the grey:
A whisper from the west
Shoots—"Add this to the rest,
Take it and try its worth: here dies another day."

So, still within this life,
Though lifted o'er its strife,
Let me discern, compare, pronounce at last,
"This rage was right i' the main,
That acquiescence vain:
The Future I may face now I have proved the Past."

For more is not reserved
To man, with soul just nerved
To act to-morrow what he learns to-day:
Here, work enough to watch
The Master work, and catch
Hints of the proper craft, tricks of the tool's true play.

As it was better, youth
Should strive, through acts uncouth,
Toward making, than repose on aught found made;
So, better, age, exempt
From strife, should know, than tempt
Further. Thou waitedst age; wait death nor be afraid!

Enough now, if the Right
And Good and Infinite
Be named here, as thou callest thy hand thine own,
With knowledge absolute,
Subject to no dispute
From fools that crowded youth, nor let thee feel alone.

Be there, for once and all,
Severed great minds from small,
Announced to each his station in the Past!
Was I, the world arraigned,
Were they, my soul disdained,
Right? Let age speak the truth and give us peace at last!

Now, who shall arbitrate?
Ten men love what I hate,
Shun what I follow, slight what I receive;

Ten, who in ears and eyes
Match me: we all surmise,
They, this thing, and I, that: whom shall my soul believe?

Not on the vulgar mass
Called "work," must sentence pass,
Things done, that took the eye and had the price;
O'er which, from level stand,
The low world laid its hand,
Found straightway to its mind, could value in a trice:

But all, the world's coarse thumb
And finger failed to plumb,
So passed in making up the main account;
All instincts immature,
All purposes unsure,
That weighed not as his work, yet swelled the man's amount:

Thoughts hardly to be packed
Into a narrow act,
Fancies that broke through language and escaped;
All I could never be,
All, men ignored in me,
This, I was worth to God, whose wheel the pitcher shaped.

Ay, note that Potter's wheel,
That metaphor! and feel
Why time spins fast, why passive lives our clay,—
Thou, to whom fools propound,
When the wine makes its round,
"Since life fleets, all is change; the Past gone, seize to-day!"

Fool! All that is, at all,
Lasts ever, past recall;
Earth changes, but thy soul and God stand sure:
What entered into thee,
That was, is, and shall be:
Time's wheel runs back or stops; Potter and clay endure.

He fixed thee mid this dance
Of plastic circumstance,
This Present, thou, forsooth, wouldst fain arrest:
Machinery just meant
To give thy soul its bent,
Try thee and turn thee forth, sufficiently impressed.

What though the earlier grooves
Which ran the laughing loves
Around thy base, no longer pause and press?
What though, about thy rim,
Skull-things in order grim
Grow out, in graver mood, obey the sterner stress?

Look not thou down but up!
To uses of a cup,
The festal board, lamp's flash and trumpet's peal,
The new wine's foaming flow,
The Master's lips aglow!
Thou, heaven's consummate cup, what needst thou with earth's
 wheel?

But I need, now as then,
Thee, God, who mouldest men;
And since, not even while the whirl was worst,
Did I,—to the wheel of life
With shapes and colours rife,
Bound dizzily,—mistake my end, to slake Thy thirst:

So, take and use Thy work!
Amend what flaws may lurk,
What strain o' the stuff, what warpings past the aim!
My times be in Thy hand!
Perfect the cup as planned!
Let age approve of youth, and death complete the same!

CONFESSIONS

I

What is he buzzing in my ears?
  "Now that I come to die,
Do I view the world as a vale of tears?"
  Ah, reverend sir, not I!

2

What I viewed there once, what I view again
  Where the physic bottles stand
On the table's edge,—is a suburb lane,
  With a wall to my bedside hand.

3

That lane sloped, much as the bottles do,
  From a house you could descry
O'er the garden-wall: is the curtain blue
  Or green to a healthy eye?

4

To mine, it serves for the old June weather
  Blue above lane and wall;
And that farthest bottle labelled "Ether"
  Is the house o'er-topping all.

5

At a terrace, somewhere near the stopper,
  There watched for me, one June,
A girl: I know, sir, it 's improper,
  My poor mind 's out of tune.

6

Only, there was a way . . . you crept
  Close by the side, to dodge
Eyes in the house, two eyes except:
  They styled their house "The Lodge."

7

What right had a lounger up their lane?
  But, by creeping very close,
With the good wall's help,—their eyes might strain
  And stretch themselves to Oes,

8

Yet never catch her and me together,
  As she left the attic, there,
By the rim of the bottle labelled "Ether,"
  And stole from stair to stair,

9

And stood by the rose-wreathed gate. Alas,
  We loved, sir—used to meet:
How sad and bad and mad it was—
  But then, how it was sweet!

"O LYRIC LOVE"

This song from The Ring and the Book, *the longest of Browning's poetic narratives, is addressed to the spirit of the poet's wife.*

O lyric Love, half-angel and half-bird
And all a wonder and a wild desire,—
Boldest of hearts that ever braved the sun,
Took sanctuary within the holier blue.
And sang a kindred soul out to his face,—
Yet human at the red-ripe of the heart—
When the first summons from the darkling earth
Reached thee amid thy chambers, blanched their blue,
And bared them of the glory—to drop down,
To toil for man, to suffer or to die,—
This is the same voice: can thy soul know change?

Hail then, and hearken from the realms of help!
Never may I commence my song, my due
To God who best taught song by gift of thee,
Except with bent head and beseeching hand—
That still, despite the distance and the dark,
What was, again may be; some interchange
Of grace, some splendour once thy very thought,
Some benediction anciently thy smile:
—Never conclude, but raising hand and head
Thither where eyes, that cannot reach, yet yearn
For all hope, all sustainment, all reward,
Their utmost up and on,—so blessing back
In those thy realms of help, that heaven thy home,
Some whiteness which, I judge, thy face makes proud,
Some wanness where, I think, thy foot may fall!

Prologue from Fifine at the Fair

1872

AMPHIBIAN

Browning's zest for new experiences never flagged. His son taught him to swim during one of the many summers they spent on the coast of Brittany. The aquatic delight expressed here seems more like that of a boy than that of a man of sixty. The passing of a butterfly—a traditional symbol of the soul—over his floating body sets him off on these philosophical musings.

The fancy I had to-day,
  Fancy which turned a fear!
I swam far out in the bay,
  Since waves laughed warm and clear.

I lay and looked at the sun,
  The noon-sun looked at me:
Between us two, no one
  Live creature, that I could see

Yes! There came floating by
  Me, who lay floating too,
Such a strange butterfly!
  Creature as dear as new:

Because the membraned wings
  So wonderful, so wide,
So sun-suffused, were things
  Like soul and naught beside.

A handbreadth overhead!
  All of the sea my own,
It owned the sky instead;
  Both of us were alone.

I never shall join its flight,
  For, naught buoys flesh in air.
If it touch the sea—good night!
  Death sure and swift waits there.

Can the insect feel the better
  For watching the uncouth play
Of limbs that slip the fetter,
  Pretend as they were not clay?

Undoubtedly I rejoice
  That the air comports so well
With a creature which had the choice
  Of the land once. Who can tell?

What if a certain soul
  Which early slipped its sheath,
And has for its home the whole
  Of heaven, thus look beneath,

Thus watch one who, in the world,
  Both lives and likes life's way,
Nor wishes the wings unfurled
  That sleep in the worm, they say?

But sometimes when the weather
  Is blue, and warm waves tempt
To free one's self of tether,
  And try a life exempt

From worldly noise and dust,
  In the sphere which overbrims
With passion and thought,—why, just
  Unable to fly, one swims!

By passion and thought upborne,
  One smiles to one's self—"They fare
Scarce better, they need not scorn
  Our sea, who live in the air!"

Emancipate through passion
  And thought, with sea for sky,
We substitute, in a fashion,
  For heaven—poetry:

Which sea, to all intent,
  Gives flesh such noon-disport
As a finer element
  Affords the spirit-sort.

Whatever they are, we seem:
  Imagine the thing they know;
All deeds they do, we dream;
  Can heaven be else but so?

And meantime, yonder streak
  Meets the horizon's verge;
That is the land, to seek
  If we tire or dread the surge:

Land the solid and safe—
  To welcome again (confess!)
When, high and dry, we chafe
  The body, and don the dress.

Does she look, pity, wonder
  At one who mimics flight,
Swims—heaven above, sea under,
  Yet always earth in sight?

From Pacchiarotto, with Other Poems

1876

PROLOGUE

Here Browning is thinking of his wife, who has been dead for more than fifteen years. The "wall" seems to symbolize the barrier that the passage of time has built up between them.

Oh, the old wall here! How I could pass
  Life in a long midsummer day,
My feet confined to a plot of grass,
  My eyes from a wall not once away!

And lush and lithe, do the creepers clothe
  Yon wall I watch, with a wealth of green:
Its bald red bricks draped, nothing loth,
  In lappets of tangle they laugh between.

Now, what is it makes pulsate the robe?
  Why tremble the sprays? What life o'erbrims
The body,—the house, no eye can probe,—
  Divined as, beneath a robe, the limbs?

And there again! But my heart may guess
  Who tripped behind; and she sang perhaps:
So, the old wall throbbed, and its life's excess
  Died out and away in the leafy wraps!

Wall upon wall are between us: life
  And song should away from heart to heart!
I—prison bird, with a ruddy strife
  At breast, and a lip whence storm-notes start—

Hold on, hope hard in the subtle thing
  That's spirit: though cloistered fast, soar free;
Account as wood, brick, stone, this ring
  Of the rueful neighbors, and—forth to thee!

HOUSE

Browning explains that the true artist declines to admit his inner life to the vulgar gaze of the public. Browning states here—as well as in other poems—that all the world needs to know about him can be gathered from the "spirit sense" of his poems.

Shall I sonnet-sing you about myself?
  Do I live in a house you would like to see?
Is it scant of gear, has it store of pelf?
  "Unlock my heart with a sonnet-key?"

Invite the world, as my betters have done?
  "Take notice: this building remains on view,
Its suites of reception every one,
  Its private apartment and bedroom too;

"For a ticket, apply to the Publisher."
  No: thanking the public, I must decline.
A peep through my window, if folk prefer;
  But, please you, no foot over threshold of mine!

I have mixed with a crowd and heard free talk
  In a foreign land where an earthquake chanced
And a house stood gaping, naught to balk
  Man's eye wherever he gazed or glanced.

The whole of the frontage shaven sheer,
  The inside gaped: exposed to day,
Right and wrong and common and queer,
  Bare, as the palm of your hand, it lay.

The owner? Oh, he had been crushed, no doubt!
  "Odd tables and chairs for a man of wealth!
What a parcel of musty old books about!
  He smoked,—no wonder he lost his health!

"I doubt if he bathed before he dressed.
  A brasier?—the pagan, he burned perfumes!
You see it is proved, what the neighbors guessed:
  His wife and himself had separate rooms."

Friends, the goodman of the house at least
  Kept house to himself till an earthquake came:
'Tis the fall of its frontage permits you feast
  On the inside arrangement you praise or blame.

Outside should suffice for evidence:
  And whoso desires to penetrate
Deeper, must dive by the spirit-sense—
  No optics like yours, at any rate!

"Hoity-toity! A street to explore,
  Your house the exception! *'With this same key*
Shakespeare unlocked his heart,' once more!"
  Did Shakespeare? If so, the less Shakespeare he!

SHOP

Disapprobation is here expressed of the shopkeeper (or any materialist) whose spirit is chained to his counter, who is so lost in his daily employment that he doesn't have any other life —hasn't anything that isn't in the show-window. Browning wants everybody to have something to feed the spirit, whether it be dreams or hobbies.

So, friend, your shop was all your house!
  Its front, astonishing the street,
Invited view from man and mouse
  To what diversity of treat
  Behind its glass—the single sheet!

What gimcracks, genuine Japanese:
   Gape-jaw and goggle-eye, the frog;
Dragons, owls, monkeys, beetles, geese;
   Some crush-nosed human-hearted dog:
   Queer names, too, such a catalogue!

I thought "And he who owns the wealth
   Which blocks the window's vastitude,
—Ah, could I peep at him by stealth
   Behind his ware, pass shop, intrude
   On house itself, what scenes were viewed!

"If wide and showy thus the shop,
   What must the habitation prove?
The true house with no name a-top—
   The mansion, distant one remove,
   Once get him off his traffic-groove!

"Pictures he likes, or books perhaps;
   And as for buying most and best,
Commend me to these city chaps!
   Or else he's social, takes his rest
   On Sundays, with a Lord for guest.

"Some suburb-palace, parked about
   And gated grandly, built last year:
The four-mile walk to keep off gout;
   Or big seat sold by bankrupt peer:
   But then he takes the rail, that's clear.

"Or, stop! I wager, taste selects
   Some out-o'-the-way, some all-unknown
Retreat: the neighborhood suspects
   Little that he who rambles lone
   Makes Rothschild tremble on his throne!"

Nowise! Nor Mayfair residence
   Fit to receive and entertain,—

Nor Hampstead villa's kind defence
  From noise and crowd, from dust and drain,—
  Nor country-box was soul's domain!

Nowise! At back of all that spread
  Of merchandise, woe's me, I find
A hole i' the wall where, heels by head,
  The owner couched, his ware behind,
  —In cupboard suited to his mind.

For why? He saw no use of life
  But, while he drove a roaring trade,
To chuckle "Customers are rife!"
  To chafe "So much hard cash outlaid,
  Yet zero in my profits made!

"This novelty costs pains, but—takes?
  Cumbers my counter! Stock no more!
This article, no such great shakes,
  Fizzes like wildfire? Underscore
  The cheap thing—thousands to the fore!"

'Twas lodging best to live most nigh
  (Cramp, coffinlike as crib might be)
Receipt of Custom; ear and eye
  Wanted no outworld: "Hear and see
  The bustle in the shop!" quoth he.

My fancy of a merchant-prince
  Was different. Through his wares we groped
Our darkling way to—not to mince
  The matter—no black den where moped
  The master if we interloped!

Shop was shop only: household-stuff?
  What did he want with comforts there?
"Walls, ceiling, floor, stay blank and rough,
  So goods on sale show rich and rare!
  'Sell and scud home,' be shop's affair!"

What might he deal in? Gems, suppose!
  Since somehow business must be done
At cost of trouble,—see, he throws
  You choice of jewels, every one,
  Good, better, best, star, moon, and sun!

Which lies within your power of purse?
  This ruby that would tip aright
Solomon's sceptre? Oh, your nurse
  Wants simply coral, the delight
  Of teething baby,—stuff to bite!

Howe'er your choice fell, straight you took
  Your purchase, prompt your money rang
On counter,—scarce the man forsook
  His study of the "Times," just swang
  Till-ward his hand that stopped the clang,—

Then off made buyer with a prize,
  Then seller to his "Times" returned;
And so did day wear, wear, till eyes
  Brightened apace, for rest was earned:
  He locked door long ere candle burned.

And whither went he? Ask himself,
  Not me! To change of scene, I think.
Once sold the ware and pursed the pelf,
  Chaffer was scarce his meat and drink,
  Nor all his music—money-chink.

Because a man has shop to mind
  In time and place, since flesh must live,
Needs spirit lack all life behind,
  All stray thoughts, fancies fugitive,
  All loves except what trade can give?

I want to know a butcher paints,
  A baker rhymes for his pursuit,

Candlestick-maker much acquaints
His soul with song, or, haply mute,
Blows out his brains upon the flute!

But—shop each day and all day long!
Friend, your good angel slept, your star
Suffered eclipse, fate did you wrong!
From where these sorts of treasures are,
There should our hearts be—Christ, how far!

PISGAH-SIGHTS

Pisgah was the mountain from which Moses was allowed to gaze into the Promised Land. How life looks if one sees all of it, how one would live if one lived it over again—these are the themes of the two simple yet profound lyrics.

I

Over the ball of it,
Peering and prying,
How I see all of it,
Life there, outlying!
Roughness and smoothness,
Shine and defilement,
Grace and uncouthness:
One reconcilement.

Orbed as appointed,
Sister with brother
Joins, ne'er disjointed
One from the other.
All's lend-and-borrow;
Good, see, wants evil,
Joy demands sorrow,
Angel weds devil!

"Which things must—*why* be?"
Vain our endeavor!

So shall things aye be
   As they were ever.
"Such things should *so* be!"
   Sage our desistence!
Rough-smooth let globe be,
   Mixed—man's existence!

Man—wise and foolish,
   Lover and scorner,
Docile and mulish—
   Keep each his corner!
Honey yet gall of it!
   There's the life lying,
And I see all of it,
   Only, I'm dying!

II

Could I but live again
   Twice my life over,
Would I once strive again?
   Would not I cover
Quietly all of it—
   Greed and ambition—
So, from the pall of it,
   Pass to fruition?

"Soft!" I'd say, "Soul mine!
   Three-score and ten years,
Let the blind mole mine
   Digging out deniers!
Let the dazed hawks soar,
   Claim the sun's rights too!
Turf 'tis thy walk's o'er,
   Foliage thy flight's to."

Only a learner,
   Quick one or slow one,

Just a discerner,
  I would teach no one.
I am earth's native:
  No rearranging it!
I be creative,
  Chopping and changing it?

March, men, my fellows!
  Those who, above me,
(Distance so mellows)
  Fancy you love me:
Those who, below me,
  (Distance makes great so)
Free to forego me,
  Fancy you hate so!

Praising, reviling,
  Worst head and best head,
Past me defiling,
  Never arrested,
Wanters, abounders,
  March, in gay mixture,
Men, my surrounders!
  I am the fixture.

So shall I fear thee,
  Mightiness yonder!
Mock-sun—more near thee,
  What is to wonder?
So shall I love thee,
  Down in the dark,—lest
Glowworm I prove thee,
  Star that now sparklest!

FEARS AND SCRUPLES

This poetic parable is difficult to understand unless one knows at the outset that the "letters" refer to the Scriptures, whose validity and authority were being attacked during Browning's lifetime, and that the "friend" whom he trusts without seeing is God.

Here's my case. Of old I used to love him,
  This same unseen friend, before I knew:
Dream there was none like him, none above him,—
  Wake to hope and trust my dream was true.

Loved I not his letters full of beauty?
  Not his actions famous far and wide?
Absent, he would know I vowed him duty;
  Present, he would find me at his side.

Pleasant fancy! for I had but letters,
  Only knew of actions by hearsay:
He himself was busied with my betters;
  What of that? My turn must come some day.

"Some day" proving—no day! Here's the puzzle.
  Passed and passed my turn is. Why complain?
He's so busied! If I could but muzzle
  People's foolish mouths that give me pain!

"Letters?" (hear them!) "You a judge of writing?
  Ask the experts! How they shake the head
O'er these characters, your friend's inditing—
  Call them forgery from A to Z!

"Actions? Where's your certain proof" (they bother)
  "He, of all you find so great and good,
He, he only, claims this, that, the other
  Action—claimed by men, a multitude?"

I can simply wish I might refute you,
  Wish my friend would,—by a word, a wink,—
Bid me stop that foolish mouth,—you brute you!
  He keeps absent,—why, I cannot think.

Never mind! Though foolishness may flout me,
One thing's sure enough: 'tis neither frost,
No, nor fire, shall freeze or burn from out me
Thanks for truth—though falsehood, gained—though lost.

All my days, I'll go the softlier, sadlier,
For that dream's sake! How forget the thrill
Through and through me as I thought "The gladlier
Lives my friend because I love him still!"

Ah, but there's a menace someone utters!
"What and if your friend at home play tricks,
Peep at hide-and-seek behind the shutters?
Mean your eyes should pierce through solid bricks?

"What and if he, frowning, wake you, dreamy?
Lay on you the blame that bricks—conceal?
Say *'At least I saw who did not see me,*
Does see now, and presently shall feel'?"

"Why, that makes your friend a monster!" say you:
"Had his house no window? At first nod,
Would you not have hailed him?" Hush, I pray you!
What if this friend happened to be—God?

HERVÉ RIEL

This poem is based on an episode which Browning had read about in an old Breton chronicle. The French fleet which had been sent to restore James II to the English throne met the Dutch and English fleets off St. Malo and was defeated after a gallant fight. D'Amfreville, leading twenty of the French vessels, was piloted into the harbor by the sailor of Croisic, Hervé Riel. This popular ballad appeared in an English magazine, and Browning donated the fee of $500 which he received for the relief of Parisian sufferers in the Franco-Prussian War.

1

On the sea and at the Hogue, sixteen hundred ninety-two,
Did the English fight the French,—woe to France!
And, the thirty-first of May, helter-skelter through the blue,
Like a crowd of frightened porpoises a shoal of sharks pursue,
Came crowding ship on ship to Saint Malo on the Rance,
With the English fleet in view.

2

'Twas the squadron that escaped, with the victor in full chase;
First and foremost of the drove, in his great ship, Damfreville;
Close on him fled, great and small,
Twenty-two good ships in all;
And they signalled to the place
"Help the winners of a race!
Get us guidance, give us harbor, take us quick—or, quicker still,
Here's the English can and will!"

3

Then the pilots of the place put out brisk and leapt on board
"Why, what hope or chance have ships like these to pass?" laughed they:
"Rocks to starboard, rocks to port, all the passage scarred and scored,
Shall the 'Formidable' here with her twelve and eighty guns
Think to make the river-mouth by the single narrow way,
Trust to enter where 'tis ticklish for a craft of twenty tons,
And with flow at full beside?
Now, 'tis slackest ebb of tide.
Reach the mooring? Rather say,
While rock stands or water runs,
Not a ship will leave the bay!"

4

Then was called a council straight.
Brief and bitter the debate:

"Here's the English at our heels; would you have them take
in tow
All that's left us of the fleet, linked together stern and bow,
For a prize to Plymouth Sound?
Better run the ships aground!"
(Ended Damfreville his speech).
"Not a minute more to wait!
Let the Captains all and each
Shove ashore, then blow up, burn the vessels on the beach!
France must undergo her fate.

5

"Give the word!" But no such word
Was ever spoke or heard;
For up stood, for out stepped, for in struck amid all these
—A Captain? A Lieutenant? A Mate—first, second, third?
No such man of mark, and meet
With his betters to compete!
But a simple Breton sailor pressed by Tourville for the
fleet,
A poor coasting-pilot, he, Hervé Riel the Croisickese.

6

And "What mockery or malice have we here?" cries Hervé Riel:
"Are you mad, you Malouins? Are you cowards, fools, or
rogues?
Talk to me of rocks and shoals, me who took the soundings, tell
On my fingers every bank, every shallow, every swell
'Twixt the offing here and Grève where the river disembogues?
Are you bought by English gold? Is it love the lying's for?
Morn and eve, night and day,
Have I piloted your bay,
Entered free and anchored fast at the foot of Solidor.
Burn the fleet and ruin France? There were worse than
fifty Hogues!
Sirs, they know I speak the truth! Sirs, believe me there's
a way!

Only let me lead the line,
  Have the biggest ship to steer,
  Get this 'Formidable' clear,
Make the others follow mine,
And I lead them, most and least, by a passage I know well,
  Right to Solidor past Grève,
    And there lay them safe and sound;
    And if one ship misbehave,
    —Keel so much as grate the ground,
Why, I've nothing but my life,—here's my head!" cries Hervé Riel.

7

Not a minute more to wait.
"Steer us in, then, small and great!
  Take the helm, lead the line, save the squadron!" cried its chief.
Captains, give the sailor place!
  He is Admiral, in brief.
Still the north-wind, by God's grace!
See the noble fellow's face
As the big ship, with a bound,
Clears the entry like a hound,
Keeps the passage as its inch of way were the wide sea's profound!
  See, safe through shoal and rock,
  How they follow in a flock,
Not a ship that misbehaves, not a keel that grates the ground,
  Not a spar that comes to grief!
The peril, see, is past,
All are harbored to the last,
And just as Hervé Riel hollas "Anchor!"—sure as fate,
Up the English come—too late!

8

So, the storm subsides to calm:
  They see the green trees wave
  On the heights o'erlooking Grève.

Hearts that bled are stanched with balm.
"Just our rapture to enhance,
  Let the English rake the bay,
Gnash their teeth and glare askance
  As they cannonade away!
'Neath rampired Solidor pleasant riding on the Rance!"
How hope succeeds despair on each Captain's countenance!
Out burst all with one accord,
  "This is Paradise for Hell!
    Let France, let France's King
    Thank the man that did the thing!"
What a shout, and all one word,
  "Hervé Riel!"
As he stepped in front once more,
  Not a symptom of surprise
  In the frank blue Breton eyes,
Just the same man as before.

9

Then said Damfreville, "My friend,
I must speak out at the end,
  Though I find the speaking hard.
Praise is deeper than the lips:
You have saved the King his ships,
  You must name your own reward.
'Faith, our sun was near eclipse!
Demand whate'er you will,
France remains your debtor still.
Ask to heart's content and have! or my name's not Damfreville."

10

Then a beam of fun outbroke
On the bearded mouth that spoke,
As the honest heart laughed through
Those frank eyes of Breton blue:
"Since I needs must say my say,
  Since on board the duty's done,
  And from Malo Roads to Croisic Point, what is it but a run?—

Since 'tis ask and have, I may—
   Since the others go ashore—
Come! A good whole holiday!
   Leave to go and see my wife, whom I call the Belle Aurore!"
   That he asked and that he got,—nothing more.

II

Name and deed alike are lost:
Not a pillar nor a post
   In his Croisic keeps alive the feat as it befell;
Not a head in white and black
On a single fishing-smack,
In memory of the man but for whom had gone to wrack
   All that France saved from the fight whence England bore the bell.
Go to Paris: rank on rank
   Search the heroes flung pell-mell
On the Louvre, face and flank!
   You shall look long enough ere you come to Hervé Riel.
So, for better and for worse,
Hervé Riel, accept my verse!
In my verse, Hervé Riel, do thou once more
Save the squadron, honor France, love thy wife the Belle Aurore!

La Saiziaz *and* The Two Poets of Croisic
1878

PROLOGUE TO LA SAIZIAZ

La Saiziaz—the sun, in the local dialect—was the name of a villa in Savoy where Browning spent the summer of 1877, and where his friend Miss Anne Egerton-Smith died.

Good, to forgive;
   Best, to forget!
   Living, we fret;
Dying, we live.

Fretless and free,
  Soul, clap thy pinion!
  Earth have dominion,
Body, o'er thee!

Wander at will,
  Day after day,—
  Wander away,
Wandering still—
Soul that canst soar!
  Body may slumber:
  Body shall cumber
Soul-flight no more.

Waft of soul's wing!
  What lies above?
  Sunshine and Love,
Skyblue and Spring!
Body hides—where?
  Ferns of all feather,
  Mosses and heather,
Yours be the care!

PROLOGUE TO THE TWO POETS OF CROISIC

Such a starved bank of moss
  Till, that May-morn,
Blue ran the flash across:
  Violets were born!

Sky—what a scowl of cloud
  Till, near and far,
Ray on ray split the shroud:
  Splendid, a star!

World—how it walled about
  Life with disgrace
Till God's own smile came out:
  That was thy face!

Dramatic Idylls

1879

IVAN IVANOVITCH

This poem, based on a legend, was written some thirty years after Browning's trip to Russia as a young man, but in its depiction of landscape and character it shows the influence of that experience. Most markedly, however, it illustrates Browning's preoccupation with complex human problems. Here, the peasant Ivan, to spare the mother a lifetime of remorse, takes vengeance into his own hands, and is absolved of guilt.

"They tell me, your carpenters," quoth I to my friend the Russ,
"Make a simple hatchet serve as a tool-box serves with us.
Arm but each man with his axe, 'tis a hammer and saw and plane
And chisel, and—what know I else? We should imitate in vain
The mastery wherewithal, by a flourish of just the adze,
He cleaves, clamps, dovetails in,—no need of our nails and brads,—
The manageable pine: 'tis said he could shave himself
With the axe,—so all adroit, now a giant and now an elf,
Does he work and play at once!"

Quoth my friend the Russ to me,
"Ay, that and more beside on occasion! It scarce may be
You never heard tell a tale told children, time out of mind,
By father and mother and nurse, for a moral that's behind,
Which children quickly seize. If the incident happened at all,
We place it in Peter's time when hearts were great not small,
Germanized, Frenchified. I wager 'tis old to you
As the story of Adam and Eve, and possibly quite as true."

In the deep of our land, 'tis said, a village from out the woods
Emerged on the great main-road 'twixt two great solitudes.
Through forestry right and left, black verst and verst of pine,

From village to village runs the road's long wide bare line.
Clearance and clearance break the else-unconquered growth
Of pine and all that breeds and broods there, leaving loth
Man's inch of masterdom,—spot of life, spirt of fire,—
To star the dark and dread, lest right and rule expire
Throughout the monstrous wild, a-hungered to resume
Its ancient sway, suck back the world into its womb:
Defrauded by man's craft which clove from North to South
This highway broad and straight e'en from the Neva's mouth
To Moscow's gates of gold. So, spot of life and spirt
Of fire aforesaid, burn, each village death-begirt
By wall and wall of pine—unprobed undreamed abyss.

Early one winter morn, in such a village as this,
Snow-whitened everywhere except the middle road
Ice-roughed by track of sledge, there worked by his abode
Ivan Ivanovitch, the carpenter, employed
On a huge shipmast trunk; his axe now trimmed and toyed
With branch and twig, and now some chop athwart the bole
Changed bole to billets, bared at once the sap and soul.
About him, watched the work his neighbours sheepskin-clad;
Each bearded mouth puffed steam, each gray eye twinkled glad
To see the sturdy arm which, never stopping play,
Proved strong man's blood still boils, freeze winter as he may.
Sudden, a burst of bells. Out of the road, on edge
Of the hamlet—horse's hoofs galloping. "How, a sledge?
What's here?" cried all as—in, up to the open space,
Workyard and market-ground, folk's common meeting-place—
Stumbled on, till he fell, in one last bound for life,
A horse: and, at his heels, a sledge held—"Dmitri's wife!
Back without Dmitri too! and children—where are they?
Only a frozen corpse!"

They drew it forth: then—"Nay,
Not dead, though like to die! Gone hence a month ago:
Home again, this rough jaunt—alone through night and snow—
What can the cause be? Hark—Droug, old horse, how he groans:

His day's done! Chafe away, keep chafing, for she moans:
She's coming to! Give here: see, motherkin, your friends!
Cheer up, all safe at home! Warm inside makes amends
For outside cold,—sup quick! Don't look as we were bears!
What is it startles you? What strange adventure stares
Up at us in your face? You know friends—which is which?
I'm Vassili, he's Sergei, Ivan Ivanovitch"—

At the word, the woman's eyes slow-wandering till they neared
The blue eyes o'er the bush of honey-colored beard,
Took in full light and sense and—torn to rags, some dream
Which hid the naked truth—O loud and long the scream
She gave, as if all power of voice within her throat
Poured itself wild away to waste in one dread note!
Then followed gasps and sobs, and then the steady flow
Of kindly tears: the brain was saved, a man might know.
Down fell her face upon the good friend's propping knee;
His broad hands smoothed her head, as fain to brush it free
From fancies, swarms that stung like bees unhived. He soothed—
"Loukeria, Louscha!"—still he, fondling, smoothed and smoothed.
At last her lips formed speech.
"Ivan, dear—you indeed!
You, just the same dear you! While I . . . Oh, intercede,
Sweet Mother, with thy Son Almighty—let his might
Bring yesterday once more, undo all done last night!
But this time yesterday, Ivan, I sat like you,
A child on either knee, and, dearer than the two,
A babe inside my arms, close to my heart—that's lost
In morsels o'er the snow! Father, Son, Holy Ghost,
Cannot you bring again my blessed yesterday?"

When no more tears would flow, she told her tale: this way.
"Maybe, a month ago,—was it not?—news came here,
They wanted, deeper down, good workmen fit to rear
A church and roof it in. 'We'll go,' my husband said:
'None understands like me to melt and mould their lead.'
So, friends here helped us off—Ivan, dear, you the first!

How gay we jingled forth, all five—(my heart will burst)—
While Dmitri shook the reins, urged Droug upon his track!

"Well, soon the month ran out, we just were coming back,
When yesterday—behold, the village was on fire!
Fire ran from house to house. What help, as, nigh and nigher,
The flames came furious? 'Haste,' cried Dmitri, 'men must do
The little good man may: to sledge and in with you,
You and our three! We check the fire by laying flat
Each building in its path,—I needs must stay for that,—
But you . . . no time for talk! Wrap round you every rug,
Cover the couple close,—you'll have the babe to hug.
No care to guide old Droug, he knows his way, by guess,
Once start him on the road: but chirrup, none the less!
The snow lies glib as glass and hard as steel, and soon
You'll have rise, fine and full, a marvel of a moon.
Hold straight up, all the same, this lighted twist of pitch!
Once home and with our friend Ivan Ivanovitch,
All's safe: I have my pay in pouch, all's right with me,
So I but find as safe you and our precious three!
Off, Droug!'—because the flames had reached us, and the men
Shouted 'But lend a hand, Dmitri—as good as ten!'

"So, in we bundled—I, and those God gave me once;
Old Droug, that's stiff at first, seemed youthful for the nonce:
He understood the case, galloping straight ahead.
Out came the moon: my twist soon dwindled, feebly red
In that unnatural day—yes, daylight, bred between
Moonlight and snow-light, lamped those grotto-depths which screen
Such devils from God's eye. Ah, pines, how straight you grow,
Nor bend one pitying branch, true breed of brutal snow!
Some undergrowth had served to keep the devils blind
While we escaped outside their border!

"Was that—wind?
Anyhow, Droug starts, stops, back go his ears, he snuffs,
Snorts,—never such a snort! then plunges, knows the sough's

Only the wind; yet, no—our breath goes up too straight!
Still the low sound,—less low, loud, louder, at a rate
There's no mistaking more! Shall I lean out—look—learn
The truth whatever it be? Pad, pad! At last, I turn—

" 'Tis the regular pad of the wolves in pursuit of the life in the sledge!
An army they are: close-packed they press like the thrust of a wedge:
They increase as they hunt: for I see, through the pine-trunks ranged each side,
Slip forth new fiend and fiend, make wider and still more wide
The four-footed steady advance. The foremost—none may pass:
They are elders and lead the line, eye and eye—green-growing brass!
But a long way distant still. Droug, save us! He does his best:
Yet they gain on us, gain, till they reach,—one reaches . . . How utter the rest?
O that Satan-faced first of the band! How he lolls out the length of his tongue,
How he laughs and lets gleam his white teeth! He is on me, his paws pry among
The wraps and the rugs! O my pair, my twin-pigeons, lie still and you seem dead!
Stepan, he shall never have you for a meal,—here's your mother instead!
No, he will not be counselled—must cry, poor Stiopka, so foolish! though first
Of my boy-brood, he was not the best: nay, neighbors have called him the worst:
He was puny, an undersized slip,—a darling to me, all the same!
But little there was to be praised in the boy, and a plenty to blame.
I loved him with heart and soul, yes—but, deal him a blow for a fault,
He would sulk for whole days. 'Foolish boy! lie still or the villain will vault,

Will snatch you from over my head!' No use! he cries, screams,
—who can hold
Fast a boy in a frenzy of fear! It follows—as I foretold!
The Satan-face snatched and snapped: I tugged, I tore—and then
His brother too needs must shriek! If one must go, 'tis men
The Tsar needs, so we hear, not ailing boys! Perhaps
My hands relaxed their grasp, got tangled in the wraps:
God, he was gone! I looked: there tumbled the cursed crew,
Each fighting for a share: too busy to pursue!
That's so far gain at least: Droug, gallop another verst
Or two, or three—God sends we beat them, arrive the first!
A mother who boasts two boys was ever accounted rich:
Some have not a boy: some have, but lose him,—God knows
which
Is worse: how pitiful to see your weakling pine
And pale and pass away! Strong brats, this pair of mine!

"O misery! for while I settle to what near seems
Content, I am 'ware again of the tramp, and again there gleams—
Point and point—the line, eyes, levelled green brassy fire!
So soon is resumed your chase? Will nothing appease, naught
tire
The furies? And yet I think—I am certain the race is slack,
And the numbers are nothing like. Not a quarter of the pack!
Feasters and those full-fed are staying behind . . . Ah, why?
We'll sorrow for that too soon! Now,—gallop, reach home, and
die,
Nor ever again leave house, to trust our life in the trap
For life—we call a sledge! Terioscha, in my lap!
Yes, I'll lie down upon you, tight-tie you with the strings
Here—of my heart! No fear, this time, your mother flings . . .
Flings? I flung? Never! But think!—a woman, after all,
Contending with a wolf! Save you I must and shall,
Terentii!

"How now? What, you still head the race,
Your eyes and tongue and teeth crave fresh food, Satan-face?
There and there! Plain I struck green fire out! Flash again?

All a poor fist can do to damage eyes proves vain!
My fist—why not crunch that? He is wanton for . . . O God,
Why give this wolf his taste? Common wolves scrape and prod
The earth till out they scratch some corpse—mere putrid flesh!
Why must this glutton leave the faded, choose the fresh?
Terentii—God, feel!—his neck keeps fast thy bag
Of holy things, saints' bones, this Satan-face will drag
Forth, and devour along with him, our Pope declared
The relics were to save from danger!

"Spurned, not spared!
'Twas through my arms, crossed arms, he—nuzzling now with snout,
Now ripping, tooth and claw—plucked, pulled Terentii out,
A prize indeed! I saw—how could I else but see?—
My precious one—I bit to hold back—pulled from me!
Up came the others, fell to dancing—did the imps!—
Skipped as they scampered round. There's one is gray, and limps:
Who knows but old bad Marpha—she always owed me spite
And envied me my births—skulks out of doors at night
And turns into a wolf, and joins the sisterhood,
And laps the youthful life, then slinks from out the wood,
Squats down at door by dawn, spins there demure as erst
—No strength, old crone,—not she!—to crawl forth half a verst!

"Well, I escaped with one: 'twixt one and none there lies
The space 'twixt heaven and hell. And see, a rose-light dyes
The endmost snow: 'tis dawn, 'tis day, 'tis safe at home!
We have outwitted you! Ay, monsters, snarl and foam,
Fight each the other fiend, disputing for a share,—
Forgetful, in your greed, our finest off we bear,
Tough Droug and I,—my babe, my boy that shall be man,
My man that shall be more, do all a hunter can
To trace and follow and find and catch and crucify
Wolves, wolfkins, all your crew! A thousand deaths shall die
The whimperingest cub that ever squeezed the teat!
'Take that!' we'll stab you with,—'the tenderness we met

When, wretches, you danced round,—not this, thank God—
not this!
Hellhounds, we balk you!'

"But—Ah, God above!—Bliss, bliss,—
Not the band, no! And yet—yes, for Droug knows him! One—
This only of them all has said 'She saves a son!'
His fellows disbelieve such luck: but he believes,
He lets them pick the bones, laugh at him in their sleeves:
He's off and after us,—one speck, one spot, one ball
Grows bigger, bound on bound,—one wolf as good as all!
Oh, but I know the trick! Have at the snaky tongue!
That's the right way with wolves! Go, tell your mates I wrung
The panting morsel out, left you to howl your worst!
Now for it—now! Ah me! I know him—thrice-accurst
Satan-face,—him to the end my foe!

"All fight's in vain:
This time the green brass points pierce to my very brain.
I fall—fall as I ought—quite on the babe I guard:
I overspread with flesh the whole of him. Too hard
To die this way, torn piecemeal? Move hence? Not I—one inch!
Gnaw through me, through and through: flat thus I lie nor
flinch!
O God, the feel of the fang furrowing my shoulder!—see!
It grinds—it grates the bone. O Kirill under me,
Could I do more? Besides he knew wolf's way to win:
I clung, closed round like wax: yet in he wedged and in,
Past my neck, past my breasts, my heart, until . . . how feels
The onion-bulb your knife parts, pushing through its peels,
Till out you scoop its clove wherein lie stalk and leaf
And bloom and seed unborn?

"That slew me: yes, in brief,
I died then, dead I lay doubtlessly till Droug stopped
Here, I suppose. I come to life, I find me propped
Thus,—how or when or why— I know not. Tell me, friends,
All was a dream: laugh quick and say the nightmare ends!

Soon I shall find my house: 'tis over there: in proof
Save for that chimney, heaped with snow, you'd see the roof
Which holds my three—my two—my one—not one?

"Life's mixed
With misery, yet we live—must live. The Satan fixed
His face on mine so fast, I took its print as pitch
Takes what it cools beneath. Ivan Ivanovitch,
'Tis you unharden me, you thaw, disperse the thing!
Only keep looking kind, the horror will not cling.
Your face smooths fast away each print of Satan. Tears.
—What good they do! Life's sweet, and all is, after-years,
Ivan Ivanovitch, I owe you! Yours am I!
May God reward you, dear!"

Down she sank. Solemnly
Ivan rose, raised his axe,—for fitly, as she knelt,
Her head lay: well-apart, each side, her arms hung,—dealt
Lightning-swift thunder-strong one blow—no need of more!
Headless she knelt on still: that pine was sound at core
(Neighbors were used to say)—cast-iron-kernelled—which
Taxed for a second stroke Ivan Ivanovitch.

The man was scant of words as strokes. "It had to be:
I could no other: God it was, bade 'Act for me!' "
Then stooping, peering round—what is it now he lacks?
A proper strip of bark wherewith to wipe his axe.
Which done, he turns, goes in, closes the door behind.
The others mute remain, watching the blood-snake wind
Into a hiding-place among the splinter-heaps.

At length, still mute, all move: one lifts—from where it steeps
Redder each ruddy rag of pine—the head: two more
Take up the dripping body: then, mute still as before,
Move in a sort of march, march on till marching ends
Opposite to the church; where halting,—who suspends,
By its long hair, the thing, deposits in its place
The piteous head: once more the body shows no trace

Of harm done: there lies whole the Louscha, maid and wife
And mother loved until this latest of her life.
Then all sit on the bank of snow which bounds a space
Kept free before the porch of judgment: just the place!

Presently all the souls, man, woman, child, which make
The village up, are found assembling for the sake
Of what is to be done. The very Jews are there:
A Gypsy-troop, though bound with horses for the Fair,
Squats with the rest. Each heart with its conception seethes
And simmers, but no tongue speaks: one may say,—none breathes.

Anon from out the church totters the Pope—the priest—
Hardly alive, so old, a hundred years at least.
With him, the Commune's head, a hoary senior too,
Starosta, that's his style,—like Equity Judge with you,—
Natural Jurisconsult: then, fenced about with furs,
Pomeschik,—Lord of the Land, who wields—and none demurs—
A power of life and death. They stoop, survey the corpse.

Then, straightened on his staff, the Starosta—the thorpe's
Sagaciousest old man—hears what you just have heard,
From Droug's first inrush, all, up to Ivan's last word—
"God bade me act for him: I dared not disobey!"

Silence—the Pomeschik broke with "A wild wrong way
Of righting wrong—if wrong there were, such wrath to rouse!
Why was not law observed? What article allows
Whoso may please to play the judge, and, judgment dealt,
Play executioner, as promptly as we pelt
To death, without appeal, the vermin whose sole fault
Has been—it dared to leave the darkness of its vault,
Intrude upon our day! Too sudden and too rash!
What was this woman's crime? Suppose the church should crash
Down where I stand, your lord: bound are my serfs to dare
Their utmost that I 'scape: yet, if the crashing scare

My children—as you are,—if sons fly, one and all,
Leave father to his fate,—poor cowards though I call
The runaways, I pause before I claim their life
Because they prized it more than mine. I would each wife
Died for her husband's sake, each son to save his sire:
'Tis glory, I applaud—scarce duty, I require.
Ivan Ivanovitch has done a deed that's named
Murder by law and me: who doubts, may speak unblamed!"

All turned to the old Pope. "Ay, children, I am old—
How old, myself have got to know no longer. Rolled
Quite round, my orb of life from infancy to age,
Seems passing back again to youth. A certain stage
At least I reach, or dream I reach, where I discern
Truer truths, laws behold more lawlike than we learn
When first we set our foot to tread the course I trod
With man to guide my steps: who leads me now is God.
'Your young men shall see visions:' and in my youth I saw
And paid obedience to man's visionary law:
'Your old men shall dream dreams:' and, in my age, a hand
Conducts me through the cloud round law to where I stand
Firm on its base,—know cause, who, before, knew effect.

"The world lies under me: and nowhere I detect
So great a gift as this—God's own—of human life.
'Shall the dead praise thee?' No! 'The whole live world is rife,
God, with thy glory,' rather! Life then, God's best of gifts,
For what shall man exchange? For life—when so he shifts
The weight and turns the scale, lets life for life restore
God's balance, sacrifice the less to gain the more,
Substitute—for low life, another's or his own—
Life large and liker God's who gave it: thus alone
May life extinguish life that life may trulier be!
How long this law descends on earth, is not for me
To trace: complexed becomes the simple, intricate
The plain, when I pursue law's winding. 'Tis the straight
Outflow of law I know and name: to law, the fount
Fresh from God's footstool, friends, follow while I remount.

"A mother bears a child: perfection is complete
So far in such a birth. Enabled to repeat
The miracle of life,—herself was born so just
A type of womankind, that God sees fit to trust
Her with the holy task of giving life in turn.
Crowned by this crowning pride, how say you, should she spurn
Regality—discrowned, unchilded, by her choice
Of barrenness exchanged for fruit which made rejoice
Creation, though life's self were lost in giving birth
To life more fresh and fit to glorify God's earth?
How say you, should the hand God trusted with life's torch
Kindled to light the world—aware of sparks that scorch,
Let fall the same? Forsooth, her flesh a fireflake stings:
The mother drops the child! Among what monstrous things
Shall she be classed? Because of motherhood, each male
Yields to his partner place, sinks proudly in the scale:
His strength owned weakness, wit—folly, and courage—fear,
Beside the female proved male's mistress—only here.
The fox-dam, hunger-pined, will slay the felon sire
Who dares assault her whelp: the beaver, stretched on fire,
Will die without a groan: no pang avails to wrest
Her young from where they hide—her sanctuary breast.
What's here then? Answer me, thou dead one, as, I trow,
Standing at God's own bar, he bids thee answer now!
Thrice crowned wast thou—each crown of pride, a child—thy
charge!
Where are they? Lost? Enough: no need that thou enlarge
On how or why the loss: life left to utter 'lost'
Condemns itself beyond appeal. The soldier's post
Guards from the foe's attack the camp he sentinels:
That he no traitor proved, this and this only tells—
Over the corpse of him trod foe to foe's success.
Yet—one by one thy crowns torn from thee—thou no less
To scare the world, shame God,—livedst! I hold he saw
The unexampled sin, ordained the novel law,
Whereof first instrument was first intelligence
Found loyal here. I hold that, failing human sense,
The very earth had oped, sky fallen, to efface

Humanity's new wrong, motherhood's first disgrace.
Earth oped not, neither fell the sky, for prompt was found
A man and man enough, head-sober and heart-sound,
Ready to hear God's voice, resolute to obey.
Ivan Ivanovich, I hold, has done, this day,
No otherwise than did, in ages long ago,
Moses when he made known the purport of that flow
Of fire athwart the law's twain-tables! I proclaim
Ivan Ivanovitch God's servant!"

At which name
Uprose that creepy whisper from out the crowd, is wont
To swell and surge and sink when fellowmen confront
A punishment that falls on fellow flesh and blood,
Appallingly beheld—shudderingly understood,
No less, to be the right, the just, the merciful.
"God's servant!" hissed the crowd.

When the Amen grew dull
And died away and left acquittal plain adjudged,
"Amen!" last sighed the lord. "There's none shall say I grudged
Escape from punishment in such a novel case.
Deferring to old age and holy life,—be grace
Granted! say I. No less, scruples might shake a sense
Firmer than I boast mine. Law's law, and evidence
Of breach therein lies plain,—blood-red-bright,—all may see!
Yet all absolve the deed: absolved the deed must be!

"And next—as mercy rules the hour—methinks 'twere well
You signify forthwith its sentence, and dispel
The doubts and fears, I judge, which busy now the head
Law puts a halter round—a halo—you, instead!
Ivan Ivanovitch—what think you he expects
Will follow from his feat? Go, tell him—law protects
Murder, for once: no need he longer keep behind
The Sacred Pictures—where skulks Innocence enshrined,
Or I missay! Go, some! You others, haste and hide
The dismal object there: get done, whate'er betide!"

So, while the youngers raised the corpse, the elders trooped
Silently to the house: where halting, some one stooped,
Listened beside the door; all there was silent too.
Then they held counsel; then pushed door and, passing through,
Stood in the murderer's presence.

Ivan Ivanovitch
Knelt, building on the floor that Kremlin rare and rich
He deftly cut and carved on lazy winter nights.
Some five young faces watched, breathlessly, as, to rights,
Piece upon piece, he reared the fabric nigh complete.
Stescha, Ivan's old mother, sat spinning by the heat
Of the oven where his wife Katia stood baking bread.
Ivan's self, as he turned his honey-colored head,
Was just in act to drop, 'twixt fir-cones,—each a dome,—
The scooped-out yellow gourd presumably the home
Of Kolokol the Big: the bell, therein to hitch,
—An acorn-cup—was ready: Ivan Ivanovitch
Turned with it in his mouth.

They told him he was free
As air to walk abroad. "How otherwise?" asked he.

CLIVE

This story, told by an old soldier to his son, relates a true episode in the life of Robert, Lord Clive, who won India for England at the Battle of Plassey, in 1757. All the dramatic tools which Browning knew so well how to use are employed in Clive: *human wills in conflict, powerful and revealing dialogue, suspense, and climax.* Clive *has always been a favorite with hero-worshiping young readers.*

I and Clive were friends—and why not? Friends! I think you
laugh, my lad.
Clive it was gave England India, while your father gives—egad,
England nothing but the graceless boy who lures him on to
speak—
"Well, Sir, you and Clive were comrades—" with a tongue
thrust in your cheek!

Very true: in my eyes, your eyes, all the world's eyes, Clive was man,
I was, am, and ever shall be—mouse, nay, mouse of all its clan
Sorriest sample, if you take the kitchen's estimate for fame;
While the man Clive—he fought Plassey, spoiled the clever foreign game,
Conquered and annexed and Englished!

Never mind! As o'er my punch
(You away) I sit of evenings,—silence, save for biscuit crunch,
Black, unbroken,—thought grows busy, thrids each pathway of old years,
Notes this forthright, that meander, till the long-past life appears
Like an outspread map of country plodded through, each mile and rood,
Once, and well remembered still,—I'm startled in my solitude
Ever and anon by—what's the sudden mocking light that breaks
On me as I slap the table till no rummer-glass but shakes
While I ask—aloud, I do believe, God help me!—"Was it thus?
Can it be that so I faltered, stopped when just one step for us—"
(Us,—you were not born, I grant, but surely some day born would be)
"—One bold step had gained a province" (figurative talk, you see)
"Got no end of wealth and honour,—yet I stood stock-still no less?"
—"For I was not Clive," you comment: but it needs no Clive to guess
Wealth were handy, honour ticklish, did no writing on the wall
Warn me "Trespasser, 'ware man-traps!" Him who braves that notice—call
Hero! none of such heroics suit myself who read plain words,
Doff my hat, and leap no barrier. Scripture says, the land's the Lord's:
Louts then—what avail the thousand, noisy in a smock-frocked ring,

All-agog to have me trespass, clear the fence, be Clive their king?
Higher warrant must you show me ere I set one foot before
T'other in that dark direction, though I stand forevermore
Poor as Job and meek as Moses. Evermore? No! By and by
Job grows rich and Moses valiant, Clive turns out less wise than I.
Don't object "Why call him friend, then?" Power is power, my boy, and still
Marks a man,—God's gift magnific, exercised for good or ill.
You've your boot now on my hearth-rug, tread what was a tiger's skin:
Rarely such a royal monster as I lodged the bullet in!
True, he murdered half a village, so his own death came to pass;
Still, for size and beauty, cunning, courage—ah, the brute he was!
Why, that Clive,—that youth, that greenhorn, that quill-driving clerk, in fine,—
He sustained a siege in Arcot . . . But the world knows! Pass the wine.
Where did I break off at? How bring Clive in? Oh, you mentioned "fear"!
Just so: and, said I, that minds me of a story you shall hear.

We were friends then, Clive and I: so, when the clouds, about the orb
Late supreme, encroaching slowly, surely, threatened to absorb
Ray by ray its noontide brilliance,—friendship might, with steadier eye
Drawing near, bear what had burned else, now no blaze—all majesty.
Too much bee's-wing floats my figure? Well, suppose a castle's new:
None presume to climb its ramparts, none find foothold sure for shoe
'Twixt those squares and squares of granite plating the impervious pile
As his scale-mail's warty iron cuirasses a crocodile.

Reels that castle thunder-smitten, storm-dismantled? From without
Scrambling up by crack and crevice, every cockney prates about
Towers—the heap he kicks now! turrets—just the measure of his cane!
Will that do? Observe moreover—(same similitude again)—
Such a castle seldom crumbles by sheer stress of cannonade:
'Tis when foes are foiled and fighting's finished that vile rains invade,
Grass o'ergrows, o'ergrows till night-birds congregating find no holes
Fit to build in like the topmost sockets made for banner-poles.
So Clive crumbled slow in London, crashed at last.

A week before,
Dining with him,—after trying churchyard chat of days of yore,—
Both of us stopped, tired as tombstones, headpiece, foot-piece, when they lean
Each to other, drowsed in fog-smoke, o'er a coffined Past between.
As I saw his head sink heavy, guessed the soul's extinguishment
By the glazing eyeball, noticed how the furtive fingers went
Where a drug-box skulked behind the honest liquor,—"One more throw
Try for Clive!" thought I: "Let's venture some good rattling question!" So—
"Come, Clive, tell us"—out I blurted—"what to tell in turn, years hence,
When my boy—suppose I have one—asks me on what evidence
I maintain my friend of Plassey proved a warrior every whit
Worth your Alexanders, Cæsars, Marlboroughs and—what said Pitt?—
Frederick the Fierce himself! Clive told me once"—I want to say—
"Which feat out of all those famous doings bore the bell away
—In his own calm estimation, mark you, not the mob's rough guess—

Which stood foremost as evincing what Clive called courageou
ness!
Come! what moment of the minute, what speck-centre in t
wide
Circle of the action saw your mortal fairly deified?
(Let alone that filthy sleep-stuff, swallow bold this wholeson
Port!)
If a friend has leave to question,—when were you most brav
in short?"

Up he arched his brows o' the instant—formidably Clive agai
"When was I most brave? I'd answer, were the instance half
plain
As another instance that's a brain-lodged crystal—curse it!-
here
Freezing when my memory touches—ugh!—the time I felt mo
fear.
Ugh! I cannot say for certain if I showed fear—anyhow,
Fear I felt, and, very likely, shuddered, since I shiver now."

"Fear!" smiled I. "Well, that's the rarer: that's a specimen
seek,
Ticket up in one's museum, *Mind-Freaks, Lord Clive's Fe*
Unique!"

Down his brows dropped. On the table painfully he pored
though
Tracing, in the stains and streaks there, thoughts encrusted lo
ago.
When he spoke 'twas like a lawyer reading word by word so
will,
Some blind jungle of a statement,—beating on and on until
Out there leaps fierce life to fight with.

"This fell in my factor-da
Desk-drudge, slaving at Saint David's, one must game,
drink, or craze.

I chose gaming: and,—because your high-flown gamesters hardly take
Umbrage at a factor's elbow if the factor pays his stake,—
I was winked at in a circle where the company was choice,
Captain This and Major That, men high of colour, loud of voice,
Yet indulgent, condescending to the modest juvenile
Who not merely risked but lost his hard-earned guineas with a smile.

"Down I sat to cards, one evening,—had for my antagonist
Somebody whose name's a secret—you'll know why—so, if you list,
Call him Cock o' the Walk, my scarlet son of Mars from head to heel!
Play commenced: and, whether Cocky fancied that a clerk must feel
Quite sufficient honor came of bending over one green baize,
I the scribe with him the warrior, guessed no penman dared to raise
Shadow of objection should the honour stay but playing end
More or less abruptly,—whether disinclined he grew to spend
Practice strictly scientific on a booby born to stare
At—not ask of—lace-and-ruffles if the hand they hide plays fair,—
Anyhow, I marked a movement when he bade me 'Cut!'

"I rose.
'Such the new manœuvre, Captain? I'm a novice: knowledge grows.
What, you force a card, you cheat, Sir?'

"Never did a thunder-clap
Cause emotion, startle Thyrsis locked with Chloe in his lap,
As my word and gesture (down I flung my cards to join the pack)
Fired the man of arms, whose visage, simply red before, turned black.

When he found his voice, he stammered 'That expression once
again!'

" 'Well, you forced a card and cheated!'

" 'Possibly a factor's brain,
Busied with his all-important balance of accounts, may deem
Weighing words superfluous trouble: *cheat* to clerkly ears may
seem
Just the joke for friends to venture: but we are not friends,
you see!
When a gentleman is joked with,—if he's good at repartee,
He rejoins, as do I—Sirrah, on your knees, withdraw in full!
Beg my pardon, or be sure a kindly bullet through your skull
Lets in light and teaches manner to what brain it finds! Choose
quick—
Have your life snuffed out or, kneeling, pray me trim yon candle-
wick!'

" 'Well, you cheated!'
"Then outbroke a howl from all the friends around.
To his feet sprang each in fury, fists were clenched and teeth
were ground.
'End it! no time like the present! Captain, yours were our dis-
grace!
No delay, begin and finish! Stand back, leave the pair a space!
Let civilians be instructed: henceforth simply ply the pen,
Fly the sword! This clerk's no swordsman? Suit him with a
pistol, then!
Even odds! A dozen paces 'twixt the most and least expert
Make a dwarf a giant's equal: nay, the dwarf, if he's alert,
Likelier hits the broader target!'

"Up we stood accordingly.
As they handed me the weapon, such was my soul's thirst to try
Then and there conclusions with this bully, tread on and stamp
out
Every spark of his existence, that,—crept close to, curled about

By that toying tempting teasing fool-forefinger's middle joint,—
Don't you guess?—the trigger yielded. Gone my chance! and at the point
Of such prime success moreover: scarce an inch above his head
Went my ball to hit the wainscot. He was living, I was dead.

"Up he marched in flaming triumph—'twas his right, mind!—up, within
Just an arm's length. 'Now, my clerkling,' chuckled Cocky with a grin
As the levelled piece quite touched me, 'Now, Sir Counting-House, repeat
That expression which I told you proved bad manners! Did I cheat?'

" 'Cheat you did, you knew you cheated, and, this moment, know as well.
As for me, my homely breeding bids you—fire and go to Hell!'

"Twice the muzzle touched my forehead. Heavy barrel, flurried wrist,
Either spoils a steady lifting. Thrice: then, 'Laugh at Hell who list,
I can't! God's no fable either. Did this boy's eye wink once? No!
There's no standing him and Hell and God all three against me,—so,
I did cheat!'

"And down he threw the pistol, out rushed—by the door
Possibly, but, as for knowledge if by chimney, roof or floor,
He effected disappearance—I'll engage no glance was sent
That way by a single starer, such a blank astonishment
Swallowed up their senses: as for speaking—mute they stood as mice.

"Mute not long, though! Such reaction, such a hubbub in a trice!
'Rogue and rascal! Who'd have thought it? What's to be expected next,

When His Majesty's Commission serves a sharper as pretext
For . . . But where's the need of wasting time now? Naught requires delay:
Punishment the Service cries for: let disgrace be wiped away
Publicly, in good broad daylight! Resignation? No, indeed!
Drum and fife must play the Rogue's-March, rank and file be freed to speed
Tardy marching on the rogue's part by appliance in the rear
—Kicks administered shall right this wronged civilian,—never fear,
Mister Clive, for—though a clerk—you bore yourself—suppose we say—
Just as would beseem a soldier?'

" 'Gentlemen, attention—pray!
First, one word!'

"I passed each speaker severally in review.
When I had precise their number, names and styles, and fully knew
Over whom my supervision thenceforth must extend,—why, then—

" 'Some five minutes since, my life lay—as you all saw, gentlemen—
At the mercy of your friend there. Not a single voice was raised
In arrest of judgment, not one tongue—before my powder blazed—
Ventured "Can it be the youngster blundered, really seemed to mark
Some irregular proceeding? We conjecture in the dark,
Guess at random,—still, for sake of fair play—what if for a freak,
In a fit of absence,—such things have been!—if our friend proved weak
—What's the phrase?—corrected fortune! Look into the case, at least!"
Who dared interpose between the altar's victim and the priest?
Yet he spared me! You eleven! Whosoever, all or each,

To the disadvantage of the man who spared me, utters speech
—To his face, behind his back,—that speaker has to do with me:
Me who promise, if positions change and mine the chance should
    be,
Not to imitate your friend and waive advantage!'

"Twenty-five
Years ago this matter happened: and 'tis certain," added Clive,
"Never, to my knowledge, did Sir Cocky have a single breath
Breathed against him: lips were closed throughout his life, or
    since his death,
For if he be dead or living I can tell no more than you.
All I know is—Cocky had one chance more; how he used it,—
    grew
Out of such unlucky habits, or relapsed, and back again
Brought the late-ejected devil with a score more in his train,—
That's for you to judge. Reprieval I procured, at any rate.
Ugh—the memory of that minute's fear makes gooseflesh rise! Why prate
Longer? You've my story, there's your instance: fear I did, you
    see!"

"Well"—I hardly kept from laughing—"if I see it, thanks must
    be
Wholly to your Lordship's candour. Not that—in a common
    case—
When a bully caught at cheating thrusts a pistol in one's face,
I should under-rate, believe me, such a trial to the nerve!
'Tis no joke, at one-and-twenty, for a youth to stand nor swerve.
Fear I naturally look for—unless, of all men alive,
I am forced to make exception when I come to Robert Clive.
Since at Arcot, Plassey, elsewhere, he and death—the whole
    world knows—
Came to somewhat closer quarters."

Quarters? Had we come to blows,
Clive and I, you had not wondered—up he sprang so, out he
    rapped

Such a round of oaths—no matter! I'll endeavour to adapt
To our modern usage words he—well, 'twas friendly license—flung
At me like so many fire-balls, fast as he could wag his tongue.

"You—a soldier? You—at Plassey? Yours the faculty to nick
Instantaneously occasion when your foe, if lightning-quick,
—At his mercy, at his malice,—has you, through some stupid inch
Undefended in your bulwark? Thus laid open,—not to flinch
—That needs courage, you'll concede me. Then, look here! Suppose the man,
Checking his advance, his weapon still extended, not a span
Distant from my temple,—curse him!—quietly had bade me, 'There!
Keep your life, calumniator!—worthless life I freely spare:
Mine you freely would have taken—murdered me and my good fame
Both at once—and all the better! Go, and thank your own bad aim
Which permits me to forgive you!' What if, with such words as these,
He had cast away his weapon? How should I have borne me, please?
Nay, I'll spare you pains and tell you. This, and only this, remained—
Pick his weapon up and use it on myself. I so had gained
Sleep the earlier, leaving England probably to pay on still
Rent and taxes for half India, tenant at the Frenchman's will."

"Such the turn," said I, "the matter takes with you? Then I abate
—No, by not one jot nor tittle,—of your act my estimate.
Fear—I wish I could detect there: courage fronts me, plain enough—
Call it desperation, madness—never mind! for here's in rough
Why, had mine been such a trial, fear had overcome disgrace.
True, disgrace were hard to bear: but such a rush against God's face

—None of that for me, Lord Plassey, since I go to church at times,
Say the creed my mother taught me! Many years in foreign climes
Rub some marks away—not all, though! We poor sinners reach life's brink,
Overlook what rolls beneath it, recklessly enough, but think
There's advantage in what's left us—ground to stand on, time to call
'Lord, have mercy!' ere we topple over—do not leap, that's all!"

Oh, he made no answer, re-absorbed into his cloud. I caught
Something like "Yes—courage: only fools will call it fear."

If aught
Comfort you, my great unhappy hero Clive, in that I heard,
Next week, how your own hand dealt you doom, and uttered just the word
"Fearfully courageous!"—this, be sure, and nothing else I groaned.
I'm no Clive, nor parson either: Clive's worst deed—we'll hope condoned.

Lyrics from Jocoseria

1883

These two lyrics from Jocoseria, *published when Browning was 71, have an amazing freshness and lilt.* Never the Time and the Place *is, deservedly, one of his most popular poems, expressing as it does the lover's most frequent complaint. Here, the "enemy" is perhaps memory which with time grows unfaithful to the old love.*

WANTING IS—WHAT?

Wanting is—what?
Summer redundant,
Blueness abundant,
—Where is the blot?

Beamy the world, yet a blank all the same,
—Framework which waits for a picture to frame:
What of the leafage, what of the flower?
Roses embowering with naught they embower!
Come then, complete incompletion, O comer,
Pant through the blueness, perfect the summer!
  Breathe but one breath
  Rose-beauty above,
  And all that was death
  Grows life, grows love,
  Grows love!

NEVER THE TIME AND THE PLACE

Never the time and the place
  And the loved one all together!
This path—how soft to pace!
  This May—what magic weather!
Where is the loved one's face?
In a dream that loved one's face meets mine,
  But the house is narrow, the place is bleak
Where, outside, rain and wind combine
  With a furtive ear, if I strive to speak,
  With a hostile eye at my flushing cheek,
With a malice that marks each word, each sign!
O enemy sly and serpentine,
  Uncoil thee from the waking man!
    Do I hold the Past
    Thus firm and fast
  Yet doubt if the Future hold I can?
This path so soft to pace shall lead
Thro' the magic of May to herself indeed!
Or narrow if needs the house must be,
Outside are the storms and strangers: we—
Oh, close, safe, warm sleep I and she,
—I and she!

Short Poems from Ferishtah's Fancies

1884

I

You groped your way across my room i' the drear dark dead of night;
At each fresh step a stumble was: but, once your lamp alight,
Easy and plain you walked again: so soon all wrong grew right!

What lay on floor to trip your foot? Each object, late awry,
Looked fitly placed, nor proved offence to footing free—for why?
The lamp showed all, discordant late, grown simple symmetry.

Be love your light and trust your guide, with these explore my heart!
No obstacle to trip you then, strike hands and souls apart!
Since rooms and hearts are furnished so,—light shows you,—needs love start?

2

So, the head aches and the limbs are faint!
Flesh is a burden—even to you!
Can I force a smile with a fancy quaint?
Why are my ailments none or few?

In the soul of me sits sluggishness:
Body so strong and will so weak:
The slave stands fit for the labor—yes,
But the master's mandate is still to seek.

You, now—what if the outside clay
Helped, not hindered the inside flame?
My dim to-morrow—your plain to-day,
Yours the achievement, mine the aim!

So were it rightly, so shall it be!
  Only, while earth we pace together
For the purpose apportioned you and me,
  Closer we tread for a common tether.

You shall sigh, "Wait for his sluggish soul!
  Shame he should lag, not lamed as I!"
May not I smile, "Ungained her goal:
  Body may reach her—by and by"?

3

Not with my Soul, Love!—bid no soul like mine
  Lap thee around nor leave the poor Sense room!
Soul,—travel-worn, toil-weary,—would confine
  Along with Soul, Soul's gains from glow and gloom,
Captures from soarings high and divings deep.
Spoil-laden Soul, how should such memories sleep?
  Take Sense, too—let me love entire and whole—
    Not with my Soul!

Eyes shall meet eyes and find no eyes between,
  Lips feed on lips, no other lips to fear!
No past, no future—so thine arms but screen
  The present from surprise! not there, 'tis here—
Not then, 'tis now:— back, memories that intrude!
Make, Love, the universe our solitude,
  And, over all the rest, oblivion roll—
    Sense quenching Soul!

4

Ask not one least word of praise!
  Words declare your eyes are bright?
What then meant that summer day's
Silence spent in one long gaze?
  Was my silence wrong or right?

Words of praise were all to seek!
  Face of you and form of you,

Did they find the praise so weak
When my lips just touched your cheek—
  Touch which let my soul come through?

Sonnets

1870-1885

GOLDONI

The eighteenth century Venetian dramatist, Carlo Goldoni, is regarded as the father of modern European comedy. Through his sparkling comedies he revealed the faults and foibles of his fellow townsmen, high and low alike. In this sonnet the poet captures the spirit of Goldoni's gay and brittle plays—and the milieu with which they dealt.

Goldoni—good, gay, sunniest of souls—
  Glassing half Venice in that verse of thine—
  What though it just reflect the shade and shine
Of common life, nor render, as it rolls,
Grandeur and gloom? Sufficient for thy shoals
  Was Carnival; Parini's depths enshrine
  Secrets unsuited to that opaline
Surface of things which laughs along thy scrolls.
There throng the people: how they come and go,
  Lisp the soft language, flaunt the bright garb—see—
On Piazza, Calle, under Portico
  And over Bridge! Dear king of Comedy,
Be honoured! Thou that didst love Venice so,
  Venice, and we who love her, all love thee!

WHY I AM A LIBERAL

Although he took no active part in politics, Browning supported the Liberal Party most of his life. This sonnet was written in response to an invitation to contribute to a volume issued in 1885 which was designed to win prestige for the then waning Liberal

Party. It may be considered as a statement of general principle by a thoroughgoing individualist who prized his own freedom rather than championship of the policies of a particular political group.

"Why?" Because all I haply can and do,
All that I am now, all I hope to be—
Whence comes it save from fortune setting free
Body and soul the purpose to pursue,
God traced for both? If fetters, not a few,
Of prejudice, convention, fall from me.
These shall I bid men—each in his degree
Also God-guided—bear, and gaily too?

But little do or can the best of us:
That little is achieved through Liberty.
Who, then, dares hold—emancipated thus—
His fellow shall continue bound? Not I
Who live, love, labour freely, nor discuss
A brother's right to freedom. That is "Why."

HELEN'S TOWER

1883

Lady Dufferin, the "Helen" of this sonnet, was a famous Victorian beauty and the center of a literary circle. She was the great-granddaughter of Richard Brinsley Sheridan. Her son, Marquis of Dufferin and Ava, built a tower in her honor in Ireland and in 1870 asked Browning to write a poem in commemoration of this event. It is not surprising that the poet, busy with Greek studies and translations at the time, should have thought of the comparison with Helen of Troy. Browning never saw fit to include this lovely sonnet in a volume of his work.

Who heard of Helen's Tower, may dream perchance
How the Greek beauty from the Scaean Gate
Gazed on old friends unanimous in hate,

Death-doomed because of her fair countenance.
Hearts would leap otherwise, at thy advance,
  Lady to whom this Tower is consecrate!
  Like hers, thy face once made all eyes elate,
Yet, unlike hers, was bless'd by every glance.

The Tower of Hate is outworn, far and strange:
  A transitory shame of long ago,
  It dies into the sand from which it sprang;
But thine, Love's rock-built Tower, shall fear no change:
  God's self laid stable earth's foundation so,
  When all the morning-stars together sang.

Asolando

1889

PROLOGUE

At the very end of his life Browning saw again the beautiful places in Italy which had thrilled him fifty years before. Recalling his acute perceptions as a young man, he finds that "the Poet's age is sad," for, while the beauties remained, the vision had dimmed. The flame was gone, the "Bush was bare."

"The Poet's age is sad: for why?
  In youth, the natural world could show
No common object but his eye
  At once involved with alien glow—
His own soul's iris-bow.

"And now a flower is just a flower:
  Man, bird, beast are but beast, bird, man—
Simply themselves, uncinct by dower
  Of dyes which, when life's day began,
Round each in glory ran."

Friend, did you need an optic glass,
  Which were your choice? A lens to drape

In ruby, emerald, chrysopras,
  Each object—or reveal its shape
Clear outlined, past escape,

The naked very thing?—so clear
  That, when you had the chance to gaze,
You found its inmost self appear
  Through outer seeming—truth ablaze,
Not falsehood's fancy-haze?

How many a year, my Asolo,
  Since—one step just from sea to land—
I found you, loved yet feared you so—
  For natural objects seemed to stand
Palpably fire-clothed! No—

No mastery of mine o'er these!
  Terror with beauty, like the Bush
Burning but unconsumed. Bend knees,
  Drop eyes to earthward! Language? Tush!
Silence 'tis awe decrees.

And now? The lambent flame is—where?
  Lost from the naked world: earth, sky,
Hill, vale, tree, flower,—Italia's rare
  O'er-running beauty crowds the eye—
But flame? The Bush is bare.

Hill, vale, tree, flower—they stand distinct,
  Nature to know and name. What then?
A Voice spoke thence which straight unlinked
  Fancy from fact: see, all's in ken:
Has once my eyelid winked?

No, for the purged ear apprehends
  Earth's import, not the eye late dazed.
The Voice said, "Call my works thy friends!
  At Nature dost thou shrink amazed?
God is it who transcends."

NOW

Out of your whole life give but a moment!
All of your life that has gone before,
All to come after it,—so you ignore,
So you make perfect the present,—condense,
In a rapture of rage, for perfection's endowment,
Thought and feeling and soul and sense—
Merged in a moment which gives me at last
You around me for once, you beneath me, above me—
Me—sure that despite of time future, time past,—
This tick of our life-time's one moment you love me!
How long such suspension may linger? Ah, Sweet—
The moment eternal—just that and no more—
When ecstasy's utmost we clutch at the core
While cheeks burn, arms open, eyes shut and lips meet!

SUMMUM BONUM

All the breath and the bloom of the year in the bag of one bee:
  All the wonder and wealth of the mine in the heart of one
    gem:
In the core of one pearl all the shade and the shine of the sea:
  Breath and bloom, shade and shine,—wonder, wealth, and—
    how far above them—
      Truth, that's brighter than gem,
      Trust, that's purer than pearl,—
Brightest truth, purest trust in the universe—all were for me
      In the kiss of one girl.

BAD DREAMS

Last night I saw you in my sleep:
  And how your charm of face was changed!
I asked, "Some love, some faith you keep?"
  You answered, "Faith gone, love estranged."

Whereat I woke—a twofold bliss:
  Waking was one, but next there came
This other: "Though I felt, for this,
  My heart break, I loved on the same."

DEVELOPMENT

While not great as a poem, Development *is a charming tribute to the poet's father. It affords us glimpses into his very sound methods of educating his gifted son: teaching the Homeric epics through dramatic play, then guiding him on to read Pope's* Homer, *and so to the study of Greek and the mastering of Aristotle's* Ethics. *The poem is interesting, too, in pointing up the controversy that raged during the nineteenth century as to the authorship of the* Iliad *and the* Odyssey.

My Father was a scholar and knew Greek.
When I was five years old, I asked him once
"What do you read about?"
                                        "The siege of Troy."
"What is a siege and what is Troy?"
                                                  Whereat
He piled up chairs and tables for a town,
Set me a-top for Priam, called our cat
—Helen, enticed away from home (he said)
By wicked Paris, who couched somewhere close
Under the footstool, being cowardly,
But whom—since she was worth the pains, poor puss—
Towzer and Tray,—our dogs, the Atreidai,—sought
By taking Troy to get possession of
—Always when great Achilles ceased to sulk,
(My pony in the stable)—forth would prance
And put to flight Hector—our page-boy's self.
This taught me who was who and what was what:
So far I rightly understood the case
At five years old: a huge delight it proved
And still proves—thanks to that instructor sage
My Father, who knew better than turn straight

Learning's full flare on weak-eyed ignorance,
Or, worse yet, leave weak eyes to grow sand-blind,
Content with darkness and vacuity.

It happened, two or three years afterward,
That—I and playmates playing at Troy's Siege—
My Father came upon our make-believe.
"How would you like to read yourself the tale
Properly told, of which I gave you first
Merely such notion as a boy could bear?
Pope, now, would give you the precise account
Of what, some day, by dint of scholarship,
You 'll hear—who knows?—from Homer's very mouth.
Learn Greek by all means, read the 'Blind Old Man,
Sweetest of Singers'—*tuphlos* which means 'blind,'
Hedistos which means 'sweetest.' Time enough!
Try, anyhow, to master him some day;
Until when, take what serves for substitute,
Read Pope, by all means!"
So I ran through Pope,
Enjoyed the tale—what history so true?
Also attacked my Primer, duly drudged,
Grew fitter thus for what was promised next—
The very thing itself, the actual words,
When I could turn—say, Buttmann to account.

Time passed, I ripened somewhat: one fine day,
"Quite ready for the Iliad, nothing less?
There 's Heine, where the big books block the shelf:
Don't skip a word, thumb well the Lexicon!"

I thumbed well and skipped nowise till I learned
Who was who, what was what, from Homer's tongue,
And there an end of learning. Had you asked
The all-accomplished scholar, twelve years old,
"Who was it wrote the Iliad?"—what a laugh!
"Why, Homer, all the world knows: of his life
Doubtless some facts exist: it 's everywhere:

We have not settled, though, his place of birth:
He begged, for certain, and was blind beside:
Seven cities claimed him—Scio, with best right,
Thinks Byron. What he wrote? Those Hymns we have.
Then there 's the 'Battle of the Frogs and Mice,'
That 's all—unless they dig 'Margites' up
(I 'd like that) nothing more remains to know."

Thus did youth spend a comfortable time;
Until—"What 's this the Germans say is fact
That Wolf found out first? It 's unpleasant work
Their chop and change, unsettling one's belief:
All the same, while we live, we learn, that 's sure."
So, I bent brow o'er *Prolegomena.*
And, after Wolf, a dozen of his like
Proved there was never any Troy at all,
Neither Besiegers nor Besieged,—nay, worse,—
No actual Homer, no authentic text,
No warrant for the fiction I, as fact,
Had treasured in my heart and soul so long—
Ay, mark you! and as fact held still, still hold,
Spite of new knowledge, in my heart of hearts
And soul of souls, fact's essence freed and fixed
From accidental fancy's guardian sheath.
Assuredly thenceforward—thank my stars!—
However it got there, deprive who could—
Wring from the shrine my precious tenantry,
Helen, Ulysses, Hector and his Spouse,
Achilles and his Friend?—though Wolf—ah, Wolf!
Why must he needs come doubting, spoil a dream?

But then "No dream 's worth waking"—Browning says:
And here 's the reason why I tell thus much.
I, now mature man, you anticipate,
May blame my Father justifiably
For letting me dream out my nonage thus,
And only by such slow and sure degrees
Permitting me to sift the grain from chaff,

Get truth and falsehood known and named as such.
Why did he ever let me dream at all,
Not bid me taste the story in its strength?
Suppose my childhood was scarce qualified
To rightly understand mythology,
Silence at least was in his power to keep:
I might have—somehow—correspondingly—
Well, who knows by what method, gained my gains,
Been taught, by forthrights not meanderings,
My aim should be to loathe, like Peleus' son,
A lie as Hell's Gate, love my wedded wife,
Like Hector, and so on with all the rest.
Could not I have excogitated this
Without believing such men really were?
That is—he might have put into my hand
The "Ethics"? In translation, if you please,
Exact, no pretty lying that improves,
To suit the modern taste: no more, no less—
The "Ethics": 't is a treatise I find hard
To read aright now that my hair is grey,
And I can manage the original.
At five years old—how ill had fared its leaves!
Now, growing double o'er the Stagirite,
At least I soil no page with bread and milk,
Nor crumple, dogs-ear and deface—boys' way.

Epilogue. 97. E !.

At the midnight in the silence of the sleep-time,
When you set your fancies free,
Will they pass to where—by death, fools ~~you~~ think, imprisoned—
Low he lies who once so loved you, whom you loved so,
—Pity me?

Oh to love so, be loved, yet so mistaken!
What had I on earth to do
With the slothful, with ~~and~~ the mawkish, the ~~and~~ unmanly?
Like the aimless, helpless, hopeless, did I drivel
—Being—who?

One who never turned his back but marched breast forward,
  Never doubted clouds would break,
Never dreamed, though right were worsted, wrong would triumph,
Held we fall to rise, are baffled to fight better,
  Sleep to wake.

No, at noonday in the bustle of man's work-time
  Greet the unseen with a cheer!
Bid him forward, breast and back as either should be,
"Strive and thrive!" cry "Speed,—fight on, fare ever
  There as here!"

Courtesy of The Morgan Library

EPILOGUE

This is Browning's last poem, a beautiful, brief, final statement of his philosophy. It was written just before the illness which caused his death, and of it Browning remarked to relatives: ". . . it's the simple truth; and as it's true it shall stand."

At the midnight in the silence of the sleep-time,
  When you set your fancies free,
Will they pass to where—by death, fools think, imprisoned—
Low he lies who once so loved you, whom you loved so,
          —Pity me?

Oh to love so, be so loved, yet so mistaken!
  What had I on earth to do
With the slothful, with the mawkish, the unmanly?
Like the aimless, helpless, hopeless, did I drivel
          —Being—who?

One who never turned his back but marched breast forward,
  Never doubted clouds would break,
Never dreamed, though right were worsted, wrong would triumph,
Held we fall to rise, are baffled to fight better,
          Sleep to wake.

No, at noonday in the bustle of man's work-time
  Greet the unseen with a cheer!
Bid him forward, breast and back as either should be,
"Strive and thrive!" cry "Speed,—fight on, fare ever
          There as here!"

Glossary

SONGS FROM PARACELSUS

Cassia-buds, etc., Oriental spices and fragrances. *Nard,* an ointment. *Arras,* a wall hanging or screen made of tapestry. *Mayne,* the river Main in Germany, the countryside Paracelsus knew as a boy.

CAVALIER TUNES

Crop-headed Parliament, Cromwell's followers cut their hair short; the Cavaliers wore theirs long. *Carles,* rustics or peasants. *Hampden, Hazelrig, Fiennes,* and *young Harry* were all enemies of the King. *Rouse,* a cheer given as they drank. *Noll's damned troopers,* Cromwell's soldiers.

MY LAST DUCHESS

Fra Pandolf and *Claus of Innsbruck* are imaginary artists.

SOLILOQUY IN A SPANISH CLOISTER

Salve tibi, hail to thee. *Oak-galls,* acorns. *Arian frustrate,* the reference is to the heresy of Arius, a fourth century priest who denied the Trinity. *Galatians,* see Galatians, 5:19-21. *Manichee,* a follower of Mani, a Persian heretic of the third century. *Belial,* Satan. *Hy, Zy, Hine,* possibly the beginning of a mystic incantation to the devil. *Plena,* etc., the wording of the prayer, *Ave Maria, gratia plena,* has been altered for the rhyme.

WARING

Monstr-inform'-ingens-horrendus, a comic rendition of Virgil's description of Polyphemus in the *Aeneid. Ichabod,* see I Samuel, 4:21: "The glory is departed from Israel." *Vishnu-land,* India, Vishnu being an ancient deity. *Avatar,* the descent of a deity to earth and his incarnation as a man or an animal. *Lambwhite-maiden,* Iphigenia, who was to be sacrificed by her father, Agamemnon, to win divine favor for his expedition to Troy. *Serpentine and syenite,* types of building stone. *Dian's fane at Taurica,* Diana's shrine at Taurus, where Iphigenia was borne to save her from death. *Caldara Polidare,* an Italian fresco painter of the Renaissance. *Purcell,* a seventeenth-century English composer. *Garrick,* the famous English actor. *Junius,* pen-name of an English political writer. *Chatterton,* the gifted English poet who died at the age of eighteen; he was the author of the *Rowley Papers,* which purported to be a fifteenth-century manuscript. *Lateen sail,* a sail peculiar to Mediterranean boats, lateen being a corruption of Latin.

IN A GONDOLA

Cruce, crucible. *Mage,* magician. *I am a Jew,* the lover is here playfully imagining. *The Three,* mentioned several times in this poem, are, according to some Browning scholars, a sub-committee of a secret tribunal of the state before whom suspected persons were brought; other authorities declare that the Three were the lady's protectors; the present editor favors the former interpretation. *Paul* and *Gian* are perhaps the lady's brothers, and *Himself* her husband. *Lido's wet accursed graves,* the Jewish cemetery at Lido, a coastal village near Venice. *Giudecca,* a Venetian canal. *Lory,* a species of parrot. *Limpet,* a mollusk that comes from the shell at the sound of water. *Schidone,* an Italian Renaissance painter. *Haste-thee-Luke,* sobriquet of Giordano, Neapolitan painter. *Castelfranco,* Giorgione, the painter, thus called from the place of his birth. *Tizian,* the great Venetian artist, Titian. *Zorzi* and *Zanze,* the lover's and the lady's servants. *Siora,* Signora.

PIED PIPER OF HAMELIN

Cham, ruler of Tartary. *Nizam,* ruler of the Indian state, Hyderabad.

PICTOR IGNOTUS

Travertine, limestone.

THE ITALIAN IN ENGLAND

Metternich, reactionary Austrian statesman of the nineteenth century; "our friend" is obviously ironic. *Duomo,* church. *Tenebrae,* darkness; the service during Holy Week commemorating the Crucifixion.

THE ENGLISHMAN IN ITALY

Piano de Sorrento, plain of Sorrento, south of Naples. *Scirocco,* usually spelled sirocco, the hot wind that blows over southern Italy from Africa. *Frails,* baskets. *Lasagne,* a kind of macaroni. *Medlar,* a fruit resembling the crab-apple. *Sorbs,* fruit of the service tree. *Lentisks,* or lentiscus, the mastic tree. *Calvano,* an adjacent mountain. *Bellini, Auber,* the former was an Italian and the latter a French composer.

THE BISHOP ORDERS HIS TOMB

Epistle-side, the right side of the altar to one who faces it. *Onion-stone,* an inferior marble which peels off in layers. *Olive-frail,* olive basket. *Jesu church,* Church of the Jesuits. *Tully,* Cicero, whose Latin was a model of purity. *See God made and eaten,* referring to the sacrament of the Holy Communion. *Ulpian,* Ulpianus, a Roman jurist whose inferior Latin was good enough for Gandolf's tomb. *Mortcloth,* funeral pall. *Elucescebat,* he was illustrious. *Term,* from the Latin *terminus,* a boundary post or stone, often surmounted by a carved figure or bust. *Thyrsus,* a wreathed wand borne by Dionysus. *Gritstone,* sandstone.

SIBRANDUS SCHAFNABURGENSIS

Matin-prime, early morning. *Arbute* and *laurustine,* arbutus and laurel. *Stonehenge,* a group of monolithic stones on Salisbury Plain, England. *Pont-levis,* drawbridge. *De profundis, accentibus laetis, Cantate,* "From the depths, with joyous accents, sing." *Trover,* finder. *Knox,* John Knox, sixteenth-century Scottish preacher and reformer. *Husband-eft,* male lizard. *Sufficit,* enough!

THE LABORATORY

Ancien Régime, the old order, before the Revolution. *Glass mask,* to prevent the chemist from inhaling poisonous fumes. *Minion,* a small woman.

THE GLOVE

Naso, Publius Ovidius Naso, Latin poet, commonly known as Ovid. *Ixion,* mythical Greek king, who seduced Hera and became the father of a race of centaurs, wild creatures who were half man and half beast. Zeus punished him by having him bound to a wheel which turned perpetually. *Clement Marot,* a poet of the court of Francis I. *Illum Juda Leonem de Tribu,* that lion of the tribe of Judah. *Marignan,* ancient name of Melegnano, a town in northern Italy. *Nemean,* referring to the lion of Nemea, slain by Hercules. *Venienti occurite morbo,* go to meet trouble. *Theorbo,* a stringed musical instrument similar to the lute.

ANOTHER WAY OF LOVE

Eadem semper, always the same.

LOVE AMONG THE RUINS

Minions, servants. *Causeys,* causeways.

BY THE FIRESIDE

John in the Desert, St. John. *Leonor,* the name is taken from Beethoven's *Fidelio. Word,* see Revelation, 21:5. *In the house,* etc., see II Corinthians, 5:1.

INSTANS TYRANNUS

Spilth, effusion. *Gravamen,* charge or complaint. *Targe,* shield. *Boss,* protuberant ornament in the center of a shield.

MY STAR

Angled spar, Iceland spar, prismatic rock crystal.

"CHILDE ROLAND TO THE DARK TOWER CAME"

Childe, a youth of noble birth. *Calcine,* reduce to ashes. *Bents,* coarse grasses. *Colloped,* ridged. *Tophet,* hell. *Apollyon,* a devil. *Dragon-penned,* dragon-pinioned. *Slug-horn,* a battle trumpet.

HOW IT STRIKES A CONTEMPORARY

Valladolid, a provincial town in northern Spain. *Ferrel,* ferrule. *Corregidor,* a Spanish magistrate. *Prado,* public square or promenade.

UP AT A VILLA—DOWN IN THE CITY

Diligence, stage coach. *Thrid,* a variant of thread. *Pulcinello-trumpet,* the trumpet blown by Pulcinello, a leading character in Commedia del Arte, to announce the arrival of these traveling players to the townspeople. *Liberal thieves,* insurgents who were plotting to undermine Austrian rule. *Seven swords,* symbolizing the seven sorrows of the Virgin. *Tax on salt,* salt was taxed in Italy at this time. *Oil passing the gate,* oil and other provisions were taxed as they entered the gates of the town. *Yellow candles,* used at funerals and in processions of penitents.

THE PATRIOT

Shambles gate, where animals were slaughtered.

MASTER HUGUES OF SAXE-GOTHA

Aloys, Jurien, Just, saints. *Breves,* musical notes. *Sciolists shent,* pretenders to knowledge rebuked. *Discept,* disagree. *One, Two, Third,* etc., the parts of a fugue disputing with each other. *Crepitant,* crackling. *Strepitant,* noisy. *Danaides,* the daughters of Danäus, mythical Greek king, who were condemned to pour water through a sieve forever. *Escobar,* a Jesuit preacher. *Est fuga, volvitur rota,* it is a flight, the wheel revolves. *Tickens,* tickings. *Tabor,* a small drum. *Mea poena,* at my risk. *Mode Palestrina,* in the fashion of the great Italian musician of the sixteenth century, who made use of the elaborations of counterpoint while preserving the gravity and solemnity suitable to church music.

ANDREA DEL SARTO

Legate, the Pope's representative. *Morello,* a mountain north of Florence. *The Urbinate,* the artist Raphael, a native of Urbino. *Giorgio Vasari,* a pupil of del Sarto's, and author of *Lives of the Painters,* which the Brownings read assiduously. *Agnolo,* original spelling of the name of Michelangelo, the greatest of the artists of the Italian Renaissance. *Francis,* Francis I of France, at whose court Andrea painted and whom he cheated by leaving for home before his commission was completed. *Cue-owl,* a small European owl. *Leonard,* Leonardo da Vinci, the great Florentine artist.

FRA LIPPO LIPPI

Carmine, the church of the Carmelites in Florence, celebrated for its murals. *Pilchard,* a fish. *St. Laurence,* a church named for the martyr who was sentenced to be burned alive on a gridiron. *Aunt Lapaccia,* the aunt who took care of Lippi when he was left an orphan. *The Eight,* Florentine magistrates. *Antiphonary,* a book of verses used by one choir in response to another. *Carmelites* and *Camaldolese,* members of two religious orders. *Giotto,* Florentine primitive painter and sculptor and friend of Dante. *Herodias,* mother of Salome and wife of Herod; it was Salome "who danced and got men's heads cut off." *Fra Angelico* and *Lorenzo* (the latter referring to Lorenzo Monaco), two Italian painters of the monastic tradition. *Guidi,* also known as Masaccio ("hulking"), an artist whom Browning incorrectly supposes to have been Lippi's pupil. *Prato,* a town near Florence, for whose church Lippi painted some of his greatest work. *Sant' Ambrogio,* the convent of St. Ambrose in Florence. *Iste perfecit opus,* this man made the work. *Hot cockles,* an old game.

"DE GUSTIBUS—"

"De gustibus non disputandum est," there is no disputing tastes. *Cicalas,* cicadas, commonly called locusts. *Liver-wing,* right arm; the King was probably the tyrannical Ferdinand II, King of Sicily and Naples.

POPULARITY

Tyre, the ancient Phoenician city from which came the much-prized Tyrian purple, a dye used for royal vestments. *Astarte,* the Syrian goddess of love and nature. *Conchs,* shells. *Hobbs, Nobbs,* etc., imitators and borrowers. *Murex,* the mollusk from which the dye was made.

SAUL

Abner, Saul's uncle and leader of his army. *Jerboa,* a small jumping rodent. *Levites,* high priests. *Paper-reeds,* reeds from which papyrus was made. *Sabaoth,* armies.

GRAMMARIAN'S FUNERAL

Crofts, fields. *Thorpes,* hamlets. *Calculus,* a medical term here, referring to gall-stone or gravel. *Tussis,* a cough. *Soul-hydroptic,* soul-thirsty. *Hoti,* that; *oun,* therefore; *enclitic de,* towards.

ONE WORD MORE

San Sisto, etc., four of Raphael's most famous Madonnas. *Guido Reni,* an Italian painter. *Bice,* short for Beatrice. *Fiesole,* hill town above Florence. *Samminiato,* San Miniato was a church near Florence. *Sinai-forehead,* the reference is to God's appearance to Moses on Mt. Sinai. *Missal-marge,* margin of a prayer-book. *Karshish, Cleon, Norbert,* Browning here enumerates some of the characters who appear in the fifty poems comprising *Men and Women.*

JAMES LEE'S WIFE

Barded and chanfroned, equipped with armor. *Quixote-mage,* whimsical magician.

PROSPICE

The title is Latin, meaning "look forward." *Arch-fear,* fear of death. *Guerdon,* reward.

YOUTH AND ART

Smith, the imaginary artist of the poem; *Gibson,* a famous English sculptor whom Browning knew in Italy. *Kate Brown,* the speaker; *Grisi,* a great operatic singer of the period whom she hoped to supplant. *Prince,* probably Prince Albert, Victoria's consort, who was interested in art. *Board,* board meeting of the Academy. *R. A.,* Royal Academy, membership in which is the highest honor accorded English artists.

ABT VOGLER

Rampired, fortified. *Protoplast,* the original creation or model.

A LIKENESS

Tipton Slasher, an English boxer. *Chablais,* Chablis is a district of France. *Rarey,* an American horse trainer. *Cruiser,* a race horse. *Sayers,* an English prize-ring figure. *Marc Antonio,* Marc Antonio Raimondi, an Italian engraver. *Festina lente,* Latin proverb, make haste slowly. *Volpato,* an Italian engraver.

HOLY-CROSS DAY

Handsel the Bishop's shaving shears, the reference is to the shearing of the beard, a sign of the converted Jew; handsel means to inaugurate, to use for the first time. *Acorned,* acorn-fed. *Chine,* spine. *Corso,* a street in Rome. *Ben Ezra,* the great medieval Jewish philosopher.

PACCHIAROTTO

Giacomo de Bartolommeo Pacchiarotto was a mediocre Italian painter of the period of the Renaissance whom Browning uses to express his views of the artist's need for privacy. In several of the poems in this volume he lashes out against his own critics, and in particular against Alfred Austin, who never lost an opportunity to attack him.

IVAN IVANOVICH

Verst, two thirds of a mile. *Droug,* friend. *Satan-faced,* according to the Russian legend, wolves were incarnations of the devil. *Stiopka,* diminutive of Stepan. *Pope,* village priest. *Starosta,* village overseer. *Pomeschik,* large landowner. *Kolokol the Big,* the great bell in the Kremlin at Moscow.

CLIVE

Plassey, the battle which won India for Britain. *Arcot,* where Clive had won a battle against Indian and French forces some years before his final victory. *Factor-days,* a factor was a business agent. *St. David's,* an outpost of the East India Company south of Madras. *Rogue's March,* played when an officer is dismissed from the army. *Thyrsis* and *Chloe,* pastoral lovers of classical literature.

JOCOSERIA

The title of this volume means jests. There was a book with this title in the elder Browning's library.

FERISHTAH'S FANCIES

Browning uses the thin disguise of a Persian sage, Ferishtah, in offering a miscellany of discursive, philosophical poems.

DEVELOPMENT

Atreidai, of the tribe of Atreus, whose sons, Agamemnon and Menelaus, led the Greeks in the siege of Troy, the object being the recapture of Helen, Menelaus' wife, stolen by Hector, son of King Priam of Troy. *Pope,* translator of the *Iliad* into English verse. *Buttmann,* German scholar, author of a Greek grammar.

Heine, Heyne, German scholar and Greek grammarian. *Prologemena,* the work in which the German scholar Wolf propounded his thesis that the Homeric epics had not been written by a single individual but were a slow accretion of folk tales, developed over many centuries. *Stagirite,* Aristotle, from his birthplace at Stagira in ancient Macedonia.

PROLOGUE TO ASOLANDO

Chrysopras, a semi-precious stone. *Bush,* the reference is to the bush which Moses saw aflame with divine fire; for the poet the divine fire is quenched, the bush is bare.

Date Due